SCOTLAND:
THE MAKING AND UNMAKING OF THE NATION
c.1100–1707

SCOTLAND:
THE MAKING AND
UNMAKING OF
THE NATION
c.1100–1707

VOLUME 5: MAJOR DOCUMENTS

Edited by

Caroline Erskine, Alan R. MacDonald and Michael Penman

DUNDEE UNIVERSITY PRESS

in association with

THE OPEN UNIVERSITY IN SCOTLAND

First published in Great Britain in 2007 by
Dundee University Press

University of Dundee
Dundee DD1 4HN

www.dundee.ac.uk/dup

ISBN 10: 1 84586 030 6
ISBN 13: 978 1 84586 030 1

British Library Cataloguing-in-Publication Data
A catalogue record for this book is available on request from the British Library

Typeset by Hewer Text UK Ltd, Edinburgh
Printed and bound in Great Britain by
CPI Antony Rowe, Chippenham and Eastbourne

Contents

PART II: EARLY MODERN SCOTLAND

Preface

This volume and the series of which it is a part represent the completion of a project which began in the mid 1990s to facilitate the study of Scottish History in Scotland and beyond. A milestone was reached in 1998 with the launch of a module in Modern Scottish History – *Modern Scottish History: 1707 to the Present*. This module, and the five volumes which accompany it, have won consistently high praise from the students who have taken it, as well as strong commendation from many professional academics. Appropriately perhaps, with the project's completion in 2007, the 300th anniversary of the parliamentary union with England, anyone who wishes to will be able to study Scottish history from c.1100 to present day by distance learning.

In 1998, the editors said that it was a particularly appropriate moment to bring Scottish history to a new and wider readership and audience. This reflected, in the first place, the outcome of the 1997 Referendum, but also the evident depth of contemporary interest, expressed in a large variety of ways, in the Scottish past. It is no less true today. Indeed, if anything, the need and desirability of doing so is only greater with the first flush of post-devolution excitement over and the place of Scottish history in universities and schools not necessarily any stronger than it was a few years ago. And while popular history books are being written and published, and from 2003 *History Scotland* has been available on newsagents' shelves, long established myths and preconceptions about the Scottish past still exert a very firm grip on general opinion and even on those who really should know better. Scottish history and Scotland deserve better than this.

These volumes aim to present recent academic research to a wider readership. As such they should be of interest to anyone with an interest in knowing about the Scottish past as well as the essential historical background to many present-day concerns and issues. They also provide a way for readers to develop their own skills as students of history, focusing on issues relating to the use (and abuse) of primary sources and the conceptual questions and challenges raised by specific topics. While we have left out some of the overtly pedagogical material which was included in the Modern Scottish History volumes, there is still plenty of discussion on sources and methods for interested readers to follow up.

The potential scope of these volumes is enormous, and this despite the fact that the sources and scholarship for the medieval and early modern periods are considerably less abundant than for the modern one. Any decision we might have taken about how to present the history of periods as long as c.1100–c.1500 and c.1500–1707 would have involved some awkward compromises. The first two volumes, comprising new essays by expert authors, start with a number of broadly chronological chapters, furnishing readers with a basic narrative. These chapters are followed by a range of more thematic ones. All the chapters are designed to offer a reasonably comprehensive introduction to recent work and, as importantly, a context or contexts for further reading and investigation. You will find there is some overlap between the chronological and thematic chapters, which offers scope for comparison between authors and for looking again at topics and themes from alternative perspectives. Some themes span the two volumes – for example, the Highland-Lowland divide, urbanisation, Scottish identity, Anglo-Scottish relations – so they can be traced over the 'long durée' and across conventional period divisions. There are no separate chapters on gender. Rather this theme has been deliberately blended in with other themes and topics. Some will not find this to their taste, but the aim is to present an inclusive, broad vision of the Scottish past, not one which segregates particular experiences. We have also chosen to include greater coverage of areas of cultural history than in the modern volumes. In part, this reflects recent trends in the writing of history – the so-called 'cultural turn' in historical studies – but also the wealth of scholarship which exists on such topics. It may also reflect something of an emancipation of scholars from the primacy of documentary sources, but then this no new thing for medievalists. Throughout both volumes a key theme which emerges, in terms of how we study the Scottish past, and also the patterns and meanings present in that past, is the importance of Scottish relationships and involvement in a broader European past. Let's hope the anniversary of the Union does not mask or detract from this theme, and the great strides which have been made in recent decades to recover this dimension to the Scottish past. The third and fourth volumes contain selected readings to accompany the topic/theme volumes, and should prove a great resource for those wishing to explore further a particular subject. The fifth volume is a collection of primary sources for the history of Scotland from c.1100 to 1707 designed to accompany the other volumes. It makes accessible documents of both local and national importance, quite a few of which have been specially transcribed for this volume. All students of history should want to read primary sources for the uniquely rich insight they furnish into the past. We also hope that they may encourage some readers to make their own forays into local archives.

This book represents a further product of the University of Dundee-Open University collaboration to offer modules in Scottish history to distance learning students. The modules are offered at honours level for undergraduates. However, all the volumes are designed to be used, singly or as a series, by anyone with an interest in Scottish history. Our hope is that they will inspire and deepen enthusiasm for the investigation of the Scottish past, perhaps even encouraging some to examine aspects of their own community history based on themes covered in the volumes.

From the outset, this project has depended on the efforts and enthusiasm of many people, and there are several major debts to acknowledge. Financial support for the development of these volumes was provided initially from the strategic fund of the Faculty of Arts and Social Sciences at the University of Dundee under the guidance of the then dean, Professor Huw Jones. His successor, Professor Chris Whatley, has been a constant supporter, and has contributed his expertise to these volumes, as well as being an editor and contributor to the Modern Scottish History volumes. The Strathmartine Trust generously provided further vital financial support to facilitate the production of these volumes. Within the Open University, invaluable supporting roles have been played by Peter Syme, Director of the Open University in Scotland, and Ian Donnachie, Reader in History at the Open University. It is the shared commitment of individuals in both institutions, stimulated by the success and quality of the Modern Scottish History course, which has driven forward the continued development of the project. John Tuckwell, who published the Modern Scottish History volumes, and who commissioned the present volumes, has been a sage and encouraging adviser to the editorial team. The authors produced their contributions to agreed formats and, for the most part, to agreed deadlines. While they are responsible for what they have written, they have also been supported by other members of the writing team and our editors. Particular thanks are also due to Mrs Johanne Phillips, the secretary and administrator of the Modern Scottish History course, to her successor Elizabeth Bryant, and to Mrs Helen Carmichael and Mrs Sara Reid, secretaries in the Department of History, University of Dundee for their administrative support. Thanks are also due to Jen Petrie who typed many of the texts for inclusion in the articles and documents volumes.

USING THIS BOOK

The primary sources in Volume 5 were chosen by the authors of the chapters in Volumes 1 and 2. They illustrate particular aspects of the periods and topics covered in those volumes, giving the reader direct access to the original records upon which historians make their judgements about the past. This volume can be read in conjunction with Volumes 1–4 but it also stands alone as an excellent collection of primary sources from medieval and early modern Scotland, some of which have never before been published.

Series Editors

Acknowledgements

The editors would like to thank the following for permission to reproduce items in this collection:

Ashgate Publishing: document 115; the Atlas Committee of the Scottish Medievalists and WFH Nicolaisen: document 4; Boydell and Brewer Ltd: document 6; the National Galleries of Scotland: docment 141; Scottish Academic Press: document 84; the Scottish Text Society: documents 58 and 160; Sir John Clerk of Penicuik: document 153; the Society of Antiquaries of Scotland: documents 42b, 44, 45; the University of St Andrews: documents 16, 33, 47, 57; the Yorkshire Archaeological Society: document 35.

Introduction

It is nearly four decades since the last major collection of sources for the teaching of medieval and early modern Scottish history was compiled and published. The late Gordon Donaldson's *Scottish Historical Documents* was widely used and, still to be superseded, it was reprinted in 1997. Yet the priorities and interests of scholars and students move on. Although extracts from many of the documents which Donaldson used can be found here, this book differs from that volume in a number of important respects. The traditional study of history tended to concentrate on high politics and the church and, while these topics rightly retain a prominent role, the ways in which they are studied have changed markedly, with much more emphasis being put on the impact of government and religion on society as a whole. The selection of documents presented here reflects that change. Approaches to the use of sources have also changed, and that is reflected particularly in the early period, but also in the fact that a significant number of the documents in this volume have never been published before. Painstaking work in the archives by a growing number of Scottish historians has brought to light previously neglected sources which have suggested new answers and raised new questions about numerous historical problems, both new and old. An increasingly broad approach to the study of Scotland's past is also being taken, with recent decades witnessing huge advances in cultural history. Thus sources which shed light on the art, architecture, literature and music of medieval and early modern Scotland can now be included. In recognition of the fact that much of Scottish life before the modern period was not recorded in written form, especially during the medieval period, material sources for the study of the past also form a part of this collection in the form of archaeological evidence.

The languages used in medieval and early modern Scotland present their own challenges and the way that each source has been presented reflects this. Some have been fully translated into modern English, while others have been glossed so that the original language is retained. The linguistic map of medieval and early modern Scotland was a complex and shifting one. At the beginning of our period, at least four languages were used in what is now Scotland: Gaelic, Latin, Scots and Old Norse, with a further two (Pictish and Cumbric) having died out by the eleventh century. Sadly, almost nothing written in Pictish, Cumbric or Old Norse survives and relatively few sources in Gaelic date from before 1600, although about half of the population of Scotland spoke that language in the later sixteenth century. Latin was reserved for legal and ecclesiastical sources, although the latter includes the records of universities and the writing of history because of the close links between the church and education in the medieval period. Most surviving sources from medieval and early modern Scotland, however, were written in the vernacular of southern and eastern Scotland, known to academics as early and middle Scots. By the fifteenth century, it was the language of central and local government (Scotland was the first country in Europe to record parliamentary statutes in the vernacular). The poets of the fifteenth century firmly established Scots as a language of elite literature and, after the Reformation, the church also adopted Scots as the language of its records. From the later sixteenth century onwards, however, and particularly after 1603, increased contact with English led to a gradual reduction in the distinctiveness of written Scots: at the end of the sixteenth century, literate English-speakers would have had difficulty understanding an act of the Scottish parliament but by 1700 they would not. It must be remembered, however, that the vast majority of the population of the Lowlands would have been relatively unaffected by this linguistic shift, as the language they spoke was largely unaffected by the written word.

This volume was compiled primarily to serve the needs of the students studying the University of Dundee–Open University Distance Learning module in Medieval and Early Modern Scottish History. It completes a five-volume set which includes two volumes of specially commissioned original essays and two volumes of reprinted historical scholarship which provide further insights into the history of medieval and early modern Scotland. Yet this volume was intended from the outset to do much more than complement the others, for it provides an immensely rich resource for lecturers, teachers and students which will allow them to engage in new ways with key themes in Scottish social, political, religious, cultural and economic life in the period from the emergence of Scotland as a kingdom until the parliamentary union with England in 1707. Each section of documents has been nominated by a historian with a particular expertise in the topic to which the sources relate. In some cases, they were chosen to focus on a specific aspect of the topic, in others to provide a range of different perspectives. They are sometimes surprising, sometimes moving, sometimes amusing, sometimes tough to interpret but always fascinating and thought-provoking.

Caroline Erskine
Alan R. MacDonald
Michael Penman

PART I

Medieval Scotland

Scotland Before 1100: Writing Scotland's Origins

DOCUMENT 1

All Items Relating to Pictland/*Alba* Found in Irish Chronicles *c.640–c.920*

Irish chronicles are the only source which can readily claim to represent contemporary evidence for events in the period when 'Pictland' and 'Picts' disappear from historical record. All Irish chronicles derive from a lost 'Chronicle of Ireland' up to 911, probably kept at Armagh or within its ambit, which had close links with Dunkeld in this period. This was continued in a text which (eventually) became what is known as the Annals of Ulster (AU), which survives in two late medieval manuscripts. The other extant Irish chronicles derive from another version of the 'Chronicle of Ireland' kept at Clonmacnoise from the mid-tenth century (which, as far as this section goes, survives best in Chronicum Scotorum *(CS) in a seventeenth-century manuscript). The paucity of contemporary information on this period is immediately apparent. A close look at this material, however, shows how Alba and 'men of Alba' replaced 'Pictland' and 'Picts' from 900. There is debate about whether Alba represents a new name, or a new kingdom, or is simply the Gaelic word for 'Pictland'.*

849 (AU):
Indrechtach, abbot of Iona, came to Ireland with the relics of Columba.
[It is assumed that Columba's relics were taken from Iona to Kells, and that this was paralleled by some of his relics being taken to Dunkeld: see Document 2 (The Chronicle of the Kings of Alba)]

858 (AU):
Cinaed son of Alpín, king of the Picts . . . died.

862 (AU):
Domnall son of Alpín, king of the Picts . . . died.

865 (AU and CS):
Cellach son of Ailill, abbot of Kildare and abbot of Iona, slept in the country of the Picts.

865 (AU):
Tuathal son of Artgus, chief bishop of Fortriu and abbot of Dunkeld, slept.

866 (AU):
Amlaíb [Ólafr] and Auisle went into Fortriu, with the foreigners of Ireland and Britain, and they raided all Pictland, and took hostages from them.

870 (AU):
Siege of Dumbarton by the Northmen, that is to say Amlaib and Ímar [Ívarr], two kings of the Northmen, besieged the fortress, and at the end of four months destroyed the fortress and plundered it.

871 (AU):
Amlaib and Ímar returned to Dublin from Britain [*Alba*] with two hundred ships, bringing away with them in captivity to Ireland a great prey of Angles and Britons and Picts.

872 (AU):
Artgal, king of the Britons of Strathclyde, was slain by counsel of Causantín son of Cinaed.

873 (AU):
Flaithbertach son of Muirchertach, abbot of Dunkeld, died.

875 (AU):
An encounter of the Picts with the Black Foreigners, and great slaughter was made of the Picts.

876 (AU and CS):
Causantín son of Cinaed, king of the Picts . . . died.

878 (AU):
Aed son of Cinaed, king of the Picts, was slain by his own people.

878 (AU&CS):
Columba's shrine, and also his relics, came to Ireland, in flight from the Foreigners. [*Presumably they came from Dunkeld: see 849 above.*]

900 (AU and CS):
Domnall son of Causantín, king of *Alba*, died.

?904 (CS):
'Ead', king of Pictland, fell fighting against the two grandsons of Ímar, and against Ceitil, with five hundred men.

904 (AU):
Ímar grandson of Ímar was killed by the men of Fortriu, and great slaughter was made about him.

918 (AU): The Foreigners of Waterford left Ireland, namely Ragnall [Rögnvaldr], king of the Black Foreigners . . . and the men of *Alba* came to meet them, and they met on the banks of the Tyne, in the north of England . . . the men of *Alba* routed the three companies that they saw, and made great slaughter of the gentiles . . . And afterwards Ragnall attacked the men of Alba in the rear, and inflicted great slaughter upon them; but neither king nor *mormaer* was lost from among them. Night stopped the battle.

SOURCE: compiled by Dauvit Broun (based mainly on Mac Airt, S and Mac Niocaill, G (eds) 1983 *The Annals of Ulster (to A.D. 1131)*. Dublin).

The Chronicle of the Kings of Alba

The Chronicle of the Kings of Alba (also known as 'The Scottish Chronicle', 'The Old Scottish Chronicle', and 'The Scottish Chronicle in the Poppleton Manuscript') is the earliest chronicle-text from Scotland to survive (albeit damaged and altered). It is full of unique information. But can it be taken at face value? In one of your exercises you will be given an opportunity to answer this question for yourself. Scholars are divided about how much can be accepted as contemporary evidence. It is found in only one manuscript originating near York about 1360 in which it forms one of a number of pieces in a collection of Scottish material: (1) A description of Scotland, with quotations from other pieces in the collection (probably written 1165x84) (2)Extracts on the origins of the Picts and Scots (but the title is 'Chronicle on the Origin of the Ancient Picts') (3) A list of Pictish kings, including an account of the foundation of Abernethy.(4) The chronicle given below (5) List of kings of Dál Riata and kings of Scots, finishing with William I (1165–1214) (6) Genealogy of William I. The names before David I (1124–53) are spelt in Gaelic (7) Version 'A' of the foundation-legend of St Andrews, but without St Andrews' claim to be archbishop.

The translation below is divided for convenience into separate 'items' according to sense and syntax. The manuscript spelling of a few names and terms is given in italics. Where an item begins with 'and', this is prefixed with * if either Latin et or ac is used (there is no difference in meaning). The dates supplied in square brackets are what may be deduced from the text in conjunction with the evidence of Irish chronicles. Additional information is supplied in square brackets in order to assist comprehension, particular when a passage is obscure (sometimes because of damage in copying). Square brackets are also used to indicate where material appears to have been omitted (probably accidentally by a copyist).

1. So *Kinadius filius Alpini* [Cinaed mac Alpín], first of the Scots, ruled this Pictland prosperously for 16 years [d. 858].
2. Pictland was named after the Picts, whom, as we have said, Kenneth destroyed; for God deigned to make them alien from, and void of, their heritage, by reason of their wickedness; because they not only spurned the Lord's mass and precept, but also did not wish to be held equal to others in the law of justice.
3. Two years before he came to Pictland, he had received the kingdom of Dál Riata.

8

4. In the seventh year of his reign [probably 849] he transported the relics of St Columba to a church that he had built.

5. *And he invaded England six times; and he seized and burned Dunbar and Melrose.

6. But the Britons burned Dunblane, and the Danes wasted Pictland to Clunie and Dunkeld.

7. He died of a tumour ultimately on the Tuesday before the Ides of February [i.e. 8 February 858], in the palace of Forteviot.

8. Domnall his brother held the kingdom for 4 years [d. 862].

9. In his time the Gaels with their king at Forteviot made [?the rights of the kingdom those of] Aed mac Echdach, [king of Dál Riata, d. 778].

10. He died in the palace of *Cinnbelathoir* on 13 April.

11. Causantín son of Cinaed reigned for 16 years [d. 876].

12. In his first year [862] Maelsechnaill king of the Irish died, and Aed son of Niall held the kingship [of Ireland].

13. *And after two years Amlaib with his Gentiles wasted Pictland, and dwelt in it from 1 January to the feast of St Patrick [17 March].

14. Again, in his third year [866] Amlaib, drawing a hundred [. . .

15. . . .] was slain by Causantín.

16. A little while afterwards, a battle was fought by him in his fourteenth year [875] at Dollar, between Danes and Scots, and the Scots were slain as far as Atholl.

17. The Northmen spent a whole year in Pictland.

18. Aed held the same [kingdom] for one year [d. 878].

19. The shortness of his [reign] has bequeathed nothing memorable to history.

20. He was slain in the *civitas* [monastery?] of *Nrurim*.

21. Eochaid son of Rhun, moreover, king of the Britons [of Dumbarton], grandson of Cinaed by his daughter, reigned for 11 years;

22. although others say that 'Ciricius' [Giric] son of . . . reigned at this time, because he became Eochaid's foster-son and guardian.

23. In his second year [879] Aed son of Niall died.

24. *And in his ninth year, on the very day of St. 'Ciricius' [Cyrus: 16 June], an eclipse of the sun occurred. Eochaid and his foster-son was [note the singular] now expelled from the kingdom.

25. Domnall son of Causantín held the kingdom for 11 years [d. 900].

26. The Northmen then wasted Pictland.

27. In his reign a battle occurred between Danes and Scots at the islands of *Solian*: the Scots had victory.

28. [He] was killed at *Opidum Fother* [Dunottar] by the Gentiles.

29. Causantín son of Aed held the kingdom for forty years.

30. And in his third year [903] the Northmen plundered Dunkeld, and all Alba.

31. But assuredly, in the following year, the Northmen were slain in *Straith hErenn* [could be either Strathearn or Strathdearn].

32. *And in his sixth year [906] King Causantín and Bishop Cellach, on the Hill of Belief near the royal *ciuitas* of Scone, undertook to preserve the laws and

disciplines of the faith, and the rights of churches and gospels equally with the Scots.

33. From that day on the hill has deserved its name, that is, the Hill of Belief.

34. *And in his eighth year [908] the most exalted king of the Irish and archbishop fell in Leinster, that is, Cormac son of Cuilennan.

35. *And in his time Dyfnwal king of the Britons [of Strathclyde] died; and Domnall son of Aed king of Ailech [in Tirconnel, Co. Donegel]; and Flann son of Maelsechnaill and Niall son of Aed who reigned for three years after Flann [as king of Ireland].

36. *And the battle of *Tinemore* took place in his eighteenth year [918], between Causantín and Ragnall, and the Scots had victory.

37. *And the battle of *Duinbrunde* [Brunanburh] in his thirty-fourth year [mistake for thirty-seventh, i.e. 937], and in it fell Causantín's son, and after one year he died.

38. Dubucan son of Indrechtach mormaer of Angus; Athelstan son of Edward *rig Saxan* ['of the king of the English']; and Eochaid son of Alpin died.

39. *And in his old age, being decrepit, he [Causantín] took the staff [i.e. entered a monastery], and served the Lord; and he gave up the kingdom to *Mael* [Mael Coluim] son of Domnall.

40. Mael Coluim son of Domnall reigned 11 years [d. 954].

41. Mael Coluim went with his army to Moray and killed Cellach.

42. In the seventh year, of his reign he plundered the English as far as the river Tees, and he seized a multitude of people and many herds of cattle: and the Scots called this the raid of *Albidosorum* [?'the raid of men of the soil', i.e. infantry-levies?], that is, *Nainndisi* [?the wretchedness].

43. But others say that Causantín made this raid, asking of the king, Mael Coluim, that the kingship should be given to him for a week's time, so that he could visit the English.

44. In fact, it was not Mael Coluim who made the raid, but Causantín incited him, as I have said.

45. Causantín died, though, in [Mael Coluim's] tenth year [952], under the crown of penitence in good old age.

46. *And the men *na Moerne* [of the Mearns] slew Mael Coluim at Fetteresso, that is, *in claideom* [the sword?].

47. *Idulfus* [Illulb] held the kingdom for 8 years [954–62].

48. In his time *opidum Eden* [Edinburgh] was evacuated, and abandoned to the Scots to the present day.

49. . . .] they were slain in Buchan by a fleet of 'Somarlidi' [Vikings].

50. *Niger* [Dub] son of Mael Coluim reigned 5 years [d. 966].

51. Fothad bishop [of the Scots] rested [i.e. died].

52. [A battle] between *Nigerum* [Dub] [and] *Caniculum* [Cuilén] upon the ridge of Crup [Duncrub] in which *Niger* [Dub] had the victory, where fell Dunchad abbot of Dunkeld and Dubduin *satrapas Athochlach* [mormaer of the men of Atholl].

53. *Niger* [Dub] was expelled from the kingdom and *Caniculus* [Cuilén] reigned for a brief time.
54. Domnal son of Cairill died.
55. *Culenring* [Cuilén] reigned for 5 years [d. 971].
56. Marcan son of Breodalach was killed in the church of St. Michael [?in St. Andrews].
57. Leot and Sluagadach went out to Rome.
58. Bishop Maelbrigte rested [i.e. died] [and] Cellach son of Ferdalach reigned [as bishop of the Scots].
59. Maelbrigte son of Dubucan died
60. Cuilén and his brother Eochaid were killed by the Britons [of Strathclyde].
61. Cinaed son of Mael Coluim reigned . . . years.
62. He immediately plundered Britain [Strathclyde] in part.
63. Cinaed's infantry were slain with very great slaughter in *Moin Uacoruar*.
64. The Scots plundered *Saxoniam* [England] to Stainmore, and to *Cluiam*, and to the lakes of *Deranni*.
65. Cinaed, moreover, walled the banks of the fords of *Forthin* [Forth].
66. After a year, Cinaed went back and plundered *Saxoniam* [England] and carried off the son of the king of the Saxons [i.e. the English].
67. It is he who founded the great monastery [*ciuitas*] of Brechin for the Lord.

SOURCE: compiled by Dauvit Broun (based partly on Anderson, AO 1922 *Early Sources of Scottish History A.D. 500–1286*. Edinburgh)

Comparison of Fordun to Early Sources on the History of Strathclyde

Fordun's Chronicle of the Scottish People *(completed no earlier than 1384) is the earliest full-length history of Scotland to survive intact. Some historians have used it as a source for the history of Strathclyde in the tenth century. Its account has almost nothing in common with contemporary or near-contemporary sources, however, and is almost wholly a work of fiction.*

Fordun's Chronicle (1384x7)

Contemporary Sources
(Note: 'Cumbrians' refers to people of Strathclyde)
908x16
Chron. of the Kings of Alba
Douenaldus (Dyfnwal) 'king of Britons' died.

915/6
Causantin son of Aed, k. of Alba, gives 'Cumbria' [Strathclyde] to *Eugenius* son of *Donaldus*, and decrees that it is to be ruled thereafter by the heir to the Scottish kingship.

934
History of the Church of Durham
King Athelstan puts Owain king of the Cumbrians to flight.
*c.*940
Life of Cathroe
Dynfwal king of the Cumbrians takes Cathroe to Leeds.

945
Mael Coluim, k. of Alba, agrees with Edmund, k. of England, that Illulb, Mael Coluim's heir and ruler of 'Cumbria', should do homage to k. Edmund and his heirs for 'Cumbria'.

945
Anglo-Saxon Chronicle [A, B, C, D]
King Edmund harries the land of the Cumbrians (a later account says that two sons of King Dyfnwal were blinded); it is then given over to Mael Coluim king of Alba.

Fordun's Chronicle (1384x7)

952 [should be 954]
Mael Coluim dies; Illulb becomes k. of
Alba and Dub, Mael Coluim's son, k. of
'Cumbria'.
970 [should be 971]
Cinaed son of Mael Coluim becomes k.
of Alba; his heir Mael Coluim son of
Dub becomes k. of 'Cumbria'.

990s
Mael Coluim son of Dub dies. Cinaed son
of Mael Coluim changes rule of succession to primogeniture, and so gets his son
Mael Coluim accepted as k. of 'Cumbria'.

1004 [should be 1005]
Mael Coluim son of Cinaed, now k. of
Alba, gives 'Cumbria' to his grandson
Donnchad [=Duncan I, son of Mael
Coluim's daughter].

Contemporary Sources

973
Anglo-Saxon Chronicle [D, E, F]
Six kings submit to King Edgar at Che-
ster [John of Worcester identifies them
as including Cinaed son of Mael Co-
luim, k. of Alba; Mael Coluim, k. of
Strathclyde, and K. Dyfnwal].
975
AU and AT [Irish Chronicles]
Domnall [Dyfnwal] son of *Eogan*
[Owain], k. of Britons, dies on pilgrim-
age/in monastic life.

997
AU and AT [Irish Chronicles]
Mael Coluim son of *Domnall* [Dyfn-
wal], k. of Britons of the north, died.

1015
Welsh Annals
Owain son of Dyfnwal dies.
1018
Symeon of Durham, *History of Kings*
Mael Coluim son of Cinaed, k. of Alba,
with Owain the Bald, king of Strathclyde,
fighting along with him, wins battle of
Carham against earl of Northumbria.

Fordun's Chronicle (1384x7)

1034

Donnchad [Duncan I] now k. of Alba;
his son Mael Coluim [Malcolm III] k. of
Cumbria.

SOURCE: compiled by Dauvit Broun.

Contemporary Sources

'Pit-' Place-Names

Place-names are invaluable as evidence for social change as well as for the history of languages in Scotland. This map of 'pit-' place-names (names like Pitlochry and Pittentaggart beginning with the word pett, meaning literally a 'portion') is evidence for the renaming or creation of settlements from the ninth century (when Pictish was being replaced by Gaelic) to the twelfth century (when Gaelic began to give way to Scots). There is a good chance that a thorough research project on these names would yield vital insights about social change that might help us to understand why people were abandoning the Pictish language and adopting Gaelic as their mother tongue in this period.

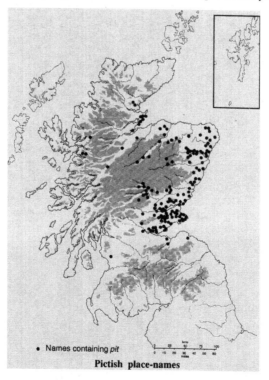

• Names containing *pit*

Pictish place-names

SOURCE: McNeill, PGB and MacQueen, HL (eds), 1996 *The Atlas of Scottish History to 1707*. Edinburgh, 51.

The Anglo-Saxon Chronicle, 1093–94

This chronicle was possibly written in the first instance for the court of King Alfred the Great of England (871–99) and continued by a number of later scribes. Overall, it covers events from AD 1 to 1154 and survives in several manuscripts which were copied from the original chronicle and then separately continued and embellished with news of local and national importance as the individual English monastic houses (Winchester, Abingdon, York etc) where the copies were kept saw fit; the label 'Anglo-Saxon' is a later addition to what was known as the Chronicum Saxonicum. *Fordun's chronicle (see Documents 1–3 above) contains a very different version of these recorded events for 1093–94, following the deaths of Malcolm III and Margaret of Scotland, making no mention of any hostility among 'Scots' to Anglo-Norman or Saxon incomers brought to the Scottish court before 1093.*

And then the Scots chose as King Donald, Malcolm's brother, and drove out all the English who were with King Malcolm before.

When Duncan, King Malcolm's [illegitimate] son, who was in king William [Rufus of England's] court – inasmuch as his father had formerly given him as a hostage to our king's father, and he had remained here ever since – heard that all this had so happened, he came to the king and did such fealty as the king would have of him; and so, with the king's consent, went to Scotland with what aid he could get of English and French, and deprived his kinsman Donald of the kingdom, and was received as king.

But afterwards some of the Scots gathered themselves together, and slew almost all his followers; and he himself escaped with few.

Thereafter they were reconciled, on the condition that he should never again introduce English or French into the land.

SOURCE: Anderson, AO (ed) 1908 *Scottish Annals from English Chroniclers AD 500 to 1286*, London.

The Anglo-Norman Impact, c.1100–c.1286

DOCUMENT 6

David I's Charter to Walter of Ryedale, *c.1150–53*

This is an early example of a royal feudal charter in Latin given under the great seal issued c.1150–3 by the chancery of King David I to one Walter of Ryedale (in Yorkshire), ancestor of the border family of Riddell: this act dates from the last years of David's reign at which time he had established his control of much of northern England following his exploitation of the English civil wars after the death of Henry I. It includes details of the lands and rights granted and a list of witnesses to the grant.

David king of Scots sends greetings to the bishops, abbots, justiciars, barons, sheriffs, grieves, ministers and all men of the whole of his land, French and English.

May those in the present and in the future know that I have given and granted to Walter of Ryedale the Whittons [Whitton and Over Whitton, in Morebattle and Hownam, Roxburghshire], half of Chatto and Lilliesleaf, by their just boundaries, with all their appurtenances which belong to them, in woodland, open country, meadows, pastures, and running water; and the shielings which are west of Riccalton, to be held by him and his heirs of me and my heirs, in fee and heritage, freely, for the service of one knight, as any one of my barons, his neighbours, who holds his fee freely, best and most freely has and holds it.

And if I or my heirs shall be unable to warrant [i.e. guarantee] the aforesaid lands to Walter or to his heirs against the claim of any other person, I and my heirs shall give Walter an exchange of equal value, to their reasonable satisfaction. Witnesses: Andrew bishop of Caithness, Walter son of Alan, Walter of Lindsay, David Uviet, Nicholas the clerk, Richard de Morville, Alexander of Seton and Alexander of St Martin. At Scone.

SOURCE: Barrow, GWS (ed) 1999 *The Charters of David I*. Woodbridge.

Foundation Charter of the Abbey of Kelso, Illuminated Initial, 1159

Sometime between 25 March and mid-May 1159, King Malcolm IV (1153–65) confirmed to the Tironensian Abbey of Kelso in the Borders all its liberties and possessions as they had been granted to that house by his royal predecessors: this was done in the pious memory of Malcolm's grandfather and predecessor, David I (1124–53). The charter itself was illuminated with an impressive initial letter depicting both David and Malcolm. It is worth analysing the symbolism of this initial on two levels: for its representation of royal office and its duties of justice, patronage and faith; and its depiction of the royal succession – it should be related to how David ensured that Malcolm followed him as king after the early death in 1152 of Malcolm's father, David's son, Prince Henry.

SOURCE: Innes, C (ed) 1846 *Liber S. Marie de Calchou.* Edinburgh, Bannatyne Club, 2 vols.

Chronicle of the Reigns of Malcolm and William

These extracts come from an anonymous contemporary Latin chronicle of the late twelfth century probably recorded at a monastic house in Scotland. The extract was written some time after William I had been captured by the English army of Henry II at Alnwick in 1174 and thus forced to give up his claims to northern English territory: this was, though, a concession which left William free to focus on asserting royal authority within his own borders.

A) MALCOLM

On 14 June [1159] Malcolm king of Scotland crossed to Normandy with 45 ships and when he had come as far as the city of Poitiers, where the king of England's army was assembled, he was honourably received by that king.

Henry king of the English then laid siege to Toulouse with a large army. Malcolm king of Scots was there and an innumerable crowd of nobles and magnates with him. King Henry girded Malcolm with the belt of knighthood in the bishop's meadow at Perigueux. The new knight made 30 young men of noble family fellows of his recent novitiate [i.e. he knighted them] and followed the king [of England] to Toulouse.

In 1160 Malcolm king of Scots returned from the army of Toulouse and when he reached the city called Perth Earl Ferteth [of Strathearn] and five other earls, angry with the king for going to Toulouse, besieged the city and wished to make the king a prisoner; but their presumption by no means prevailed.

B) WILLIAM

William king of Scotland and his brother David, with earls and barons of the land and with a large powerful army, penetrated into Ross and there built two castles, one called Dunskeath, the other 'Etherdover' (1180).

While the king of Scotland was staying with his lord the king of England in Normandy, Donald son of William son of (King) Duncan (II), who had often claimed the kingship of Scotland and carried out numerous plundering raids in the Scottish kingdom, landed in Scotland at the invitation of certain powerful men of that kingdom, laying waste and burning all the territory he could reach, putting men to flight and slaying all whom he could capture (1181).

William king of Scotland, having assembled a great host, advanced into Moray to make war on his enemy whose name was Mach Willam. He claimed to be born of royal stock and claimed the kingship of Scotland by right of his parents. He inflicted much damage upon King William with the consent and by the advice of earls and barons of the Scottish realm.

King William judged that he must kill Mach Willam or at least drive him from the kingdom, or else he himself would lose his kingdom. Having set off to Moray he appointed commanders and officers over the host and declared to the people 'I shall go forth with you' to which the people answered 'Do not go yourself; it would be best for you to be in command in the city, with us.' The king replied 'I shall do whatever you judge to be right.'

The king therefore remained in the castle called 'Ylvernis' and sent his earls and barons, with Scots and men of Galloway, to make war upon his enemy. When they had set off treachery arose among them, for some of them loved the king while others loved him not at all. The former wished to press on, the latter to hold back. While they argued, it was agreed that the leaders would stay behind while they sent out scouts to search for food supplies. About 3000 [?] warlike young men were chosen and sent ahead to seek out the king's enemy.

Among these was the household of Roland Uhtred's son (lord of Galloway) to whose judgement all deferred. Approaching the aforesaid William's [correctly Donald's] army they attacked and slew [Donald] and many of his host – the rest they put to flight, sharing out the spoils among themselves, and they cut off [Donald's] head and presented it to the king.

With him laid low, a great peace prevailed within the kingdom of Scotland. No-one lamented his death (1187).

SOURCE: Lawrie, AC (ed) 1910 *Annals of the Reigns of Malcolm and William, Kings of Scotland AD 1153–1214*. Glasgow.

Alexander II and the Isles, 1249

This extract comes from a late-thirteenth-century Norse saga history, Hakon, Hakon's Son's Saga. *The extract looks back to events of the 1240s but was written after Scotland gained ostensible control of the Western Isles after the Battle of Largs (1263) and through the resulting Treaty of Perth (1266).*

Alexander, the king of the Scots, was very covetous of dominion in the Hebrides, and constantly sent men to Norway to demand the purchase of the lands. This summer, the Scottish king drew an army together, and prepared for his journey into the Hebrides. He made it plain to his men that he intended not to turn back until he had acquired all the Norwegian king's dominion that he claims for himself, to the west of the Solundar Sea [the North Sea]. King Alexander sent word to King Ewen saying that he wished to meet him. But this meeting did not take place before four earls in Scotland had pledged their faith to Ewen that he should go in truce from that meeting. But when the kings met, the Scottish king required that King Ewen would give up Biarnaborg into his power, and three other castles which he held of King Hakon, and the rest of the dominion that the king of Norway had assigned to him. The king of the Scots said that he would give him a much larger dominion in Scotland; and along with it his friendship. They all pressed this upon King Ewen but he would on no account break his oaths to the king of Norway. Upon that King Ewen went away.

When King Alexander lay in Kerrera Sound he dreamed a dream: and he thought that three men came to him. He thought that one wore royal apparel; this man was very frowning, and red-faced, and stout in figure. The second man seemed to him tall and slender and youthful, the fairest of men and nobly dressed. The third was by far the largest in figure, and the most frowning, of them all. He was very bald in front. He spoke to the king and asked whether he intended to go plundering to the Hebrides. He thought he answered that that was certain. The dream-man bade him turn back, and said to him that they would not hear of anything else.

The king told his dream; and men begged him to turn back, but he would not do that. And but little later he fell ill, and died. Then the Scots broke up the levy and conveyed the king's body up into Scotland. The Hebrideans say that these men who appeared to the king in his sleep must have been St Olaf, king of Norway; and St Magnus, earl of the Orkneys; and St Columba. (1249).

SOURCE: 'Hakon, Hakon's Son's Saga' in Unger, CA (ed) and Anderson, AO (trans.) 1922 *Early Sources of Scottish History*. Edinburgh.

DOCUMENT 10

Alexander III and the Issue of Homage to England, 1278

These extracts are preserved in the Scottish Rolls *of the English royal government, i.e. documents relevant to England's dealings with Scotland which were enrolled together by English royal clerks in Westminster. These documents are safe-conducts detailing the conditions of Alexander III's passage to Edward I's court and the terms under which the Scottish king was recorded as having given his homage for his English lands (an oath held over from Edward I's accession in 1272) and how the English officials allegedly reserved their king's right to ask for homage for Scotland itself. Significantly, however, the Scots had a very different version of Alexander III's reply, asserting that their king had refused to give homage for Scotland by insisting that he held it of 'no-one but God alone': both the English and Scottish versions of the exchanges of 1278 may have been altered during the Wars of Independence.*

In the parliament of King Edward at Westminster at Michaelmas in the sixth year of the king's reign [1278] . . . Alexander king of Scotland . . . came to Edward king of England in the king's chamber at Westminster . . . to become his liegeman and to do homage to him; and he did so in the following words: 'I Alexander, king of Scotland, become the liegeman of Lord Edward, king of England, against all men.'

And the King of England received the homage of the king of Scotland, reserving the right and claim of the king of England, and of his heirs, to the homage of the king of Scotland and of his heirs for the kingdom of Scotland, when they wish to discuss this. And the king of Scotland . . . offered his fealty to the king of England and asked the king of England that he might swear fealty by the mouth of Robert Bruce earl of Carrick. And the king of England granted it to the king of Scotland as an act of special grace in the circumstances. Then Robert was asked by the king of Scotland to do this and thereupon . . . he swore fealty to the king of England in the name of and on behalf of the king of Scotland in the following words: 'I, Alexander, king of Scotland, will keep true faith with Edward, king of England, in matters of life and limb and of earthly honour, and will faithfully perform the services due for the lands and tenements that I hold of the king of England.'

SOURCE: Bain, J (ed) 1884 *Calendar of Documents Relating to Scotland*. Edinburgh, ii, nos. 120, 122, 125–6, 128.

The Wars of Independence

DOCUMENT 11

The Treaty of Salisbury, 1289

This treaty was agreed on 6 November 1289 between the Guardians of Scotland (now just four, following the deaths of the earls of Buchan and Fife) and the community of that realm and the kings of Norway and England. Significantly, it reveals much about the state not only of international relations but of the tension within Scotland at this time, presumably still caused by Bruce v. Balliol/Comyn rivalry over the kingship or, at least, over who should marry Margaret, Maid of Norway. The Scots were right to insist on Margaret's arrival while 'free and quit' of marriage contracts: by May of 1290 Edward I had secretly secured a papal dispensation for Margaret to wed his son, Edward of Caernarfon, some two months before the Scots, English and Norwegians finally agreed a marriage treaty at Birgham.

. . . the aforesaid Queen and heir of the kingdom of Scotland shall come to the kingdom of Scotland before the Feast of All Saints next to come, free and quit of all contract of marriage and espousal; and this the aforesaid Norwegian envoys promise faithfully they will cause to be done within the foresaid term, so far as in them it lies . . . [and] the said king of England faithfully promises that if the aforesaid Lady shall come into his hands or custody free and quit of all contract of marriage and espousal, then when the kingdom of Scotland shall have been fully settled in quietness and peace, so that the Lady herself may come there safely, and stay there, and when the king of England shall be so requested by the people of Scotland, the said king will send the same Lady to Scotland, as free and quit of all contracts, as is said above, as he received her . . .

SOURCE: Rymer, T 1726–35 *Foedera, conventiones, literae, et cujuscunque generis Acta Publica* . . . London, i, 719–20.

Wallace and Murray's Letter to the Merchants of Lübeck, 11 October 1297

This famous letter was preserved in the Lübeck archives, Germany, and recently exhibited in Scotland. (It created quite a controversy in 1998 when it was not included in the 'Story of Scotland' display at the then new Museum of Scotland – the press mistakenly thought academics had assumed it had been destroyed during World War II bombing.) It is the only documentary evidence that Andrew Murray shared the responsibility of guardianship with Wallace following their victory at Stirling (11 September 1297) and until Murray died of wounds.

Andrew de Moray and William Wallace, the Generals of the army of the realm of Scotland, and the Community of the same realm, to the prudent and discreet men and well-beloved friends, the Mayors and Commons of Lübeck and Hamburg, greeting, and increase ever of sincere friendship.

We have learned from trustworthy merchants of the said realm of Scotland that you, of your own goodwill, lend your counsel, aid, and favour in all matters and transactions touching us and the said merchants, although we on our part have previously done nothing to deserve such good offices; and all the more on that account are we bound to tender you our thanks and to make a worthy return. To do so we willingly engage ourselves to you, requesting that you will make it known among your merchants that they can have safe access to all the ports of the realm of Scotland with their merchandise; for the realm of Scotland, thank God, has been recovered by war from the power of the English. Farewell.

Given at Hadsington [Haddington], in Scotland on October 11, in the year of Grace 1297.

We further request you to have the goodness to forward the business of John Burnet and John Frere, merchants of ours, as you would wish us to forward the business of merchants of yours. Farewell. Given as above.

SOURCE: Murison, AF 1898 *Sir William Wallace*. Edinburgh, 93.

An English Spy's Report of a Scottish War Council at Peebles, August 1299

Following the Scots' defeat at the Battle of Falkirk, Wallace stepped down as Guardian and by mid-1299 had set out for Paris (where he was detained for almost a year) and possibly Rome in an ultimately unsuccessful attempt to secure John Balliol's release from papal custody. Wallace's actions worsened the rifts among the Scots still active in their resistance to Edward I: these were reported by an English spy.

At the Council, Sir David Graham demanded the lands and goods of Sir William Wallace because he was leaving the kingdom without the leave or approval of the Guardians. And Sir Malcolm, Sir William's brother, answered that neither his lands nor his goods should be given away, for they were protected by the peace in which Wallace had left the kingdom, since he was leaving to work for the good of the kingdom. At this, the two knights gave the lie to each other and drew their daggers. And since Sir David Graham was of Sir John Comyn's following and Sir Malcolm Wallace of the earl of Carrick's following, it was reported to the earl of Buchan and John Comyn that a fight had broken out without their knowing it; and John Comyn leaped at the earl of Carrick and seized him by the throat, and the earl of Buchan turned on the bishop of St Andrews, declaring that treason and lèse-majesté were being plotted. Eventually [James] Stewart and others came between them and quietened them . . . so it was ordained then that the bishop of St Andrews should have all the castles in his hands as principal captain, and the earl of Carrick and John Comyn be with him as joint guardians of the kingdom . . .

SOURCE: Bain, J (ed) 1884 *Calendar of Documents Relating to Scotland*. Edinburgh, ii, no. 1978.

Edward I's Orders About Bruce, *c.*November 1306 x 20 March 1307

These orders to Edward's officers in Scotland following Bruce's murder of Comyn, his seizure of the throne in 1306 and his flight to the west are preserved in the Scottish Rolls of the English royal government, i.e. documents dealing with the English occupation regime in Scotland which were enrolled together by clerks in Westminster.

The K. and Council order that all present at the death of Sir John Comyn, or of counsel and assent thereto, shall be drawn and hanged. Those . . . found in Scotland without the King's permission, or their resetters, shall be hanged or their heads cut off. All rebels in the war previous to the battle of Methven, or in the battle, or after, and who surrender, shall be sent to such prisons as the King orders, and not released until the King's pleasure is taken. Those of Robert de Brus's party, or who advised in any way the rising against the King, by preaching to the people, are to be arrested, whether clerks or laymen, and imprisoned till the King's pleasure is known. The poor commons of Scotland, who have been forced to rise against the King in this war, shall be held to ransom as the Guardian shall see their offences require. This ordinance is in three parts, one to remain in the Wardrobe, another with the Bishop of Chester the treasurer, and another with Sir Robert de la Warde seneschal of the Household.

SOURCE: Bain, J (ed) 1884 *Calendar of Documents Relating to Scotland.* Edinburgh, ii, no. 1908.

The Declaration of Arbroath, 6 April 1320

This famous Latin document survives as the Scottish 'file' version or copy of the original sent to the Pope (now lost): this file copy is now held in the National Archives of Scotland in Edinburgh. Following the Scots' breach of a papal truce in 1318 – when they recaptured Berwick-upon-Tweed – Bruce was again excommunicated and by 1319 summoned to appear, along with some of his bishops, at the papacy in Avignon by John XXII. Rather than attend in person (by May 1320) Bruce's government arranged for this letter to be sent in the name of the nobles of Scotland accompanied at the same time by letters from Robert I himself and from his clerics (both these letters are now lost). The drawing up and sending of these documents may have been discussed at a Council held at Newbattle in March 1320, just weeks before the so-called 'Soules Conspiracy' was exposed. There is debate as to the authorship of the nobles' letter with suggestions ranging from Abbot Bernard of Arbroath (then Robert I's chancellor) or clerks in his service, to St Andrews clerics like Alexander Kinninmund, later bishop of Aberdeen. The document was witnessed/sealed by the following Scottish nobles: Duncan earl of Fife; Thomas Randolph earl of Moray, lord of Man and Annandale; Patrick earl of March; Malise earl of Strathearn; Malcolm earl of Lennox; William earl of Ross; Magnus earl of Caithness and Orkney; William earl of Sutherland; Walter Steward of Scotland; William Soules, butler; James lord of Douglas; Roger Mowbray; David lord of Brechin; David Graham; Ingram Umfraville; John Menteith; Alexander Fraser; Gilbert Hay, constable; Robert Keith, marischal; Henry Sinclair; John Graham; David Lindsay; William Oliphant; Patrick Graham; John Fenton; William Abernethy; David Weymss; William Muschet; Fergus of Ardrossan; Eustace Maxwell; William Ramsay; William Mowat; Alan Murray; Donald Campbell; John Cameron; Reginald Cheyne; Alexander Seton; Andrew Leslie; Alexander Strachan; Alan of Callendar; Alexander Lamberton; Edward Keith; Martin Campbell; John Inchmartin; Thomas Menzies; John Durant; Thomas Morham; Robert Mowat.

Our nation hath hitherto lived in freedom and peace, with the protection of the papal see, till the magnificent King Edward, father of the present King of England, under the colour of friendship and alliance, did inflict us with innumerable oppressions, at the time we were without a king and expected no fraud or deceit, and when the people were unacquainted with arms and invasions. It is impossible for anyone whose own experience hath not informed him, to describe or fully to understand the injuries, blood, and violence, the destructions, fire, imprisonments of prelates, slaughter, and robbery committed upon holy persons and religious houses, and a vast multitude of other barbarities which that king executed on this people, sparing neither age, nor sex, nor religion, nor rank of man.

But at length it pleased God, who only healeth wounds, to restore us to liberty from these innumerable calamities, by our most valiant Prince and King, Lord Robert, who for the delivering of his people and his own rightful inheritance from the enemies' hand, like another Joshua, hath most cheerfully undergone all manner of toil, fatigue, hardship, and hazard. Divine Providence, the right of succession, and the customs and laws of the kingdom, which we will maintain till death, and the due and lawful consent and assent of all the people, make him our king and prince. To him we are obliged and resolved to adhere in all things, both on account of his right and his merit, as the person who hath restored the people's safety, in defence of their liberties. But after all, if this prince shall leave those principles which he hath so nobly pursued, and consent that we or our kingdom be subjected to the king or people of England, we will immediately endeavour to expel him as our enemy, and as the subverter of both his own and our rights, and will choose another king who will defend our liberties; for as long as one hundred of us remain alive, we will never consent to subject ourselves to the English. For it is not glory, it is not riches, neither is it honour, but it is liberty alone that we fight and contend for, which no honest man will lose but with his life.

For these reasons, most reverend Father, we earnestly pray and entreat your Holiness that you may be pleased, with a sincere and cordial piety, to consider that with Him whose Vicar on earth you are, there is no respect of Jew, nor Greek, nor English; and that, with a tender and fatherly eye, you may look upon the calamities and straits brought upon us and the church of God by the English; and that you may admonish and exhort the King of England to rest satisfied with his own dominions, since his kingdom of old was sufficient for seven or more kings, and to suffer us to live in peace in that narrow spot of Scotland, beyond which we have no habitation, and desire nothing but our own. And we on our part, so far as we are able, consistently with the national interest, are willing to do everything that may procure our peace.

It is your concernment, most Holy Father, to interpose in this, when you see how far the violence and barbarity of the pagan is let loose to rage against Christendom for punishing the sins of the Christians, and how much they daily encroach upon the Christian territories. And it is your interest to notice that there be no ground given for reflecting on your memory, if you suffer any part of the Church to come under a scandal or eclipse, which we pray God may prevent during your times.

Let it, therefore, please your Holiness to exhort the Christian princes not to make the wars between them and their neighbours a pretext for not going to the relief of the Holy Land, since that is not the true cause of the impediment, but the real ground of it is that they have a much nearer prospect of advantage, and far less opposition, in the subjecting of their weaker neighbours; and God, who is ignorant of nothing, knows with how much cheerfulness both our king and we would go thither, if the King of England would leave us in peace, and we now testify and declare it to the Vicar of Christ and to all Christendom.

But if your Holiness shall be too credulous of the English misrepresentations, and not give fair credit to what we have said, nor desist from favouring them to our destruction, we must believe that the Most High will lay to your charge all the blood, loss of souls, and other calamities that may ensue between us and them.

By granting our just desires, your Holiness will always oblige us, where our duty shall require it, to endeavour to satisfy you, as becomes the obedient sons of the Vicar of Christ. We commit our cause to Him who is the supreme king and judge, we cast the burden of our cares upon Him, and hope for such an issue as may give strength and courage to us, and bring our enemies to nought. May the Almighty long preserve your Holiness to His church.

SOURCE: Mackintosh, J 1878 *The History of Civilisation in Scotland*. London, i, 325–8.

Stewart Monarchy: 1371–1513

DOCUMENT 16

Walter Bower's *Scotichronicon* – the Events of 1390

Walter Bower (c.1385–1449) was the abbot of the Augustinian island abbey of Inchcolm in the Forth and also rose to be a tax collector and parliamentarian for James I (1406–37) of whom he had a high opinion as a 'lawgiver' king able to assert royal authority against over-mighty magnates. Bower wrote his Scotichronicon, continuing and embellishing the earlier chronicle of John of Fordun and adding an original history for events after c.1383 (although he also drew on fourteenth-century sources used by chronicler Andrew Wyntoun c.1400–22). Writing in the 1440s, one of Bower's concerns was to use his history as a 'mirror', or book of advice, for the then child king, James II (1437–60), urging him to take a strong hand against his noble subjects and to end the civil strife which had characterised the period after the murder of James I in 1437. Here Bower details the events of 1390, two years after Robert Stewart, earl of Fife, had seized the office of King's Lieutenant from his brother, John Stewart, earl of Carrick, who had in turn shoved aside his ailing father, King Robert II, in a coup in Council in 1384. Note the timing of the events described.

And so the kingdom of Scotland was at peace and great tranquillity had been established, when King Robert II the peacemaker, the son of peace, was struck by sudden illness, and ended his life at his castle of Dundonald. He was buried in royal fashion at Scone. He died on 19 April 1390 . . . in that same year Sir Alexander Stewart, earl of Buchan and a son of the said king, burned the cathedral of Moray at Elgin [17 June], which was then an ornament to the whole country . . . [when] the body of the most highly regarded King Robert II had been placed in its tomb and the kingdom had been entrusted to the guardianship of his son (that is Robert his second son), John earl of Carrick, the first born son of the dead king was crowned at Scone in the royal manner on the eve of the Assumption of Our Lady [14 August] following, 1390 (which was a Sunday). He was thereafter with the consent of the estates known as King Robert III . . .

SOURCE: Watt, DER *et al* (ed) 1987–99 *Scotichronicon – Walter Bower*. Aberdeen, vii, 445–7; viii, 3.

Appointment of David, Duke of Rothesay, as Lieutenant, 1399

This is an act of Council at Edinburgh (i.e. not a full parliament, which only a king could call) recorded in middle Scots on 27 January 1399. As Steven Boardman has shown, however, the real decision behind this change of office was probably taken at a meeting at Falkland Castle in Fife in November 1398 involving key magnates such as the dukes of Rothesay and Albany (who was earl of Fife), the earls of Douglas and Crawford, the queen and the bishop of St Andrews. This was the fourth appointment of a King's Lieutenant to be made during the reigns of the first two Stewart kings, Robert II and Robert III, following the appointments of 1384, 1388 and 1390: these appointments had been justified by the claim that the king (or, as in 1388, his heir) was infirm and unable to exercise office. It was of course Albany, acting in concert with the fourth earl of Douglas to protect their magnatial interests, who would be responsible for Rothesay's death in prison at Falkland in 1401–02.

Qwhar it is deliveryt that the mysgovernance of the Realme and the defaut of the kepying of the common law sulde be imput to the kynge and his officers. And therefore gife [if] it lykeis oure lorde the kynge til excuse his defuates he may at his lyking gerr [cause] calle his officers to the quhilkis [which] he hes giffen commission and accuse thai in presence of his consail. And thair answer herde, the consail sal be redy to juge thair defautes, syn na man aw [ought] to be codnampynt qwhil [until] he be callit and accusit.

Item sen it is welesene and kennyt that oure lorde the kynge for sekness of his person may nocht travail to governe the Realme na restreygne trespassours and rebellours, It is sene to the consaill maste expedient that the duc of Rothesay be the kyngis lieutenande generally throch all the kynrike for the terme of thre yher hafande fwl powers and commission of the kyng to governe the lande in al thyng as the kynge suld do in his persone gife he warr present that is to say to punnys trespassours till restreygne trespassours and to trete and remitte with the condicions efter folowande that is to say that he be oblygit be his lettres and sworne til governe his person and the office til hym committit with the consail general. And in thai with the consail of wyse men and lele [*twenty-one councillors named*]. The quhilke consail generale and special sal be obligit be thair lettres and sworne til gife hym lele consail for the common profit nocht hafande ee [eye] to fede [feud] na frendschyp. Ande in efter the Duc be sworne to fulfil efter his powers all thingis that the kyng in his crowning wes sworne for til do to holy kyrke and the pepyl . . . That is to say the fredume and the rycht of the kirke to kepe undamyste, the lawys and the lovable custumes to gerr be kepit to the peil, manslayers reifers and all mysdoers thruch strynthe til restreygnhe and punisye . . . And at the kynge be obliste that he sal nocht lette his office na the execucion of it be na contremandmentit as sumqwile has been seen.

SOURCE: 1814–75 *Acts of the Parliaments of Scotland*. Edinburgh, i, 572.

The Murder of James I, 20–21 February 1437

One of the earliest recorded accounts of the death of James I came from an English scribe, John Shirley, who may have copied some of his account from a contemporary news-sheet approved by James I's widow, Joan Beaufort. Shirley details the leading role of Sir Robert Graham and his confederates in the murder, some months after Graham had failed in an attempt to arrest James I in a parliament in October 1436 (following the failed siege of Roxburgh Castle). Recent scholarship has shown that as well as being motivated to revenge himself upon James as the destroyer in 1425 of Graham's former patrons – the Albany Stewarts – Graham was also motivated by Walter Stewart, earl of Atholl, with whose lands James was interfering. This contemporary evidence is also largely confirmed by Bower's account which firmly blamed the earl of Atholl and Graham for the king's violent end.

Perth Blackfriars: . . . Therewithal that odious and false traitor Sir Robert Graham, seeing the King laboured so sore with those two false traitors which he had cast under his feet, and that he waxed faint and was weary, and that he was weaponless, the more pity was, descended down also unto the King, with an horrible and mortal weapon in his hand. And then the King cried him mercy. 'Thou cruel tyrant,' quoth Graham to him. 'Thou hadst never mercy of lords born of thy blood, nor of none other gentlemen that came in thy danger, therefore no mercy shalt thou have here.' . . . and therewithal he smote him through the body, and therewithal the good King fell down.

SOURCE: Thompson, T 1893 *A History of the Scottish People*. London.

DOCUMENT 19

Oaths Taken in Parliament, 1445

This is an act of parliament at Perth recording, in middle Scots, oaths given in the course of a ceremony on 14 June 1445. The same parliament, dominated by William, eighth earl of Douglas, and his associates, had had the 'majority' or official adulthood of James II declared (he was fifteen but his official majority should not have begun until he was twenty-five). This came as the dust settled on an intermittent civil war, fought especially hard between 1443 and 1445, which had seen the Douglases and Crichtons and their allies struggle for control of the crown following the murder of James I in 1437: this conflict had seen a number of sieges, attacks on the lands of the diocese of St Andrews and the death of the king's mother. It also followed a period of notable patronage, distributed in the young king's name, with the earl of Douglas's brothers also receiving earldoms (Moray and Ormond) and a number of other nobles being 'promoted' to be Lords of Parliament.

A) FORM OF THE OATH OF THE KING TO HIS THREE ESTATES

I sal be lele and trew to God and Haly Kirk, and to the thre Estaitis of my realm. And ilk estate kepe, defende and governe in thair awn fredome and privilege at my gudly power, efter the lawis and custumis of the realm. The law, custume and statutes of the realm neythir to eik [add to], nor to mynis [diminish] without the consent of the Thre Estaitis. And nathing to wirk, na use tuiching the commoun profit of the realm, but [without] consent of the Three Estaitis. The law and statuts, maid be my forebearis, keip and use in all puncts, at all my power, till all my leigis in all things, sa that thai repung [turn] nocht agane the faith. Sa help me God.

B) OATH OF THE BARONS

I . . . becum your man as my king, in landis lif, licht and lym, and wardis honour fewtie and lawtie aganis all that leif and dee may; your consale celand [keeping] that ye schaw to me. The best consale gevand, geif ye charge me. Your scaith nor dishonour to heir, no se, bot I sall lat it, at al my gudlie power, and warn yow thereof. Sa help me God.

SOURCE: British Library MS Harley 4700, cited in Pinkerton, J 1797 *The History of Scotland*. London, i, 476–7.

The Auchinleck Chronicle

*This anonymous chronicle, written in middle Scots, is crucially our only contem-
porary Scottish source for many of the turbulent events of the 1440s and 1450s –
from the 'Black Dinner' through to James II's murderous clashes with the Black
Douglases. It is now preserved in incomplete and disordered form in the* Asloan
Manuscript, *part of the collection of Alexander Boswell of Auchinleck.*

(1452) The samyn yere thar was ane parliament haldin in Edinburgh the xii day of
junii be king James the secund and thair was forfaltit [forfeited] alexander lyndesaye
the erll of craufurd . . . bath land lyf and gudis And in that samyn parliament thar
was put on the parliament hous dure ane letter under sir James of Douglas sele . . .
declynand fra the kyng sayand that thai held nocht of him nor wald nocht hald with
hym . . . calland tham tratouris that war his secret counsall and than this parliament
continewit for xv dayis and chargit all maner of man till be at Edinburgh baith on fut
and hors . . . under the pane of ded and tinsall [loss] of thair landis . . .

   Item thair was syndry landis gevin to syndry men in this parliament be the kingis
secret counsall . . . the quilk [which] men demyt [deemed] wald nocht stand.

SOURCE: McGladdery, C 1992 *James II*. Edinburgh, appendix 2.

The Western *Gàidhealtachd* in the Middle Ages

DOCUMENT 21

John of Fordun's Description of the Highlands and Islands

Fordun, probably an Aberdeenshire cleric, assembled his Latin chronicle history of the kingdom from its origins to his present between the 1360s and 1380s, drawing on and embellishing earlier histories, annals and king-lists. This (in)famous description of the differences between the Lowlands and the Highlands is to be found in Fordun's early sections describing Scotland. However, it is surely much influenced also by Fordun's personal knowledge, and perhaps experience, of violence inflicted by 'caterans' – Gaelic militarised forces – in northern and north-eastern Scotland after 1371 (violence which was complained about repeatedly in parliament at that time).

A) CHAPTER VII: SCOTIA: ITS NATURE AND EXTENT, NOW AND FORMERLY

Scotia is so named after the Scottish tribes by which it is inhabited. At first, it began from the Scottish firth on the south, and, later on, from the river Humber, where Albania also began. Afterwards, however, it commenced at the wall Thirlwal, which Severus had built to the river Tyne. But now it begins at the river Tweed, the northern boundary of England, and, stretching rather less than four hundred miles in length, in a north-westerly direction, is bounded by the Pentland Firth, where a fearfully dangerous whirlpool sucks in and belches back the waters every hour. It is a country strong by nature, and difficult and toilsome of access. In some parts, it towers into mountains; in others, it sinks down into plains. For lofty mountains stretch through the midst of it, from end to end, as do the tall Alps through Europe; and these mountains formerly separated the Scots from the Picts, and their kingdoms from each other. Impassable as they are on horseback, save in very few places, they can hardly be crossed even on foot, both on account of the snow always lying on them, except in summertime only; and by reason of the boulders torn off the beetling crags, and the deep hollows in their midst. Along the foot of these mountains are vast woods, full of stags, roe-deer, and other wild animals and beasts of various kinds; and these forests oftentimes afford a strong and safe protection to the cattle of the inhabitants against the depredations of their enemies; for the herds in those parts, they say, are accustomed, from use, whenever they hear the shouts of men or women, and if suddenly attacked by dogs, to flock hastily into the woods.

Numberless springs also well up, and burst forth down the hills and the sloping ridges of the mountains, and, trickling down with sweetest sound, in crystal rivulets between flowery banks, flow together through the level vales, and give birth to many streams; and these again to large rivers, in which Scotia marvellously abounds, beyond any other country; and at their mouths, where they rejoin the sea, she has noble and secure harbours.

B) CHAPTER VIII: LOWLANDS AND HIGHLANDS OF SCOTIA, AND WHAT IS CONTAINED IN THEM

Scotia, also, has tracts of land bordering on the sea, pretty level and rich, with green meadows, and fertile and productive fields of corn and barley, and well adapted for growing beans, pease, and all other produce; destitute, however, of wine and oil, though by no means so of honey and wax. But in the upland districts, and along the highlands, the fields are less productive, except only in oats and barley. The country is, there, very hideous, interspersed with moors and marshy fields, muddy and dirty; it is, however, full of pasturage grass for cattle, and comely with verdure in the glens, along the watercourses. This region abounds in wool-bearing sheep, and in horses; and its soil is grassy, feeds cattle and wild beasts, is rich in milk and wool, and manifold in its wealth of fish, in sea, river, and lake. It is also noted for birds of many sorts. There noble falcons of soaring flight and boundless courage, are to be found, and hawks of matchless daring. Marble of two or three colours, that is, black, variegated, and white, as well as alabaster, is also found there. It also produces a great deal of iron and lead, and nearly all metals. The land of the Scots, says *Erodotus*, in the fertility of its soil, in its pleasant groves, in the rivers and springs by which it is watered, in the number of its flocks of all kinds, and its horses, where its shore rejoices in inhabitants, is not inferior to the soil of even Britain itself. *Isidore* tells us:- Scotia, with respect to the wholesomeness of its air and climate, is a very mild country; there is little or no excessive heat in summer, or cold in winter; – and he has written of Scotia in nearly the same terms as of Hibernia. In Scotland, the longest days, at midsummer, are of eighteen hours, or more; and, in midwinter, the shortest are not of fully six; while in the island of Meroë, the capital of the Ethiopians, the longest day is of twelve hours; in Alexandria, in Egypt, of thirteen; and in Italy, of fifteen. In the island of Thule, again, the day lasts all through the six summer months, and the night, likewise, all through the six winter months.

C) THE NATIONS OF SCOTIA, AND THEIR LANGUAGES, DISTINCT – THEIR DIFFERENT MANNERS AND CUSTOMS

The manners and customs of the Scots vary with the diversity of their speech. For two languages are spoken amongst them, the Scottish and the Teutonic; the latter of which is the language of those who occupy the seaboard and plains, while the race of Scottish speech inhabits the highlands and outlying islands. The people of the coast are of domestic and civilized habits, trusty, patient, and urbane, decent in their attire, affable, and peaceful, devout in Divine worship, yet always prone to resist a wrong at the hand of their enemies. The highlanders and people of the islands, on the other hand, are a savage and untamed nation, rude and independent, given to rapine, ease-loving, of a docile and warm disposition, comely in person, but unsightly in dress, hostile to the English people and language, and, owing to diversity of speech, even to their own nation, and exceedingly cruel. They are, however, faithful and obedient to their king and country, and easily made to submit to law, if properly governed. *Solinus*, the historian, in describing the manners and customs of the Scottish nation of the olden time, says:- In its social observances, the Scottish nation was always rugged and warlike. For, when males were born to them, the fathers were wont to offer them their first food on the point of a sword, so that they should desire to die not otherwise than under arms, in battle for liberty; and when, afterwards, they are grown up, and able to fight, the victors, after drinking the blood of the slain, besmear their faces with it. For they are a high-spirited race, of sparing diet, of a fierce mettle, of a wild and stern countenance, rugged in address, but affable and kind to their own people, given to sports and hunting, and to ease rather than toil. The Scottish nation, writes *Isidore*, is that, originally, which was once in Ireland, and resembles the Irish in all things – in language, manners, and character. For the Scots are a light-minded nation, fierce in spirit, savage towards their foes, who would almost as soon die as be enslaved, and account it sloth to die in bed, deeming it glorious and manly to slay, or be slain by, the foe in the field; a nation of sparing diet, sustaining hunger very long and rarely indulging in food before sunset; contenting themselves, moreover, with meat, and food prepared from milk. And though they are, by nature, a people of, generally, rather graceful figure, and goodly face, yet their peculiar dress much disfigures them.

SOURCE: Skene, FJH and Skene, WF (ed and trans) 1872 *John of Fordun's Chronicle of the Scottish Nation*. Edinburgh, iv, 36–8.

Annals of Somerled

These annals come from various anonymous contemporary Latin and Gaelic chronicles from the Scottish Lowlands and Borders and, significantly, Ireland.

A) CHRONICLE OF HOLYROOD, 1153

On that day, in Scotland, Somerled and his nephews, the sons of Malcolm [Macheth], having allied themselves with very many men, rebelled against king Malcolm; and perturbed and disquieted Scotland in great part.

B) CHRONICLE OF MAN, c.*1156*

In the year 1156, a naval battle was fought between Godfrey and Somerled on the night of the Lord's Epiphany; and great slaughter took place, of men on either side. And when day dawned they made peace; and they divided the kingdom of the islands between them, and the kingdom became bipartite from that day to the present time. And this was the cause of the downfall of the kingdom of the islands, from the time when the sons of Somerled took possession of it.

C) CHRONICLE OF MAN, 1158

In the year 1158, Somerled came to Man with fifty-three ships, and fought a battle with Godfrey, and routed him; and wasted the whole island, and went away. And Godfrey sailed over to Norway, to seek help against Somerled.

D) CHRONICLE OF MELROSE, 1159

Somerled, Gilla-Adamnain's son, and [Somerled's] son, were killed. And along with him, slaughter [was made] of the men of Argyll and of Kintyre, and of the men of the Hebrides, and the Foreigners of Dublin.

E) TIGERNACH'S CONTINUATOR, 1164

Somerled, Gillabrigte's son, king of the Hebrides and of Kintyre, and his son Gillabrigte, were slain by the men of Scotland; and a slaughter was made of the Foreigners of Dublin along with them.

F) CHRONICLE OF MELROSE, 1164

Somerled, the regulus of Argyll, wickedly rebelling for now twelve years against Malcolm, the king of the Scots, his natural lord, after he had landed at Renfrew, bringing a large army from Ireland and various places, was at last through divine vengeance slain there, along with his son, and innumerable people, by a few of his fellow-provincials.

G) CARMEN DE MORTE SUMERLEDI, 1164

How by very few was slain Somerled Sitebi, the king, with his immense army.

When by death's law King David had been enclosed in his coffin, the treachery of hostile Scots became at once apparent. Hebrideans (?) and Argyllsmen, supported by a force of Scots, raged, and slew the righteous, with cruel hand. The righteous hastened, and appeased the fury of the wicked men, who were raging and destroying cities and churches.

Peace was broken, violence renewed. The strong drove out the weak. The enemy slew and injured with fire and sword their miserable victims. Gardens, fields, ploughed lands, were ravaged and laid waste; barbarous hands mastered and menaced the meek.

The people of Glasgow, wounded, fled from the sword-strokes. But when the clergy dispersed, Mark remained alone, grumbling, within the hard walls of the church; and enduring hard mischance. There he wept and lamented the days of former prosperity. But, though not far away, the modest and upright Bishop Herbert was suffering and grieving along with him. [Herbert] implored Kentigern to pray to the King above, for [the attainment of] his captives' hopes; and he cursed the enemy.

While he was praying, and yearning for an answer to his prayers; and while his supplications were without result, as they were without cessation, he began to disparage in words the Scottish saints, and piously to rebuke the blessed Kentigern. After these insults had been stilled, and almost forgotten, Kentigern did not forget the bishop's cry. After a long time, he recalled the bishop, to take vengeance, and wipe out the disgrace of the Scottish saints. Immediately he took the bishop (an old man, venerable and estimable) who forsook his righteous bed, and like a youth, strenuously and willingly, travelled with his attendants, by night and by day, as quickly as was possible. But while he went, without knowing why he was so eager to go, [he did so] because, with Elias, he was inspired from heaven. This was proved by one who asked him quickly to return, to deliver and save himself from the hand of the hostile Somerled, foul with treachery, the most cruel enemy, who was conspiring and striving against the Lord's servants: and who suddenly landed with an immense company of satellites, and threatened to destroy the whole kingdom. When he heard this on his way, [Herbert] groaned in spirit, and said: 'Who urges me now to go, or to return?'

And he called upon Solomon, a warlike young knight; and Elias, who often helped him upon the way.

'Let us hasten, let us assist the desolate of our country; and let us pray, and check their misery. The teacher and ruler ought to fight for his country. Let us hurry and fight; the victory is ours; because God, who is ever with me, defends his flock and his people in battle, though not with spear or sword.'

The defenders, having heard of the bishop's arrival, became very bold, like dragons or lions: although Somerled and a thousand enemies were ready for battle against a hundred of the innocent, yet [the latter] advanced and made an attack upon the ranks of the treacherous men of Argyll, those ill-starred soldiers.

Hear a marvel! To the terrible, the battle was terrible. Heather and furze-bushes, moving their heads; burnt thyme, and branches; brambles and ferns, caused panic, appearing to the enemy as soldiers. Never in this life had such miracles been heard. Shadows of thyme and ordure were bulwarks of defence.

And in the first cleft of battle the baleful leader fell. Wounded by a [thrown] spear, slain by the sword, Somerled died.

And the raging wave swallowed his son, and the wounded of many thousand fugitives: because when this fierce leader was struck down, the wicked took to flight; and very many were slaughtered, both on sea and on land. When they wished to enter their ships among the blood-tinged waves, they were drowned in troops, alternately, in the water. Rout and slaughter were made of thousands of the traitors; while none of their assailants was wounded or killed.

Thus the enemies' ranks were deluded and repelled; and the whole kingdom with loud voices praised Kentigern.

A priest cut off the head of the unfortunate leader Somerled, and gave it into the bishop's hands. As his custom was, he went piously on seeing the head of his enemy; saying, 'The Scottish saints are truly to be praised.' And he attributed the victory to the blessed Kentigern; whose memory keep ye always, and befittingly.

This, which he saw and heard, William has composed; and he has dedicated it to Kentigern's honour and glory.

SOURCE: Lawrie, AC (ed) 1910 *Annals of the Reigns of Malcolm and William, Kings of Scotland AD 1153–1214*. Glasgow.

The Moray Chronicler, c.1398

This anonymous northern chronicle, recorded in the Registrum *of the diocese of Moray based at Elgin Cathedral, surely reflected upon a decade in which lawlessness in the north seemed to be a running theme, from the burning of the cathedral at Elgin by Alexander Stewart, the 'Wolf of Badenoch', in the uncertain weeks after the death of Robert II in 1390, to the campaigns of the earls of Carrick and Fife in the north to deal with the caterans of the Wolf and his sons c.1397–98.*

In those days there was no law in Scotland, but he who was stronger oppressed him who was weaker and the whole realm was a den of thieves; murders, herschips and fire-raising and all other misdeeds remained unpunished; and justice, as if outlawed, lay in exile outwith the bounds of the realm.

SOURCE: Innes, C (ed) 1837 *Registrum Episcopatus Moraviensis*. Edinburgh, Bannatyne Club.

The Battle of Harlaw, 1411

This extract comes from the Extracta e variis cronicis Scocie, *a late-fifteenth-century Latin chronicle which was a continuation of Abbot Walter Bower's* Scotichronicon *of the 1440s. Bower, the abbot of the Augustinian island abbey of Inchcolm in the Forth, had worked for the governments of the duke of Albany and James I, both of whom had sought to assert their authority over perceived Highland lawlessness in the north; by the late fifteenth century, however, the author of the* Extracta *could also have called upon his knowledge of the attempts of James III and James IV to forfeit and break the MacDonald Lords of the Isles who, as earls of Ross from the early fifteenth century, had threatened royal authority in the north-east. The origins of the rise of the MacDonalds of Islay as Lords of the Isles lay in the power vacuum created in the west by the Wars of Independence and the MacDonalds' subsequent push of their lordship into north-western mainland Scotland, in particular through Lochaber and the Great Glen and the earldom of Ross and lordship of Urquhart, challenging royal authority there after the decline of the fortunes of the Wolf of Badenoch. Harlaw was just twenty miles or so west of Aberdeen and the earl of Mar (who commanded the royal forces) was the illegitimate son of the Wolf.*

The battle of Harlaw took place in Mar, on the vigil of St James the Apostle [24 July] in the year of the Lord 1411, because Donald of the Isles, with ten thousand islesmen and his men of Ross, made a warlike invasion, ravaging all the land and intending to sack the town of Aberdeen and subject the whole country as far as the Tay to his dominion. He was manfully resisted by Alexander Stewart, earl of Mar, with Sir Alexander Ogilvy, sheriff of Angus . . . and with all the men he could raise from Mar, Garioch, Angus, Mearns and Buchan . . . Donald himself was put to flight . . . On the other side [Mar's] were slain . . . the warlike Robert David[son], provost of Aberdeen, with many of his fellow burgesses.

SOURCE: Dickinson, WC 1952 *A Source Book of Scottish History*. London, i, 170–1.

Acts of Justice in the North and West, 1504

These acts of parliament were passed thirty years after James III had forfeited the MacDonalds of the earldom of Ross in 1476 and a decade after James IV had forfeited the MacDonalds' Lordship of the Isles in 1493 and then attempted to assert royal authority in the north and north-west through galley expeditions to the region. After 1500, however, James IV left the enforcement of the law in this quarter of his realm to local lords like the Campbell earls of Argyll and the Gordon earls of Huntly – these houses were granted so-called 'lieutenancies of fire and sword'; but here James's government also sought to establish sheriffdoms first considered in the reign of John Balliol (1292–6).

Item because thair hes bene greit abusione of justice in the north partis and west partis of the realme sic as the northt Ilis and south Ilis for lak and falt of justice airis justicis and schreffis and tharthrou the pepill ar almaist gane wilde, it is tharfor statute and ordanit for the acquietting of the pepill be justice that thair be in tyme tocum justicis and schreffis depute in thai partis as eftir followis; that is to say that the justicis and schreffis of the northt Ilis haif thair sait and place for administratioun of justice in Invernes or Dingwale as the materis occuris to be decernyt be the saidis officiaris, and that ane uther justice and schreff be maid and deput for the south Ilis and thai partis, and to hif his place and sait for administratioun of justice in the Tarbart or at Lochkinkerane at the will and plesour of the saidis officiaris as the materis occuris.

SOURCE: 1814–75 *Acts of the Parliaments of Scotland.* Edinburgh, ii, 249.

The Medieval Church

DOCUMENT 26

A Miracle of St Margaret

This extract comes from The Life of St Margaret *by Turgot, prior of Durham (d. c.1114) and Queen Margaret of Scotland's confessor. Although Turgot – writing his work for Matilda, wife of King Henry I of England and Margaret's daughter – greatly praised Margaret for reforms of the church that he claims she oversaw in Scotland after c.1070 (including her foundation of a Benedictine monastery at Dunfermline), he recorded only one miracle associated with the queen. In the end it was left to Dunfermline clerics of the thirteenth century to record over forty miracles of Margaret which were then used c.1249–50 to secure her canonisation in 1251.*

She had had a book of gospels, adorned with jewels and gold; and in it the figures of the four evangelists were decorated with painting, interspersed with gold; and also every capital letter glowed all in gold. This volume she had always cherished very dearly, beyond the others in which she had been accustomed to read and study. This volume she was carrying [that is, a servant was carrying], when she chanced to be crossing a ford; and the book, being not carefully enough wrapped up in cloths, fell into the middle of the water. The carrier, not knowing this, concluded unconcernedly the journey that he had begun: and he first learned what he had lost, when he wished afterwards to produce the book. It was long sought without being found. At last it was found lying open in the bottom of the river, its leaves being constantly kept in motion by the current of the water; and the little sheets of silk that had covered the golden letters to prevent their being dimmed by contact with the leaves, had been torn out by the rapidity of the river. Who would have thought the book worth anything any longer? Who would have believed that even one letter in it would have remained visible? But indeed it was drawn out from the middle of the river entire, undecayed, unhurt, so that it appeared not to have been touched by the water at all. The whiteness of the leaves, and the unimpaired beauty of the letters throughout, remained as they had been before it had fallen into the river; except that in parts of the last leaves some mark of moisture could just be seen. The book was brought back and the miracle related to the queen; and she returned thanks to Christ, and cherished the volume much more dearly than before.

SOURCE: Anderson, AO 1922 *Early Sources of Scottish History*. Edinburgh, ii, 80–1.

Thirteenth-century Statutes of the Scottish Church

These acts were drawn up by various general councils of the Scottish church headed by the bishops of Scotland. Scotland (which had twelve bishoprics in all, although Galloway/Whithorn was loyal to England and the archbishopric of York until c.1350) had been made a 'special daughter' of the papacy in 1189 and then, in 1225, had also been given the right to hold inter-diocesan meetings without at the same time having a supervisory archbishop (although the Scottish church and crown had tried and failed throughout the eleventh and twelfth centuries to secure an archbishopric – or 'metropolitan' status – for St Andrews).

A) PAPAL BULL DIRECTING THE SCOTTISH CHURCH TO HOLD PROVINCIAL COUNCILS

Honorius, bishop, servant of the servants of God, to his venerable brethren all the bishops of the kingdom of Scotland, greeting and apostolic benediction. Certain of you lately made known to our ears that since you had not an archbishop by whose authority you might be able to celebrate a provincial council, it happens in the kingdom of Scotland, because it is so remote from the Apostolic See, that the statutes of the General Council are disregarded and very many irregularities are committed and remain unpunished. Now, since provincial councils ought not to be omitted, in which care should be had, in the fear of God, to correct excesses and to reform morals, and in which the canonical rules should be read over and recorded – especially those which were laid down in the same general council – we command you, by apostolic writing, that, since you are known not to have a metropolitan, you celebrate a provincial council by our authority. Dated at Tivoli, on the fourteenth before the Kalends of June. In the ninth year of our pontificate.

B) THIRTEENTH-CENTURY STATUTE OF A PROVINCIAL COUNCIL

We, the prelates of the Scottish church . . . ordain that every year all bishops and abbots and priors of priories shall religiously assemble . . . for the holding of a council on a certain day to be duly intimated to them by the conservator of the council; so that they may be able to remain at the same council for three days, if need be.

And we ordain firstly that every year the duty of preaching be laid on one of the bishops one after the other, [to be performed] at the next council by himself or by another to be proposed [by him], beginning with the bishop of Saint Andrews; and that by choice of the others one of the bishops be appointed conservator of the statutes of the council . . .

SOURCE: Dickinson, WC 1952 *A Source Book of Scottish History*. London, i, 73–5.

The Translation of St Margaret, 1251

In 1251, after a campaign for papal canonisation, the remains of Queen Margaret were translated to a new tomb at the Benedictine Abbey of Dunfermline: another Scottish source asserts that when the participants tried to move Margaret's body beyond that of her husband, Malcolm III, at the high altar, they were (miraculously) unable to, and could only lay them together. It is important to compare this act of Scottish royal devotion with what was happening in England at this time where Henry III had invested much time and money in elevating the cult of his predecessor king, St Edmund the Confessor, at Westminster Abbey.

. . . in the second year of King Alexander III, on the 19th of June 12[51], this king, and the queen his mother, with bishops and abbots, earls and barons, and other good men, both clerics and laymen, in great numbers, met at Dunfermline, and took up, in great state, the bones of the blessed Margaret, sometime queen of Scots, out of the stone monument where they had lain through a long course of years; and these they laid, with the deepest devoutness, in a shrine of deal, set with gold and precious stones.

SOURCE: Skene, FJH and Skene, WF (ed and trans) 1872 *John of Fordun's Chronicle of the Scots Nation.* Edinburgh, ii, 290–1.

A Miracle at Canterbury, 1445

Although most ordinary and elite Scots would have worshipped and sought divine intercession at local shrines, altars and churches, many also sought the help of God and the saints further afield, with pilgrimage to important shrines in England (Canterbury and Walsingham), France (St John's tomb at Amiens) and the Holy Land remaining popular throughout the later middle ages. This report of a miracle for such a Scottish pilgrim comes from an official contemporary ecclesiastical source.

. . . Alexander Stephenson, born at Aberdeen in Scotland, twenty-four years old, suffered severely from contracted feet, with vile worms lurking in them . . . after making a vow at a place of pilgrimage of the Virgin called Seton [East Lothian], he made his way to the shrine of the holy martyr Thomas and there, in full view of men, the glorious athlete of God, first wringing horrible shrieks from him, restored his feet to him on the second day of May last . . . We have received fullest proof of this event, since the said Alexander then went with the grace of God on pilgrimage to the Holy Blood at Wilsnack, in fulfilment of his vow, and then returned to the shrine of the holy martyr Thomas . . . we had previously, under the guidance of the divine clemency, taken the oaths of the aforesaid Alexander, of Alexander Art gentleman, of Robert Davidson, and John Thomason, of the aforementioned town in Scotland . . .

SOURCE: Sheppard, JB (ed) 1887–9 *Litterae Cantuariensis*. London, iii, 191–2.

Erection of the Archbishopric of St Andrews, 1472

This is a Papal 'Bull', issued at Rome on 13 August 1472, finally raising St Andrews to an archbishopric. This was secured by Patrick Graham who had acted outwith the orders of King James III: on returning home, Graham incurred the king's wrath and was hounded out of office to be replaced by royal favourite, William Scheves, while a number of the other bishops of Scotland – including Glasgow – sought and secured papal exemptions over the diocese from St Andrews' authority.

Sixtus . . . Since in the famed realm of Scotland, in which a large number of notable cathedral churches are known, there is said to be no metropolitan church, and for that reason for every case which the inhabitants of that realm wish to plead against their ordinaries at the time, and for the appeals which they, oppressed in their courts, put forward, they must, not without very grave perils, inconveniences and expenses, have recourse to the Roman *curia* or abandon their rights untried, and it sometimes happens that these cases are drawn to a forbidden court and dealt with there, and the same ordinaries because of the lack of a Metropolitan and the distance of the Roman *curia* have a more free opportunity for overburdening and overstepping their power with impunity, thinking it is easier to do illicit things, and excesses and crimes which are wont to be punished by the metropolitans in their provinces in the aforesaid kingdom often remain unpunished: and since the venerable church of St Andrew of the said kingdom is distinguished and famous among the other churches of the kingdom, for a celebrated city and ample diocese in which our dearest son in Christ, James, king of Scotland, and his predecessors, kings of Scotland for the time, were wont frequently to make residence with their court, and surrounded by a well-watered plain, adorned by the pleasantness of clergy and people and worthy to be of a deserved metropolitan prelacy:

We . . . erect the aforesaid church and episcopal seat of St Andrews into a metropolitan and the archiepiscopal seat of the whole realm aforesaid, and we honour it in like manner and adorn it by the gift of special grace by the title of metropolitan dignity and archiepiscopal honour, and we assign to it Glasgow, Dunkeld, Aberdeen, Moray, Brechin, Dunblane, Ross, Caithness, Whithorn, Lismore, Sodor or the Isles and Orkney, the churches of the said realm, with their cities, dioceses, rights and all pertinents, and the whole aforesaid realm for its archiepiscopal province, and the prelates of the same churches for its suffragans and all the clergy of the cities and dioceses aforesaid for its provincials and we subject them to it in respect of archiepiscopal rights . . . so that the archbishop of St Andrews shall claim for himself metropolitan and archiepiscopal right in the said kingdom and in each of the aforesaid cities and dioceses, and that the bishops of Glasgow, Dunkeld, Aberdeen, Moray, Brechin, Dunblane, Ross, Caithness, Whithorn, Lismore, Sodor or the Isles and Orkney shall be obliged to him in all and sundry as their metropolitan and archbishop and shall be bound in those things in which suffragans are held to their archbishop and shall be bound according to canonical sanctions:

And we decree that to our venerable brother Patrick, bishop of St Andrews, and to his successors, bishops of St Andrews for the time, shall be assigned the pall and cross in token of the plenitude of pontifical office and the archiepiscopal dignity, and the church of St Andrew as a metropolitan; and that the said present bishop and those who will be in their time bishops of St Andrews ought to be esteemed and in all future times called and named archbishops of St Andrews, ought to wear the archiepiscopal and metropolitan insignia, and be able to do, conduct, exercise, pursue and administer the rights, jurisdictions and all and sundry things which metropolitans can of right do and exercise in their cities, dioceses and provinces . . .

We ordain that the archbishop and church of St Andrews aforesaid and also the beloved sons the chapter of the same church of St Andrew shall hold and enjoy all and sundry privileges, exemptions, immunities, apostolic graces and indults and any other things which archbishops, metropolitan churches and their chapters can in any way use and enjoy from custom or of right; and that the aforesaid suffragans, their clergy and people altogether shall show reverence and honour to their said arch-bishop and metropolitan . . .

Given at Rome at St Peter's 13 August 1472, in the first year of our pontificate.

SOURCE: Dickinson, WC 1952 *A Source Book of Scottish History*. London, i, 92–4.

Scotland and Europe

Jurisdictional Disputes at Sea, 1246 and 1275

Tensions over ships and their cargo were often high between England and Scotland in the later middle ages, both before and after the Wars of Independence: these incidents were recorded in the Scottish Rolls *kept by the English administration.*

A) 1246

The King of Scotland has guaranteed by his envoys sent to the King of England, that he will satisfy the merchants of Bordeaux [by 29 September] for all debts that they can reasonably show due by his men of Perth . . . the bailiffs of Lynn . . . are commanded to deliver all the vessels and goods arrested on that account, to the said men of Perth.

B) 15 AUGUST 1275

Alexander III King of Scots to the King of England, informs him that he has learned that certain men of a baron of his, Alexander Macdougall of Argyll . . . touching . . . Bristol, were arrested there with their vessel and goods on suspicion of piracy . . . begs the King of England to cause the bailiffs of Bristol to permit the men freely to depart for Scotland with their goods.

SOURCE: Bain, J (ed) 1884 *Calendar of Documents Relating to Scotland.* Edinburgh, i, no. 1694; ii, no. 55.

Jean Froissart's Description of Scotland, *c*.1385

Froissart was a Hainault (now part of France) chronicler and poet of chivalry and romance in France, England, Spain, Scotland and elsewhere in Europe during the Hundred Years War between England and France and their respective allies, and was patronised by both the French and English kings. Froissart also visited Scotland in 1365, staying with David II, and later talked to Scottish knights visiting the Continent in the 1370s and 1380s. All this contact enabled him to include considerable Scottish material in the various manuscripts of his Chroniques *of the late fourteenth century, and to use Scotland as some of the setting of an epic poem,* Méliador.

Edinburgh, notwithstanding it is the residence of the king, and is the Paris of Scotland, is not such a town as Tournai or Valenciennes; for there are not in the whole town four thousand houses. Several of the French lords were therefore obliged to take up their lodgings in the neighbouring villages, and at Dunfermline, Kelso, Dunbar, Dalkeith and in other villages. News was soon spread through Scotland that a large body of men-at-arms from France were arrived in the country. Some began to murmur and say, 'What devil has brought them here? Or who has sent for them? Cannot we carry on our wars with England without their assistance? We shall never do any effectual good as long as they are with us. Let them be told to return again, for we are sufficiently numerous in Scotland to fight our own quarrels, and do not want their company. We neither understand their language nor they ours, and we cannot converse together. They will very soon eat up and destroy all we have in this country, and will do us more harm, if we allow them to remain amongst us, than the English could in battle. If the English do burn our houses, what consequence is it to us? We can rebuild them cheap enough, for we only require three days to do so, provided we have five or six poles and boughs to cover them.' Such was the conversation of the Scots on the arrival of the French: they did not esteem them, but hated them in their hearts, and abused them with their tongues as much as they could, like rude and worthless people as they are. I must, however, say that, considering all things, it was not right for so many of the nobility to have come at this season to Scotland: it would have been better to have sent twenty or thirty knights from France, than so large a body as five hundred or a thousand. The reason is clear. In Scotland you will never find a man of worth: they are like savages, who wish not to be acquainted with any one, and are too envious of the good fortune of others, and suspicious of losing anything themselves, for their country is very poor.

When the English make inroads thither, as they have very frequently done, they order their provisions, if they wish to live, to follow close at their backs; for nothing is to be had in that country without great difficulty. There is neither iron to shoe horses, nor leather to make harness, saddles, or bridles: all these things come ready made from Flanders by sea; and, should these fail, there is none to be had in the country. When these barons and knights of France, who had been used to handsome hotels, ornamented apartments, and castles with good soft beds to repose on, saw themselves in such poverty, they began to laugh, and to say before the admiral, 'What could have brought us hither? We have never known till now what was meant by poverty and hard living . . .'

SOURCE: Hume Brown, P (ed) 1891 *Early Travellers in Scotland*. Edinburgh, 10–11.

Bower's *Scotichronicon* – a Scot Killed on Crusade, 1391

Many Scottish knights participated in the Reisen *crusades to northern Europe (Prussia/north-western Germany-Poland-Lithuania, where the populace was still pagan) throughout the fourteenth century up to 1410 (and the defeat there of the Teutonic knights) and thus made a name for themselves in European chivalric circles. Here Bower describes the violent end of an illegitimate son of Archibald the Grim, third earl of Douglas. Many border knights – including the Douglases – ran up large travel and hotel bills attending these regular crusades.*

In that year [1391] the noble William de Douglas knight of Nithsdale was treacherously killed by Englishmen on the bridge at Danzig in Prussia. He had been chosen as admiral in charge of 240 ships to fight the pagans, and at that time had been advanced to the table of honour of the Master of Prussia by proclamation of the heralds as superior to all others. The [English] lord of Clifford envied his prowess, and hired some Englishmen at a price to expunge his memory from the earth. On this account, because as a result of animosity which had arisen between them on some occasion or other, Clifford challenged Sir William to a duel, and once the day for defending himself had been fixed, the said Sir William in the interval crossed over to France to arrange for more reliable arms for himself. When he heard this, Clifford thought that the said Sir William was stealing away as he did not dare appear at the agreed place at the time arranged for the fight, and for this reason Clifford wrongly slandered him. When Douglas found out about this, he sought and obtained a safe-conduct, and appeared at the place and time arranged. But Clifford was cloaked with excuses, and cravenly refused to appear on account of Douglas's immense strength. The said Sir William returned to Prussia, where he was surrounded by a crowd of Englishmen and treacherously killed. Because of his death that crusade was halted.

SOURCE: Watt, DER *et al* (ed) 1987–99 *Scotichronicon – Walter Bower*. Aberdeen, vii, 447–9.

The Marriage of Princess Margaret to the Dauphin, 1436

In 1428 James I contracted a marriage treaty with France for his eldest daughter to wed the Dauphin. However, it was not until 1436, once the girl was ten, and Scotland at war with England, that James finally committed to send her to France. Margaret was the first of James's six daughters, all of whom were used to contract marriage with continental allies of France.

In the year 1436 the King of Scots sent his first born daughter Margaret to France, with a notable company of lords, knights and counsellors, most worthily boden, in such seemly apparel and so honourably marshalled that never within living memory has so strong an army, so gloriously arrayed or so nobly led, been sent out of Scotland. As head of the company, to contract the marriage between the foresaid parties, were Lord John Crennach bishop of Brechin, and the lord earl of Orkney, Lord Sinclair, Admiral of Scotland, together with fifty more gentle knights and squires and their companies and also with a strong armed fleet to escort her safely, for fear of the English, to the King of France. And in the said fleet there were three thousand fencible men, well graithed. Now she was a maid of ten years, clad in most noble and costly raiment seemly in body and very lovely in face.

SOURCE: Skene, FJH (ed) 1877 *Liber Pluscardensis*. Edinburgh, i, 380–2.

Inventory of a Scottish Ship at Hull, 1466

This customs document is preserved in the National Archives (Kew) and was recorded by John Dey and Robert Percy, collectors of Hull. At the time of this inventory, England was riven by the Lancastrian v. Yorkist wars in which Scotland – during the minority of James III (1460–69) – had at first aided the exiled Lancastrians of Henry VI (and thus regained Berwick-upon-Tweed from 1461– 82) but then made a long truce with the Yorkists of Edward IV. By the later fifteenth century, Scottish wool and other exports had declined markedly from fourteenth-century levels.

Ship of Donkan Rowe called *Maryknyght* of Leith, arrived 29 November
The same Donkan, alien: 5 barrels salmon; 2 barrels salt; 100 [or 120] salted fish £4 13s 4d
Thomas Colthyrd, alien: 3 barrels salmon; 120 stockfish £2 10s 0d
John Neleson, alien: 6 barrels salmon £4 0s 0d
John Doughty, alien: 7 barrels salmon; 13 barrels [fish?] oil; 6 barrels white herrings; 3 barrels salt £14 0s 0d
John Trowlopp: 6 lasts 8 barrels salmon; 11 barrels white herring; 18 'salthyddes' £50 0s 0d
Nicholas Parcur: 12 barrels white herrings; 4 barrels salmon £8 0s 0d

Ship of Donkan Rowe called *Maryknyght* of Leith, departed last day of January
The same Donkan alien: 10 quarts malt £2 0s 0d
John Nelleson, alien: 40 quarts malt £8 0s 0d
John Doughty, alien: 9 barrels bitumen £1 16s 8d
The same John, alien: 2 woollen cloths without grain £2 0s 0d
John van Breeme, alien: 1 last bitumen, 10 quarts malt £4 8s 0d
John Trowlopp, alien [*sic*]: 100 quarts malt £20 0s 0d

SOURCE: Childs, W (ed) 1986 *The Customs Accounts of Hull, 1453–1490*. Leeds, Yorkshire Archaeological Society, 97–120.

Townlife and Trade

DOCUMENT 36

Leges Burgorum

The Leges Burgorum *(laws and customs of the royal burghs of Scotland) were laid down in Latin in the twlefth century by the successive regimes of David I, Malcolm IV and William I, and drew heavily on English borough practice.*

A) ON INHERITANCE

If a man or a woman that is burgess die in the burgh, whether they make a testament or not, of all the goods the heir shall have these necessary things pertaining to his house, i.e. the best table with the frame supporting it, a table cloth, a towel, a basin, a washing-vessel, the best bed with the sheets and all the rest of the cloths that pertain to it, and the best feather bed (or a wool bed if there be no feather bed), a brewing-vat and implements, a vat for fermenting wort, a barrel, a cauldron, a kettle, a gridiron, a porringer, a chimney, a pitcher, a crook. These things ought not to be left in legacy away from the house. Also whatever be built, set or sown shall remain with the ground. Also he shall have a chest, a shearing hook, a plough, a horse or ox-drawn wagon, a cart, a wagon, a brass pot, a pan, a roasting iron, a griddle, a mortar, a pestle, a drinking cup, a large wooden platter, a cup, 12 spoons, a seat, a bench, a stool, a balance and weights, a spade, an axe. And if the land be heritage all the said things are known to pertain to heritable right, nevertheless the burgess if he is in his power of health may sell all these things if he be constrained by necessity or poverty, and that shall be witnessed by the burgesses. And of all these said things and all others of household, the best pertains to the heir.

B) ON BREWING

What woman that will brew ale to sell shall brew all the year through after the custom of the town. And if she does not, she shall be suspended from her office for the space of a year and a day. And she shall make good and satisfactory ale as time asks. And if she makes evil ale and does against the custom of the town and be convicted of it, she shall give to her fine 8s and then suffer the law of the town, that is to say be put on the cuckstool, and two-thirds of the ale shall be given to the poor folk, and the third part sent to the brethren of the hospital. And the same such doom shall be done of mead as of ale. And each brewster shall put her alewand outside her house at her window or above her door that it might be visible commonly to all men, the which if she does not she shall pay for her fault 4d.

58

c) ON SELLING PROPERTY

Each man who is in the state of health in which he has full power to dispose of his goods, may sell or give the lands he has of conquest in the burgh to whomever he wish. But if, because of need, he must sell his heritage land he shall offer that land to the nearest heirs at three head courts. And if they wish to buy that land, they shall provide the person who needs to sell the land with meat and clothes such as are necessary. The clothing shall be of a grey or white hue. And if they will not do so, or have not the power to do so, it shall be lawful to him to sell the land as best he may. And if the heir be outwith the kingdom in the next kingdom, he ought to wait for him 40 days. And if the heir be in a further kingdom next to that kingdom he ought to wait for him twice 40 days, and so of other further kingdoms. And if the heir be absent for evil will or malice longer than the foresaid terms assigned to him, it shall be lawful to the man in necessity to dispose of his land where he may best have success.

SOURCE: 1868 *Ancient Laws and Customs of the Burghs of Scotland, 1124–1424.* Edinburgh, Scottish Burgh Records Society, i.

David II's General Charter of Burghal Rights, 28 March 1364

After his release from English captivity in 1357 David II had to pay a large ransom to Edward III (100,000 merks, or more than ten times annual royal income) and to do so required the support of his subjects through parliamentary grants of extra-ordinary taxation. This meant that the royal burghs became an increasingly important element in parliament – the 'third estate' – from then on, especially as the customs revenue was so dependent on a healthy return from the export of Scottish wool and hides, and Edinburgh now had to compete with English-occupied Berwick-upon-Tweed as a port for the export of produce from the valuable Scottish Border abbeys like Melrose.

David, by the grace of God king of Scots, to all upright men of his land, churchmen and laymen, greeting: know that we, with [consent of our] council, have granted to our beloved Scottish burgesses free leave to buy and sell everywhere within the liberties of their own burghs, but forbidding any of them to buy or sell within the bounds of the liberty of another burgh without license. Also we forbid any bishop, prior or other churchman, any earl, baron or other lay man, whatsoever may be his rank, to buy or sell wool, skins, hides or other merchandise under any pretext, save only from [or to] the merchants, effectively, and without guile, all such merchandise at the market-place and cross of the burgh, and to pay there the king's customs.

SOURCE: Marwick, JD (ed) 1866 *Records of the Convention of the Royal Burghs of Scotland*. Edinburgh, i, 538.

Acts of Parliament 1366 and 1370

With David II's need for ransom finance (see Document 37 above) came a greater need for control of customs and specie: the affairs of the burghs were all the more closely regulated by the three estates as a result.

A) 1366

In the council held at Perth on [14 January 1366], among other acts it was ordained that there shall be a tron for weighing the wool in royal burghs through all the ports of the kingdom, having been duly and fitly set up by the chamberlain. And there should be a tronar in each place who should take one penny on the part of the king from each sack. And there should also be a clerk at the tron, who, as it seems to the lords of council, shall conveniently be clerk of the king's cocket; for the custumars ought, as it seems to them, to have their clerk at their own expense; for whom (namely, both the custumars and the tronar) the same clerk of the cocket ought to be keeper of the counter-roll.

B) 1370

[Parliament, 10 February 1370] And because it has been perceived that the removal of money in this way, namely gold or silver, is intolerable, inasmuch as, unless it is prevented and altogether given up by everyone, it will not be possible to have the money for the payment of the ransom nor for the necessary expenses of the king and community, they deliver and from common deliberation require our lord king that he shall allow such persons contravening the statute, either in the past or the future, to be punished, and he should not remit, reduce or lighten in any way any custom of this kind for anyone; and that concerning this point indictment should be taken and accusation made by the justiciar concerning those who dwell within the realm. And they deliver that if anybody shall conceal money being exported, he shall incur the same penalty which by law a wool merchant or other person of merchandise ought to incur for having concealed custom, namely paying 20 shillings of the penny concealed, except that if any foreigner shall carry any money into the kingdom which he shall be able to prove he carried from another kingdom, he shall still freely enjoy and re-export that money without paying any custom.

SOURCE: 1814–75 *Acts of the Parliaments of Scotland*. Edinburgh, i, 497, 508–9.

A ruling of Edinburgh Burgh Court, 1475

This legal decision was recorded in the vernacular but has been translated into modern English. By the later fifteenth century most royal burghs had seen the development of craft guilds, organisations of individual crafts who sought to regulate their profession through rules of apprenticeships, property, pricing and collective identity and worship: these craft guilds increasingly vied with merchant guilds for control of burgh councils.

To all and sundry whom it concerns to whose knowledge these present letters shall come, the provost, bailies and council of Edinburgh greeting in God everlasting. To you universally we make it known that there appeared before us in our tolbooth, we sitting in judgment, the best and worthiest persons of the whole craft of the websters [weavers] within the said burgh, who presented to us their bill of supplication, in the which was contained certain statutes and articles made and advised with them for the honour and loving of God almighty, and of his mother the Virgin Mary, and of St Severan and for the supplying and upholding of divine service and outfitting of their altar of St Severan founded and upheld by them in St Giles' Kirk and for the governance of their works and labour and good rule both for worship of the realm, common profit and loyalty of the craftsmen and for other various and many causes of good motive; the which bill we have seen, heard, and ordered read, and therewith being well-advised, considering their desires of us therein to have our benevolence, assistance and leave thereof, and to have our affirmation and ratification thereupon so far as in us is or may be, we therefore have considered the said desires and statutes and find them consistent with reason, honour and worship to God and holy kirk, profitable of the realm and craft; and these are the desires and statutes: In the first, that the whole craftsmen may yearly choose themselves a deacon as other craftsmen do, who shall rule and govern the craft in all good rules as concerns them; to the which deacon all the rest of the craft shall obey in all lawful and honest things concerning the craft; and this deacon to be chosen by the freemen of the craft that are burgesses, and none others to have voice therein. Item, that no man occupy the craft as master until he be made burgess and freeman, and to be examined by the deacon and masters of the craft if he be worthy, and that he shall have good and sufficient materials and equipment to be seen and considered by four men of the craft; this being so he shall pay 2 merks and two pounds of wax to the altar foresaid. Item, no masters shall take an apprentice for shorter terms than five years, and shall pay at his entry to the said altar 5s, or less as can be treated with the craftsmen if he is unable to do so, and whoever takes him for less than those 5 years shall pay 20s when this is proven. Item no master shall take any other master's apprentice in his service, nor another man's feed servant until he be freed, or else have leave of his master to whom he owes service, under the penalty of 10s and a pound of wax, and to restore the apprentice or servant again. Item, that no man takes on hand to receive nor work another man's woven yarn, nor work without permission, but he shall pay one pound of wax or the price thereof. Item, each man or woman that occupies the craft shall give the priest his meat, and each week give to the altar a penny, to be gathered by the deacon, and each feed servant shall give in the year 4d; and also that those persons who disobey the deacon and will not obey the ordinance of the craft statutes for the good thereof, as oft as he disobeys he shall pay one pound of wax or the price thereof, and to be taken without favour. Item that no woman shall occupy the craft as for a master to hold workhouse but if she be a freeman's wife. Item that no man shall take equipment to her for fear of spoiling of the work but if it be a freeman, and who that does shall pay a pound of wax when it can be proven therewith. The which statutes, articles and all points contained therein we find them lovable to God and the holy kirk, and therefore we admit the same, and for us and our successors we the said provost, bailies and council of Edinburgh approve and ratify in all points and articles as is above written, insofar as is in our power, and this to all and sundry whom it concerns we make it known by these our letters; and for the more witnessing to the same we have hung our common seal of cause at Edinburgh the last day of January the year of our Lord 1475.

SOURCE: Marwick, JD (ed) 1869 *Extracts from the Records of the Burgh of Edinburgh 1403–1528*. Edinburgh, Scottish Burgh Records Society, 33–4.

'Quhy Will Ye, Merchantis of Renoun'

The following are stanzas from a satirical poem in middle Scots by the court makar William Dunbar (c.1460–1514). Edinburgh dominated Scotland's trade and paid the largest share of customs and urban taxation income from the loss of Berwick-upon-Tweed in the fourteenth century right through to the eighteenth century.

Quhy will ye, merchantis of renoun,	Quhy: why
Lat Edinburgh, your nobill toun,	
For laik of reformatioun	laik: lack
The commone proffeitt tyine and fame?	lose common prosperity and reputation
Think ye not schame	
That onie uther regioun	
Sall with dishonour hurt your name?	Sall: shall
May nane pas throw your principall gaittis,	gaittis: streets
For stink of haddockis and scattis,	scattis: fish
For cryis of carlingis and debaittis,	carlingis: old women
For feusum flyttingis of defame.	feusum flyttingis: foul quarrels
Think ye not schame,	
Befoir strangeris of all estaittis,	estaittis: ranks
That sic dishonour hurt your name?	sic: such
At your hie Croce, quhar gold and silk	hie Croce: market cross
Sould be, thair is bot crudis and milk,	crudis: curds
And at your Trone bot cokill and wilk,	cokill and wilk: cockles and whelks
Pansches, pudingis of Jok and Jame.	Pansches . . . Jame: low status puddings
Think ye not schame,	
Sen as the world sayis that ilk,	since the whole world says the same
In hurt and sclander of your name?	
Your burgh of beggeris is ane nest,	
To schout thai swenyouris will not rest.	thai swenyouris: those scoundrels
All honest folk they do molest,	
Sa piteuslie thai cry and rame.	rame: clamour
Think ye not schame,	
That for the poore hes nothing drest,	nothing drest: made no provision
In hurt and sclander of your name?	

Your proffeit daylie dois incres,
Your godlies workis les and les.
Through streittis nane may mak progres,
For cry of cruikit, blind and lame.
      Think ye not schame,
That ye sic substance dois posses,   substance: wealth
And will not win ane bettir name?
. . .

Thairfoir strangeris and leigis treit,   leigis: king's subjects; treit: welcome
Tak not over meikle for thair meit,   over meikle: too much; meit: food
And gar your merchandis be discreit.   gar: cause; discreit: wise
That na extortiounes be, proclame   to prevent all extortions, denounce all
      All fraud and schame.   fraud and shameful conduct
Keip ordour and poore neichtbouris beit, beit: assist
That ye may gett ane bettir name!

SOURCE: Small, J (ed) 1893 *The Poems of William Dunbar*. Edinburgh, ii, 261–3.

Medieval Archaeology

DOCUMENT 41

Development of Inchcolm Abbey

These plans illustrate the evolution over time of the island Augustinian abbey of Inchcolm in the Forth from the twelfth century through to the fifteenth century, the time of Abbot Walter Bower, the great chronicler, whose Scotichronicon *recorded many of the occasions on which Inchcolm was attacked by the English or embellished by Scottish patrons.*

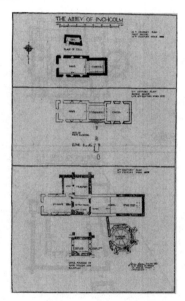

Inchcolm Abbey: twelfth- and
thirteenth-century plans

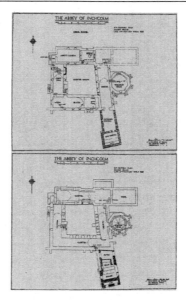

Inchcolm Abbey: fourteenth-century plans

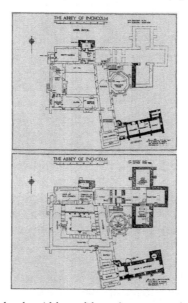

Inchcolm Abbey: fifteenth-century plans

SOURCE: Paterson, JW 1925–26 'The development of Inchcolm Abbey' in *The Proceedings of the Society of Antiquaries of Scotland*, vol. 60, 227–56. Also available on-line: http://ads.ahds.ac.uk/catalogue/ARCHway/toc.cfm?rcn=1340&-vol=60

DOCUMENT 42

Description of Kelso Abbey, 1517, and Archaeological Excavations of 1971–72

This description of the great Tironensian Border abbey of Kelso, transferred there from Selkirk by David I in 1126 and close by the royal burgh of Roxburgh (which was held by England from 1332 to 1347), was related by John Duncan, a cleric of Glasgow diocese, and given to a papal notary recording an inspection of Kelso Abbey in 1517. By that time Kelso had suffered badly through repeated war damage and an absentee abbot and would soon pass into commendatorship – being granted by the crown into the care of a lay administrator. Excavations in 1971–72 revealed much which broadly confirms the abbey's historical experience.

A) DESCRIPTION OF KELSO ABBEY, 1517

The church or monastery of Calco took its name from the small town of that name by which it stands. Its dedication is to St Mary . . . It is in the diocese of St Andrews, but is wholly exempt from any jurisdiction of the archbishop and is directly subject to the Apostolic See . . . It lies on the bank of a certain stream which is called in their language the Tweed and which today divides Scotland from the English . . .

The monastery itself is double, for not only is it conventual, having a convent of monks, but it is also a ministry; for it possesses a wide parish with the accompanying cure of souls which the Abbot is accustomed to exercise through a secular presbyter-vicar, removable at his pleasure. The Abbot exercises episcopal jurisdiction over his parishioners himself.

The church, in size and shape, resembles that of St Augustine de Urbe, except that at each end it has two high chapels on each side, like wings, which give the church the likeness of a double cross. Its fabric is of squared grey stone, and it is very old indeed. It has three doorways, one towards the west, in the fore-part, and the other two at the sides. It is divided into three naves by a double row of columns. The entire roof of the church is wooden, and its outer covering is of leaden sheets. The ground within is partly paved with stone and partly floored with bare earth. It has two towers, one at the first entrance to the church, the other in the inner part of the choir; both are square in plan and are crowned by pyramidal roofs like the tower of the Basilica of St Peter. The first contains many sweet-sounding bells, the other, at the choir, is empty on account of decay and age. The church is divided by a transverse wall into two parts; the outer part is open to all, especially parishioners both women and men, who there hear masses and receive all sacraments from their parochial

68

vicar. The other part, the back of the church, takes only monks who chant and celebrate the divine office. Laymen do not go in except at the time of Divine Service, and then only men but on some of their solemn festivals of the year women are also admitted. In this furthest-back part, at the head of the church, there is an old wooden choir.

The high altar is at the head of the choir, facing east, and on this several choral masses are celebrated daily, one for the founder and the other according to the current feast or holiday. There are besides, in the whole church, twelve or thirteen altars on which several masses are said daily, both by monks and by secular chaplains. In the middle of the church, on that wall which divides the monks from the parishioners, there is a platform of wood; here stands the altar of the Holy Rood, on which the Body of Christ is reserved and assiduously worshipped, and there is great worship and devotion of the parishioners. On the same platform there is also an organ of tin. The sacristy is on the right-hand side of the choir; in it are kept a silver cross, many chalices and vessels of silver, and other sufficiently precious ornaments belonging to the altar and the priests, as well as the mitre and pastoral staff.

The cemetery is on the north, large and square, and enclosed with a low wall to keep out beasts. It is joined to the church. The cloister . . . is on the south and is also joined to the church; it is spacious and square in shape, and is partly covered with lead and partly unroofed through the fury and impiety of enemies. In the cloister there is, on the one side, the chapter-house and the dormitory and on the other two refectories, a greater and lesser. The cloister has a wide court round which are many houses and lodgings; there also are guest-quarters common to both English and Scots. There are granaries and other places where merchants and the neighbours store their corn, wares and goods and keep them safe from enemies. There is also an orchard and a beautiful garden.

In the cloister there is usually the Abbot, the Prior, and the Superior; and in time of peace thirty-six or forty professed monks reside there. The town by which the monastery stands is called Calco, as has been said, or rather, in their common tongue, Chelso; it contains not more than sixty dwellings and is subject to the Abbot in respect of both temporal and spiritual jurisdiction. Nearly all the inhabitants are husbandmen and cultivators of the fields of the monastery, and none of them pays tithe or dues; on the contrary they receive payment from the Abbot, that they may be able to withstand and repel from the monastery the continual attacks of enemies.

The Abbey has, in addition, three or four other hamlets under it from which it receives tithes. It also holds the patronage of many parish churches from the vicars of which it receives part of the fruits. The Abbot's house is separate from that of the monks, but their table is in common.

Its value is somewhat uncertain because of the continual raids and pillaging of enemies and robbers, but by common opinion it is estimated at 1,500 ducats or thereabouts: and its fruits consist in church dues, tithes, provisions and rentals.

B) EXCAVATIONS, 1971–72

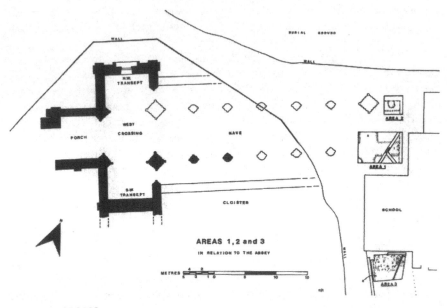

CONCLUSIONS

The paucity of building-stone and foundation material from the excavations serves to illustrate archaeologically what is implied in the documentary evidence. The structure that housed the Tironensian monks of Kelso, situated as it was four miles from the troubled border, was a natural target for destructive forces throughout its four centuries of history; indeed, for a time after the Wars of Independence, it had even to be abandoned and it is subsequent to this or some similar event that the rebuilding with burnt limestone boulders can best be ascribed. Facing-stone is noticeable by its absence though one has only to walk around the burgh to discover whither it strayed. More puzzling perhaps is the complete absence of rubble foundations at the inter-section of the foundation-trenches in Area 1 and this poses the problem of the opposing fates with which the two ends of the church met. The W end still towers like 'some antique Titan . . .' above the surrounding cluster of houses whilst the E end would appear to have been thoroughly robbed. The Duke of Hertford's resolve in 1545 to 'rase and deface this house of Kelso so as the enemy shal have lytell commoditie of the same' would seem to have included the total uprooting of the foundations at the E end – but why did his forces, and subsequent pillagers, stop there? A reference in John Duncan's deposition to the Vatican in 1517 provides the probable answer: 'The church is divided by a transverse wall into two parts; the outer part is open to all, especially parishioners both women and men, who there hear masses and receive all sacraments from their parochial vicar. The other part, the back of the church, takes only monks who chant and celebrate the Divine Office.'

The Abbey church was bipartite for it served both the monks to its S side and the inhabitants of the burgh and parish on the N, and, long after the last monk had been dislodged from the E end, the W end continued in use as a parish church. It would appear from this that both the English armies and the reformers of 1560 simply desired to debase the monks and destroy only that which was wholly monastic. One fears for the legacy that would have been left us had the abbey church been totally immune from secular contact.

The location of substantial foundations in Area 3 and their apparent relation with the robbed-out trenches in Area 1 would indicate that this was on the alignment of the E cloistral range, yet this perhaps creates more problems than it solves. The nave of the church would have to be limited to one of six bays, which is exceedingly stunted. For an Abbey of such importance and great wealth one would have expected at least two more, yet trenching further to the E revealed nothing to substantiate this. The lack of stratigraphy and the absence of stratified material, coupled with the relatively small area excavated, forbids any positive statement: only by further excavation in the Manse garden to the S could this be resolved. The idea of such a short nave may seem strangely unacceptable yet this strangeness extends to the whole building. The existence of W as well as E transepts makes it unique in Scotland and a rarity over Britain as a whole. Even with only six bays, the length of the church from the W porch to the start of the E crossing is over 52.0m which is 5.0m longer than the equivalent portion at Arbroath Abbey, also a Tironensian House of substantial proportions.

SOURCE: a) 1956 *An Inventory of the Ancient and Historical Monuments of Roxburghshire*. Edinburgh, i, 240–1; b) Tabraham, C 1971–72 'Excavations at Kelso Abbey, Roxburghshire', in *Proceedings of the Society of Antiquaries of Scotland*, vol. 104, 248–51; available in full on line at: http://ads.ahds.ac.uk/catalogue/library/psas/

Medieval Coin Hoards

The presence of so many English coins in these hoards should not necessarily be taken as remarkable, as England had a far greater moneyed economy with more specie in circulation. Indeed, Scotland repeatedly had to pass parliamentary acts against the exportation of Scottish specie, so low were its gold and silver reserves: the Scottish crown began to mint gold coins only c.1357 and also frequently indulged in reducing the precious metal content of its coinage after 1367.

A) KILKERRAN TREASURE TROVE

In April 1892, while a grave was being dug in an unused part of the churchyard of Kilkerran, in Kintyre, a number of coins were discovered. These were found lying among ashes, shells, and peat debris, about five to six feet below the present surface. The hoard consisted of 72 coins and fragments, of which 38 were English and 34 Scottish: 6 of the former and 22 of the latter were added to the Museum collection. The following is a list of the coins:-

Scottish

Robert III, 1390–1406
1. Groat, Perth, Burns, No. 21, fig. 364
2. Half Groat, Edinburgh, an unpublished variety, Obverse treasure of 7 arcs pointed with trefoils.
   +ROBERTVS : D : GRA : REX : SCOTORV.
   Reverse variety, No. 7, fig. 354, wg. 23.5 grs.

James I, 1406–1437
3. Groat, Edinburgh

James II, 1437–1460
4. Groat, Edinburgh, fragment, 2nd variety of the Crown groats.

James III, 1460–1488
5–9. Groats, Edinburgh, Thistle heads and mullets on Reverse as Nos. 6 and 7, figs. 577 and 578
10–15. Groats, Edinburgh, varieties of No. 11, fig. 581

16–17. Half Groats, Edinburgh, same issue No. 3, fig. 585
18–19. Groats, Edinburgh, Mullets of 5 points, No. 25, fig. 605
20–21. Groats, Edinburgh, Mullets of 5 points, No. 26, fig. 606
22. Half Groat, Edinburgh, Mullets of 5 points, No. 6, fig. 607
Groats, ¾ face crown and pellets on Reverse.
23. Groats, ¾ face crown, No. 34, fig. 638
24–25. Groats, ¾ face variety, No. 36, fig. 638
26–28. Groats, ¾ face, No. 41, fig. 641
29. Groats, ¾ face, No. 44, fig. 641
30. Groats, Aberdeen, No. 55, fig. 646
31. Half Groat, Edinburgh, same issue, No. 9A, fig. 648
32. Half Groat, Edinburgh, same issue, No. 11, fig. 648
33. Plack, fragment, fig. 571

James IV, 1488–1513
34. Groat, Edinburgh, No. 5, fig. 658

English

Edward III, 1327–1377
1–2. Groats, London
3–10. Half Groats, London, all in poor condition

Henry VI, 1422–1461
11–14. Groats, London
15–17. Half Groats, London
18–25. Groats, Calais, annulet each side of neck
26. Groats, Calais, rosette and mascle coinage
27–28. Half Groats, Calais, annulet each side of neck
29–30. Half Groats, Calais, rosette and mascle coinage

Edward IV, 1461–1483
31. Groat, Coventry, Rud V or 4
32. Groat, Bristol, Rud V or 8
33–35. Groat, London, with M.M. Obv. Cross, Rev. Sun, pierced cross and crown
36. Half Groat, London, M.M. crown, quatrefoil each side of neck
37. Groat, London, M.M. boar's head Hks 356

Henry VII, 1485–1509
38. Groat, London, arched crown similar to Hks 371

B) KINGHORNIE TREASURE TROVE

About the middle of October 1893, while a man was ploughing a field at King-hornie, near Bervie, in Kincardineshire, his plough struck an earthen jar, filled with coins, scattering them in all directions. Curiously enough, this jar, when thus discovered, was lying over the site of a chapel erected by David II, in 1342, in gratitude for his escape from shipwreck along with his Queen, Johanna, on the 4th of May of the previous year. Only a small portion, numbering 437 coins, of this hoard, and consisting of Sterlings of the Edward I, II, and III series, were forwarded from the Exchequer for examination; but I am informed by Mr H. Linton, Bervie, who has kindly furnished me with particulars of the finding of the coins, that the number found considerably exceeded 1000, and that also pennies of John Balliol and Alexander III were among them. The following is a list of the mints:-

Edward I, II and III Sterlings

Berwick	20
Bristol	11
Canterbury	85
Chester	1
Durham	62
Kingston	1
Lincoln	5
London	214
Newcastle	14
Robert de Hadley	1
St Edmundsbury	7
York	9
Uncertain	6
Foreign Sterling	1
Total:	437 coins

C) CLEUCHHEAD, ROXBURGHSHIRE

The following coins were turned up on the 24th November 1897 while ploughing a field on the farm of Cleuchhead, on the Wolfelee estate, Jedburgh. They were found about 6 inches below the surface in the Hill End Field, at a spot 17 yards from the Hill End Plantation, and 100 yards from the 'Old Roman Road'. The coins, as examined by me, numbered 138, and were nearly all foreign deniers.

John II, Count of Hainault, 1280–1305

1.   *Obv.* + I COMES HAVONIE
       Rev. VALENCHENENS
       Valenciennes,   24

2. *Obv.* As no. 1
    Rev. MONETA MONTES
    Mons,   22
3. *Obv.* As no. 1
    Rev. MELBODIENSIS
    Maubeuge,   5

John I, II, and III, Dukes of Braband, 1260–1356
4. *Obv.* + I DVX LIMBVRGIE
    Rev. DVX BRABANTIE
    Five slight varieties of obverse,   13

John, Seigneur of Louvain, 1253–1318
5. *Obv.* + IOHES DE LOVANIO
    Rev. DNS DEHARS' TEL   6

Guy, Count of Flanders, 1251–1290
6. *Obv.* + G COMES FLANDIS
    Rev. SIGNVM CRVCIS   11

Guy, Count of Flanders, as Marquis of Namur
7. *Obv.* + MARCHIO NAMVRC
    Rev. G COMES FLADRE
    A saltire at each side of the neck,
    an open quatrefoil in the third
    quarter of the reverse   5
8. As no. 7, but without the saltires
    at the sides of the neck; three pellets
    in each quarter of the reverse   2
9. *Obv.* + G MARCHIO NAMVR
    Rev. MONETA MONTES   1

John of Namur?
10. *Obv.* + OIH COMES HANON
    Rev. MONETA NVMVR   1

Arnold, Count of Loos, 1280
11. *Obv.* + COMES ARNOLDVS
    Rev. MONETA COMITIS   4
12. As last, with three cinquefoils in
    the third quarter of the reverse   1
13. *Obv.* + ARNOLDVS COMES
    Rev. As no. 11

Bishops of Cambray
William D'Avesnes, 1292–1295

14.	*Obv.* + GVILLS EPISCOPVS	
	Rev. CAMERACENSIS	8

Guido, etc.

15.	*Obv.* + GUIDO EPISCOPVS	
	Rev. As last	19
16.	Obv. + MONETA CAPIAVLI	
	Rev. As last	
	An eagle in one quarter of	
	the reverse	2
Uncertain and illegible		12

TOTAL	138

SOURCE: a) 1894–95, *Proceedings of the Society of Antiquaries of Scotland*, vol. 5, 275–7; b) & c) 1897–98, *Proceedings of the Society of Antiquaries of Scotland*, vol 32, 295–6. Available in full for consultation online at: http://ads.ahds.ac.uk/catalogue/library/psas/

Excavation of a Cemetery at Holyrood Abbey, Edinburgh

These extracts from an archaeological report of 1998 by Susan Bain detail some of the findings of a 1995 excavation of fourteenth- and fifteenth-century graves found to the west of the abbey church at Holyrood. The conclusions drawn by the archaeologists from the survey of the human remains found there have much to tell historians about the quality of life of late medieval Scots and about urban life.

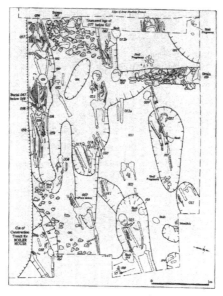

Composite plan of Trench A (showing features from all phases)

SUMMARY

Several factors have limited the scope of this report. The lack of complete skeletons (only four were 80–100% complete) and the universal abrasion and fragmentation of the bones prohibited more precise age-at-death, sex, and living stature determinations, as well as pathological diagnoses. The 33 individuals (51 including commingled remains) were varied and informative, but such a small sample cannot be used to formulate robust theories on the demography of the population, nor be reliably comparable with other cemetery populations.

Nonetheless, osteological analysis has revealed some insights into the demography of the Abbey and its burgh of Canongate. Nearly 50% of the cemetery population are sub-adults, as is the case among other contemporary Scottish skeletal samples. Glasgow Cathedral is an exception as, here, there were relatively few children. The Glasgow sample is thought to be made up primarily of elite individuals, however, thus excluding children. In contrast, the sample from Holyrood Abbey appears to represent the burgh of Canongate and not the convent of the Abbey or the royal household. The high proportion of young adults at Holyrood supports this proposal, since individuals of a higher social/economic status, having once survived childhood diseases, would generally have lived much longer than their less privileged contemporaries. Stature averages for women (1.55m) and men (1.65m) were generally comparable to other Scottish samples, though men were slightly shorter than the norm, perhaps reflecting differences in health and diet, or possible misidentification of sex in some individuals.

Pathological analysis recorded evidence for frequent dental disease related to diet, hygiene and development, diffuse non-specific infection related to general immune stress, and degenerative joint disorders of the lower vertebrae and appendiculars, apparently resulting from natural ageing and mechanical stresses.

The numerous caries, periodontal disease and calculus suggest that a starchy diet and poor oral hygiene was the norm at Holyrood and would have led eventually to total tooth loss, as seen on one mandible from the commingled remains. Dental attrition was pronounced, but corresponded to other ageing results, so that the rate of wear and the general diet were similar to that of Miles' (1963) prehistoric British population.

Skeletal pathology was not unlike that seen in other urban medieval populations. The frequency (45%) and location (tibia and fibula) of periostitis of the skeletal remains from Holyrood is typical of urban populations. In fact, the location of degenerative joint disease primarily on the lower vertebrae and the diathroidal joints of the legs, and the mature age of the individuals most extensively affected, corresponds with the pattern of this general disorder among 20th-century urban populations, as well as other medieval samples.

The pathology of the sample also reveals information on the population's response to illness. The evidence of metabolic disorder and dental malformation of one sub-adult (Sk 53) related to possible intestinal illness, the sinusitis of a child (Sk 24) and the tympania dehiscence of an infant (Sk 20) all attest to the ill-health of children in medieval Scotland. The chronic illnesses of the children is a tale of suffering, but it also implies that they had some form of medical care permitting survival beyond the acute phase of the disease. The osteoarthritis of Sk 55, chronic osteomyelitis of Sk 10 and osteochondritis dissecans of four women (Sk 16, 32, 38 & 56) demonstrate the tenacity of some individuals in the face of painful and debilitating illnesses.

CONCLUSIONS

The small scale of the excavation obviously limited the amount of information retrieved and subsequently limits the conclusions one can draw. Nevertheless, some illumination of important events in the history of the Abbey and Palace can be derived from the archaeological record.

The early feature, a possible ditch, may have been the western boundary of an early churchyard pre-dating the Abbey but, pending further evidence for this, it must be considered more likely that it was a primary boundary to the Abbey precinct. The deliberate infilling of the ditch is interpreted as part of a programme of improvements, including drainage and enclosure, in the 14th century, reflecting the ongoing development of a major Abbey, provided with royal apartments and suitable to serve as a political as well as religious centre.

English invasions during the 14th century directly involved Holyrood on three occasions. The most serious episode was in 1322, when construction of the Abbey suffered a setback at the hands of Edward II's army. Historical records do not describe the effects of the attack in detail, but materials recovered from the excavation suggest that stained glass windows were smashed and architectural details damaged. Probably those fragments which were suitable for reuse were recovered but enough was left amongst the buried debris to offer a glimpse of the grisaille decoration of the original windows.

The human remains are typical of an urban medieval cemetery population, with articulated, supine skeletons lying amongst the disarticulated remains of earlier burials. From the limited sample available, it seems that all age groups and both sexes are equally represented. This suggests that these burials are neither from the monastic convent nor the royal household, but represent a more diverse and less elite population. This lends support to the identification of the area north and west of the Abbey church as the parish cemetery of Canongate; but the cemetery is also likely to include Abbey tenants and artisans employed on the construction of its buildings, as such a task could be a lifetime's occupation. The convent of the Abbey and the royal household would also have employed many people to attend to their needs, and these too may be potential occupants of the cemetery.

The continuing status of Holyroodhouse as an official royal residence in the post-medieval period is represented by the construction of a new range attached to the great tower in the 1670s. After the demolition of this building in the mid 19th century, the excavated area was occupied by a boilerhouse, a more prosaic reminder that Holyroodhouse was again a favoured royal residence, as the grounds were improved and the apartments modernized in the reign of Queen Victoria. Holyroodhouse today is still a royal residence, but also a major tourist attraction. The present excavation was a consequence of further upgrading and landscaping which allowed private gardens to be opened to the public. The excavation of substantial medieval deposits indicates that equally informative deposits survive in other areas of the present garden and paved forecourt.

SOURCE: Bain, S 1998 'Excavations of a medieval cemetery at Holyrood Abbey, Edinburgh', in *Proceedings of the Society of Antiquaries of Scotland*, vol. 128, 1047–77; available in full online at: http://ads.ahds.ac.uk/catalogue/library/psas/

Excavation of Burgage Plot Backlands in Medieval Perth

These extracts from an archaeological report of 1996 by Adrian Cox detail some of the findings from two excavations undertaken as part of the ongoing archaeological assessment of the royal burgh of Perth. The extracts focus on the findings drawn from the study of grain-drying kilns found in the backlands off Meal Vennel and (as above) have much to reveal to historians about the nature and quality of urban life in late medieval Scotland and the value of archaeological evidence.

Primary activity on the site was represented by three grain-drying kilns. These keyhole-shaped features were all similar in construction and each appeared to have a flue to the north or north-west (along with scorched clay floor layers and some ash deposits). Lines of stake-holes within the kilns are thought to have supported a wattle and clay lining. The southernmost kiln was rebuilt at least once to a slightly larger plan, and its flue contained large amounts of heavily burnt daub. This may suggest that the kiln was surrounded by either a wall or roof-like structure. Environmental samples taken from one of the kiln floors, and from the flue of another, revealed the presence of wood charcoal, oats and barley.

Adjacent to the kilns was a complex feature consisting of two gullies and two pits. The fills contained both organic and burnt material, the latter in the form of slag and daub. The eastern gully also produced the earliest horseshoe from the site, of a type dating to the mid-13th century. However, the function of this feature is uncertain. Nearby, a number of pits contained a mixture of both industrial waste in the form of iron slag, and domestic refuse. The presence of goat and cattle horncores suggest some horn working took place in the area.

One side of a large cut feature was recorded running along the street frontage, with a silt fill including some ash, slag, burnt daub and antler offcuts. This feature was interpreted as a large boundary ditch, since it was on the same alignment as the street. To the south of this but at a slightly higher level was a narrow north/south cut, containing some residual material including a retouched flint scraper. This feature may also have been a ditch but, since it appeared to terminate at its northern extent, was probably not a recut of the earlier ditch. It was, however, on the same alignment as the boundary ditch. To one side of the earlier ditch was a wattle fence line and remnants of a square structure, consisting of five or more lines of wattle that may have formed the lining at the base of a well shaft.

Over 1300 sherds of pottery were recovered from this phase. The imported wares were dominated by Scarborough/Yorkshire ware and Low Countries Greywares and Redwares.

A small assemblage of antler offcuts was recovered from deposits in the main excavation area, indicating small-scale antler-working. One of these may represent an unfinished artefact or a core piece from which slices have been taken.

Fragments of quernstones associated with this phase of activity contribute to the evidence for grain-drying and processing activities. Three conjoining quernstone fragments were recovered from the fill of a gulley and another fragment came from a double post-hole, in which it may have been reused as packing. Samples from the grain-drying kilns revealed the presence of wood charcoal, oats and barley. The clay linings of the kilns were tempered with grass or straw. The presence of hammerscale in samples taken from the southern end of the site may indicate that iron working activities were taking place in the vicinity.

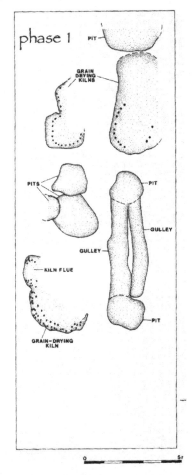

Meal Vennel: Phase 1: principal features

On the whole, the features in Phase 1 would tend to indicate grain drying and processing as the main activity along with some ironworking in the area. The first activity may have given rise to the name Meal Vennel. The ditch running parallel to the street frontage could represent the early town boundary, with the kilns being located beyond this boundary as they would have represented a considerable fire risk.

Meal Vennel: Phase 1: kiln, looking south-east

Keyhole-shaped grain-drying kilns are not uncommon and may be either wattle- or stone-lined structures. Examples have been excavated on rural sites at Barbush Quarry Dunblane, Perthshire, Capo, Kincardineshire, and Abercairney, Perthshire. Such structures remained in use until the end of the last century, especially on Orkney and Shetland. There, the kilns were heated by a peat fire within the flue and the grain was placed on a wood and straw drying floor suspended above the the base of the kiln.

SOURCE: Coleman, R 1996 'Burgage plots of medieval Perth: the evidence from excavations at Canal Street', in *Proceedings of the Society of Antiquaries of Scotland*, vol. 126, 689–732; avaliable in full online at: http://ads.ahds.ac.uk/catalogue/library/psas

Rural Society and Economy

DOCUMENT 46

Royal Grants of Agricultural Resources in the Twelfth Century

These two charters were granted by Malcolm IV (1153–65) under his great seal to monastic houses both founded by his grandfather, David I (1124–53), who would later be described by James I as 'ane sair sanct for the croun' because of his pious generosity in terms of land and natural resources to the religious orders. Such grants to monastic houses were invaluable not only for the daily support of the house through the income it thus received 'in kind' (i.e. crops, livestock and goods, rather than cash rent), but also in affording hospitality to pilgrims and important travellers – including the crown.

A) SCONE

Malcolm, King of Scots etc . . . Let all present and to come know that I have granted the teind of the whole parish of Scone, in grain, cheese and fish and all other things from which teind is rendered; at the Queen's ferry free passage for the abbot and canons of Scone and their own men and stock without payment of any toll or charge; freedom to take material in the king's woods throughout the whole of Scotland, where it is convenient for them, for the construction of the church of Scone and their houses . . . the serfs of the lands who, being freed and discharged by the said canons, have lawfully departed from them . . . and from every ploughgate of the whole land of the foresaid church of Scone, for the said canons' conveth, each year at the feast of All Saints, one cow, two swine, four measures of meal, ten thrives of oats, ten hens, twelve sheep, ten bundles of candles, four pennies of soap and twenty halves of cheese.

B) CALLANDER

Malcolm, King of Scots etc. Let all present and to come know that I have granted, and by this my charter confirmed, to God and the church of Newbattle and the monks serving God there a saltpan in Callander, gifted by King David, my grandfather, and common easement in pastures and waters, and fuel for the same saltpan in the wood of Callander, with common pasture in perpetual alms, free and quit of all custom and secular exaction.

SOURCE: Translated from the original Latin by GWS Barrow.

Bower's *Scotichronicon* on the Black Death and Other Afflictions

Walter Bower, abbot of Inchcolm and officer of James I (see Documents 16 and 24 above), wrote his great chronicle in the 1440s and drew on the works of Fordun and Wyntoun and other lost sources for his history of the events of the fourteenth century. These extracts should be related to what historians like Alexander Grant, Ranald Nicholson and Ian Whyte tell us about the general European economic downturn of the later middle ages and the mini 'Ice Age' of the fourteenth and fifteenth centuries, all of which adversely affected Scotland's society and economy.

[In 1336] there was a great scarcity of food nearly everywhere in the kingdom. Because of the strife and disturbance, and also because of the tangled severity of the feuds and fights of both peoples of England and Scotland which had been conducted on both sides in various ways, such a severe famine resulted that many people from the kingdom of Scotland left their native soil and settled with people in England or abroad. Their descendants still remain there. Others, however, who stayed in their native country, ate pods in the manner of pigs for want of food, and swelling up all over after a short time, they ended their lives wretchedly . . . there was such a great fowl pest that people altogether shrank from eating or even looking at all their cocks and hens on the grounds that they were unclean and riddled with leprosy. And therefore nearly all that species was destroyed.

In 1349 there was a great pestilence and mortality among men in the kingdom of Scotland, and it also ranged over a wide area during many earlier and later years throughout the whole world, such as had nowhere been heard of or written down in history books for the information of future generations from the beginning of the world until now. Such was the severity of that plague that nearly one-third of the whole human race was obliged to pay the debt of nature. The way in which this painful death happened by the divine will was strange and unusual; once the swollen inflammation of the flesh had taken hold, life in this world hardly lasted for a further two days. Wherever it happened, it affected for the most part the middling and lesser folk, and seldom the magnates. Everyone trembled at it with such fearful dread that children would not dare to visit their parents suffering in the last extremity; instead they fearfully shunned the contagion as they would flee before a serpent. In this year it so pleased the Lord that twenty-four professed canons of the house of St Andrews were called from the troubles of this present life, as is the way of all flesh . . . these plagues occur from time to time because of the sins of mankind.

In 1358 on the eve of the feast of Our Lady's Nativity flooding of rain and water suddenly burst out in parts of Lothian in such quantity and of such a kind as have not been seen from the days of Noah to the present. Its extent was such that the rising water overflowed channels, embankments and reservoirs, and spread into fields, villages, towns and monasteries. By its force it threw down from the foundations and demolished stone walls and the strongest bridges, as well as built up areas and the most substantial of houses. Likewise the violent flow dragged tall oaks and strong trees sited near rivers, uprooted by the flood water, all the way to where rivers joined the sea. It was also responsible for removing from human use from places near and far and destroying corn that had been cut and spread out where it had been cut for drying.

[In 1362] a second extremely severe mortality began on the feast of the Purification of Our Lady and lasted until Christmas immediately following. It spread its strength and virulence as much among nobles and magnates as among the common people and other persons of intermediate rank, to such an extent that it seemed to men at the time that nearly a third of the human race that remained after the first pestilence were forced to render their debt to nature.

[In 1420] a sickness by which not only magnates but also numberless men of the people were snuffed out was called 'le qwhew' by the common people. The physicians say that it was caused by an inequality or excess in the preceding winter, spring and summer, for the winter was very dry and northern, spring was rainy like autumn, and so it was inevitable that in summer fevers, eye-inflammations and dysenteries became acute, especially in damp places.

SOURCE: Watt, DER *et al* (ed) 1987–99 *Scotichronicon – Walter Bower*. Aberdeen, vii, 127, 157, 273, 311-1-3, 319; viii, 11.

Description of Scotland in the 1430s

This description was written by Italian papal legate Aeneas Sylvius, the future Pope Pius II, who visited the court of James I (1406–37) from his native Tuscany. Aeneas's visit was even recorded visually in a late-fifteenth-century fresco which still survives in Siena (and is reproduced in a number of books on James I).

A) FROM DE EUROPA, SYLVIUS'S GEOGRAPHICAL DESCRIPTION OF VARIOUS COUNTRIES OF EUROPE

Scotland is the remotest part of that island in which England is situated. It stretches in a northerly direction, possesses no large rivers, and is separated from England by a mountain. Here I once lived in the season of winter, when the sun illuminates the earth little more than three hours. At that time James (I) was king, robust of person, and oppressed by his excessive corpulence. Formerly made a captive by the English, he had been kept a prisoner for eleven years; and on his return (with an English wife) he was eventually slain by his own subjects. After his death had been fully avenged, his son succeeded him in the kingdom. I had previously heard that there was a tree in Scotland, that growing on the banks of rivers produced fruits in the form of geese, which, as they approached ripeness dropped off of their own accord, some on the ground and some into the water; that those which fell on the ground rotted, but that those submerged in the water immediately assumed life, and swam about under the water, and flew into the air with feathers and wings. When I made enquiries regarding this story, I learned that the miracle was always referred to some place further off, and that this famous tree was to be found not in Scotland but in the Orkney Islands, though the miracle had been represented to me as taking place among the Scots. In this country I saw the poor, who almost in a state of nakedness begged at the church doors, depart with joy in their faces on receiving stones as alms. This stone, whether by reason of sulphurous or some fatter matter which it contains, is burned instead of wood, of which the country is destitute.

B) FROM SYLVIUS'S *COMMENTARII RERUM MEMORABILIUM*

Aeneas found the following facts relating to Scotland worthy of mention. Scotland makes part of the same island as England, stretching northwards 200 miles with a breadth of 50. Its climate being cold, it produces few crops, and is scantily supplied with wood. A sulphurous stone dug from the earth is used by the people for fuel. The towns have no walls, and the houses are for the most part constructed without lime. The roofs of the houses in the country are made of turf, and the doors of the humbler dwellings are made of the hide of oxen. The common people are poor, and destitute of all refinement. They eat flesh and fish to repletion, and bread only as a dainty. The men are small in stature, bold and forward in temper; the women, fair in complexion, comely and pleasing, but not distinguished for their chastity, giving their kisses more readily than Italian women their hands.

There is no wine in the country unless what is imported. All the horses are amblers, and are of small size. A few are kept for breeding, the rest being gelded. They are never touched either with an iron brush or a wooden comb, and they are managed without bit. The oysters of the country are larger than those found in England. Hides, wood, salted fish, and pearls are exported to Flanders. Nothing pleases the Scots more than abuse of the English. There are said to be two distinct countries in Scotland – the one cultivated, the other covered with forests and possessing no tilled·land. The Scots who live in the wooded region speak a language of their own, and sometimes use the bark of trees for food. There are no wolves in Scotland. The crow is unusual in the country, and consequently the tree in which it builds is the king's property. At the winter solstice in Scotland [the season when Aeneas was there] the day is not above four hours long.

His business in the country being finished, when he was on the point of departure, the captain who had brought him to Scotland came to him with the offer of a berth he had previously occupied. Aeneas, thinking rather of his former dangers than divining fresh ones, replied: 'If he has no right to accuse Neptune, who has twice risked his life, what shall we say of him who should suffer shipwreck thrice? For my part I prefer the tender mercies of man to those of the sea.' So saying he dismissed the sailor, and decided to make his journey homewards through England. As it happened, the ship, which sailed immediately afterwards, had hardly left the harbour when she foundered in a storm and went down in sight of the shore. The master (who was returning to Flanders to celebrate his second marriage) was lost with all his crew save four, who escaped to the shore by floating on boards. On hearing of this disaster Aeneas at once concluded that he owed his life to the special goodness of God.

Disguising himself as a merchant, he now made his way through Scotland into England. A river, which descends from a lofty mountain, forms the boundary of the two countries. Crossing this river in a boat, he turned aside to a large town, where he alighted at a farm-house. Here with the priest of the place, and the host, he was entertained to supper. There was abundance of hens, geese, and various relishes, but no wine or bread. During the supper the women from surrounding houses flocked to look on as if they had never seen such a sight before, and stared at Aeneas, as in Italy the people stare at an Ethiopian or an Indian. 'Of what religion is he,' they ask; 'what has brought him here; is he acquainted with the Christian religion?' Having been cautioned beforehand, Aeneas had provided himself with a number of loaves and a measure of wine at a nearby monastery. When these were laid on the board, the wonder of the barbarians was greater than ever, since wine and white bread were sights they had never seen before. Pregnant women and their husbands approaching the table handled the bread and smelt the wine, and prayed that a portion might be given them. As there was no avoiding it, the whole had to be distributed amongst them.

At two o'clock in the morning (for the meal was protracted to that hour), the priest and the landlord, rising hastily, quitted the house, leaving Aeneas behind. 'They were going,' they said, 'to a distant keep for fear of the Scots, who for the purposes of plunder were in the habit of crossing the river at ebb-tide during the night.' Aeneas besought eagerly to accompany them; but they gave no heed to his entreaties. They were equally deaf to the prayers of the women, though there were many handsome ones amongst them, both married and unmarried. They give out that strangers are safe in the hands of the Scots; and as for the women, they do not regard outrage done to them as any great misfortune.

Accordingly, with two male domestics and his guide, Aeneas was left among some hundred women who, forming a circle round the first, spent the night in cleansing hemp, and in lively conversation carried on through an interpreter. A great part of the night had thus passed, when an uproar arose from the barking of dogs and the cackling of geese. The women at once fled in all directions and the guide along with them. The confusion was as complete as if the enemy was at the door. To Aeneas the thought occurred that his best course was to await the event in bed – that is to say, in the stable; since, ignorant as he was of the country, any attempt to escape would have placed him at the mercy of the first marauder he met. In no long time, however, the women returned, and announced through the interpreter that there was no need for alarm, and that the newcomers were friends and not enemies. At daybreak Aeneas continued his journey, and reached Newcastle, which is said to have been built by Caesar. Here for the first time it seemed to him that he once more beheld civilisation, and a country with a habitable aspect; for Scotland and that part of England adjoining it bear no resemblance to Italy, but are nothing but a rugged wilderness, unvisited by the genial sun.

SOURCE: Hume Brown, P (ed) 1891 *Early Travellers in Scotland*. Edinburgh, 25–9.

Acts of Parliament Governing Rural Life in the Fifteenth Century

Dating mostly from the reign of James I (1406–37) – held to have been a great 'law-giver king' – these acts may in fact be based on earlier (now lost) acts: the forthcoming new edition of the Records of the Parliaments of Scotland *by scholars based at St Andrews University should illuminate many more such acts.*

A) THE SELLING OF HORSES, 1424

It is ordained that no horse be sold out of the realm till at least they be three years old, under pain of escheat of them to the king.

B) STEALING GREENWOOD AND BREAKING ORCHARDS, 1424

It is ordained that the Justice Clerk inquire at the receiving of the Interdictment of them that by night steal greenwood or peel the bark of trees, destroying wood; and whoever is convicted before the Justice of such trespass shall pay xl shillings to the king for break of law and compensation to the party injured. And also the said clerk shall inquire of breakers of men's orchards and stealers of fruit and destroyers of rabbit-warrens and of dovecotes, who shall be punished as is ordained of the stealers of greenwood.

C) THE SOWING OF PEAS AND BEANS, 1427

Our sovereign lord the king, with consent of the whole parliament, ordained that through all the realm each man tilling with a plough of eight oxen shall sow at the least each year a firlot of wheat, half a firlot of peas, and xl beans, under the pain of x shillings to the baron of the land that he dwells in, as often as he be found guilty. And if the baron sows not the said corn in like manner in his demesnes he shall pay to the king xl shillings. And if the baron shall be found negligent in raising the fine on his husbandmen, there shall be raised on him xl shillings as oft times as he default, without remission.

D) THE WHELPS OF WOLVES, 1427

It is statute and ordained by the king, with consent of his whole council, that each baron within his barony at the proper time of the year shall cause his servants to seek the whelps of the wolves and cause them to slay them. And the baron shall give to the man that slays one in his barony and brings the baron his head ii shillings. And when the baron ordains to hunt and chase the wolves, the tenants shall rise with the baron. And that the barons hunt in these baronies and chase the wolves four times a year and as often as any wolf is seen within the barony. And that no man seek the wolves with shooting except only in the times of hunting them.

E) SALMON, 1431

The king and the whole parliament have statute and ordained that no salmon be sold nor bartered with any man that has it out of the realm except for English money only – that is to say, gold or silver for the one half and Gascon wine or such like good penny's worth for the other half.

F) SORNERS AND OTHER IDLE PERSONS, 1449

It is ordained that for the putting away of sorners, *ourlyars*, and masterful beggars with horses and hounds and other goods, that all officiars, both sheriffs, barons, alderman, and bailies as well within burgh as without, take an inquisition at each court that they hold of the foresaid things, and, if any such be found, that their horses, hounds, and other goods be escheated to the king, and their persons put in the king's ward till the king has said his will to them. And also that the said sheriffs, bailies, and officiars inquire at each court if there be any that make them fools that are not, bards, or other such runner-about. And if any such be found that they be put in the king's ward or in his irons for their own trespass as long as they have any goods of their own to live upon. And from [the time that] they have nought to live upon that their ears be nailed to the trone [the public beam for weighing] or to another tree and cut off and banished the country. And thereafter, if they be found guilty again, that they be hanged.

G) THE THRESHING OF CORN, 1452

It is statute and ordained by our sovereign lord the king and by advice of the lords now present with him that all manner of men that have corn unthreshed cause it to be threshed out before the last day of May next to come, under the pain of escheat of the corn to the king, that happens then to be unthreshed, as well within barns as without.

H) THE IMPORTATION OF VICTUAL, 1454

For the inbringing of victuals it is ordained that strangers that bring in victuals be favourably treated and thankfully paid for the victuals. And that there be no new custom taken of them, and that there be no more victuals taken to the king's port except only as much as will serve his household. And right so if Scottish merchants bring in victuals out of England, that they be favourably treated as said is.

I) THE PLANTATION OF WOODS AND HEDGES, 1447

Anent plantation of woods and hedges and sowing of broom, the lords think it speedful that the king charge all his freeholders, both spiritual and temporal . . . that they statute and ordain that all the tenants plant woods and trees, make hedges and sow broom . . . in places convenient therefor, under such pain and fine as the baron or lord shall notify.

J) THE PRESERVATION OF WILD BIRDS, 1447

Anent the preservation of birds and wild fowls that are fit to eat for the sustentation of man, such as partridge, plovers, wild ducks, and such like fowls, it is ordained that no man destroy their nests nor their eggs, nor yet slay wild birds in moulting time when they may not fly; and that all men according to their power destroy nests, eggs, and young of birds of prey.

K) ROOKS' NESTS, 1447

Anent rooks, crows, and other birds of prey, as herons, buzzards, hawks, and *myttals* [a kind of hawk], the which destroy both corn and wild birds, such as partridges, plovers, and others, and as to the rooks and crows building in orchards, kirkyards, or other places, it is seen speedful that they to whom such trees pertain prevent them from building, and destroy them with all their power, and in no wise let the birds fly away. And where it is proved that they build and that the birds are flown and the nests found in the trees, at Beltane the trees shall be forfeit to the king, except they be redeemed again, and they that own the said trees [shall be mulcted] in v shillings fine to the king. And that the said birds of prey be utterly destroyed by all manner of means, by all ingenuity and manner of way that may be found thereto, for the slaughter of them shall cause great multitude of divers kinds of wild birds for man's sustenance.

L) GREEN WOOD AND MOOR-BURNING, 1503

Anent the article of green wood, because that the wood of Scotland is utterly destroyed by the fine thereof being so small, it is statute and ordained that the fine of green wood to any man for selling or burning in time to come be v li. [i.e. £5], and that both of Regality and Royalty the old fine of green wood to the destroyers of it otherwise stand in effect as before; and that the fine of moor-burning after the month of March be likewise v li. in all times to come.

SOURCE: Hume Brown, P 1893 *Scotland Before 1700 from Contemporary Records*. Edinburgh, 20–32.

Act of Parliament Concerning 'Feu-ferme', 1458

Feu-ferme was the process by which lands were 'set' or leased out in return for a perpetual fixed annual money-rent (under which lands could be passed by tenants to their heirs): this process developed and increased from the later fifteenth century as a way of increasing the annual revenue from burgh, royal and ecclesiastical lands. This should also be related to the increasing need of the crown in this period for an income suitable for supporting a lavish Renaissance court as well as everyday household government and foreign policy and the reciprocal need of the estates in parliament to ensure that the crown did not resort to regular taxation or forfeitures to find this money.

1458 – Item anentis feuferme, the lordis thinkis speidfull that the king begyne and gif exempill to the laif and quhat prelate, barone or frehaldare that can accorde with his tenande apone setting of feuferme of his awin lande in all or in part; our soverane lorde sall ratify and appreif the said assedacioun sa that gif the tenandry happynnis to be in warde in the kingis handis; the saide tenande sall remane with his feuferme unremovyt payande to the king siklik ferme endurande the warde as he did to the lorde sa that it be set to a competent avail without prejudice to the king.

SOURCE: 1814–75 *Acts of the Parliaments of Scotland*. Edinburgh, ii, 49.

Medieval Architecture

DOCUMENT 51

Description of Scotland in the 1490s

This description was written in 1498 by Pedro de Ayala, the Spanish Ambassador to the court of James IV (1488–1513): Ayala had originally been sent to 'stall' James with false offers of a Spanish marriage if he would desist from aggression towards Henry VII and England; but James clearly impressed Ayala and won him round to the idea of even advocating a Scottish-Spanish match (although this may also have had something to do with the fact that James opened and read Ayala's correspondence and instructions!).

The king is twenty-five years and some months old. He is of noble stature, neither tall nor short, and as handsome in complexion and shape as a man can be. His address is very agreeable. He speaks the following languages: Latin, very well; French, German, Flemish, Italian, and Spanish; Spanish as well as the Marquis, but he pronounces it more distinctly. He likes very much to receive Spanish letters. His own Scotch language is as different from English as Aragonese from Castilian. The king speaks, besides, the language of the savages who live in some parts of Scotland and on the islands. It is as different from Scotch as Biscayan is from Castilian. His knowledge of languages is wonderful. He is well read in the Bible and in some other devout books. He is a good historian. He has read many Latin and French histories, and profited by them, as he has a very good memory. He never cuts his hair or his beard. It becomes him very well.

He fears God, and observes all the precepts of the Church. He does not eat meat on Wednesdays and Fridays. He would not ride on Sundays for any consideration, not even to mass. He says all his prayers. Before transacting any business he hears two masses. After mass he has a cantata sung, during which he sometimes despatches very urgent business. He gives alms liberally but is a severe judge, especially in the case of murderers. He has a great predilection for priests, and receives advice from them, especially from the Friars Observant, with whom he confesses. Rarely, even in joking, a word escapes him that is not the truth. He prides himself much upon it, and says it does not seem to him well for kings to swear their treaties as they do now. The oath of a king should be his royal word, as was the case in bygone ages. He is neither prodigal nor avaricious, but liberal when occasion requires. He is courageous, even more than a king should be. I am a good witness of it. I have seen him often undertake most dangerous things in the last wars. I sometimes clung to his skirts and succeeded in keeping him back. On such occasions he does not take the least care of himself. He is not a good captain, because he begins to fight before he has given his orders. He said to me that his subjects serve him with their persons and goods, in just and unjust quarrels, exactly as he likes, and that, therefore, he does not think it right to begin any warlike undertaking without being himself the first in danger. His deeds are as good as his words. For this reason, and because he is a very humane prince, he is much loved. He is active and works hard. When he is not at war he hunts in the mountains. I tell your Highnesses the truth when I say that God has worked a miracle in him, for I have never seen a man so temperate in eating and drinking out of Spain. Indeed, such a thing seems to be superhuman in these countries. He lends a willing ear to his counsellors, and decides nothing without asking them; but in great matters he acts according to his own judgment, and, in my opinion, he generally makes a right decision. I recognise him perfectly in the conclusion of the last peace, which was made against the wishes of the majority in his kingdom.

I can say with truth that he esteems himself as much as though he were lord of the world. He loves war so much that I fear, judging by the provocation he receives, the peace will not last long. War is profitable to him and to the country.

I will give an account of his revenues. Although I do not know them to a certainty, I do not think that I shall be far wrong. I shall estimate them a little below their real amount. He has a revenue from arable and pasture lands, which are let by leases of three years. The farmers pay a fine upon entry. This rent is said to amount to 50,000 pounds Scotch, each pound Scotch being worth one Castiliano. I rather believe that it amounts to 40,000 ducats.

Another revenue is that from the customs. The import duties are insignificant, but the exports yield a considerable sum of money, because there are three principal articles of export, that is to say, wool, hides, and fish. The customs are worth about 25,000 ducats a year. They have much increased, and still continue to increase. Another revenue is that derived from the administration of the law. His predecessors farmed it out to certain persons called justices, like our *corregidores*. The king does not like to farm the administration of the law, because justice is not well adminis-tered in that way. It is said that this revenue amounts to more than 30,000 ducats, but I will put it down at only 25,000 ducats.

He has another revenue from his wards, which is very considerable, and which offers good opportunities for rewarding his servants. If lords, or gentlemen of the middle class, in whatever part of the kingdom they may be, die and leave children under twenty-two years of age, the king is the guardian of them. He receives all their revenues till they come of age. He lets or sells such guardianships. He even sells the marriages of his wards, male and female. When the ward comes of age, and the king gives him the title of his father, or brother, or testator, he pays the amount of one or two years' rent, or any other sum that is agreed upon, into the exchequer of the king. I am told that this is the richest source of revenue, but I will estimate it at only 20,000 ducats.

He enjoys one year's revenue from the bishoprics and abbacies for the presenta-tion. He likewise receives all the revenues of them during the vacancy of the see. The same is the case with respect to other livings, for they are all in his gift. I do not know to how much this amounts. He has a rent from the fisheries, not in money, but in kind, for his kitchen, and likewise from meat and poultry, &c. This is his income, according to what I have been able to ascertain, and to what I have seen. He is in want of nothing, judging from the manner in which he lives, but he is not able to put money into his strong boxes. I shall speak hereafter of this.

The country is large. Your Highnesses know that these kingdoms form an island. Judging by what I have read in books and seen on maps, and also by my own experience, I should think that both kingdoms are of equal extent. In the same proportion that England is longer than Scotland, Scotland is wider than England; thus the quantity of land is the same. Neither is the quality very different in the two countries, but the Scotch are not industrious, and the people are poor. They spend all their time in wars, and when there is no war they fight with one another. It must, however, be observed, that since the present king succeeded to the throne they do not dare to quarrel so much with one another as formerly, especially since he came of age. They have learnt by experience that he executes the law without respect to rich or poor. I am told that Scotland has improved so much during his reign that it is worth three times more now than formerly, on account of foreigners having come to the country, and taught them how to live. They have more meat, in great and small animals, than they want, and plenty of wool and hides.

Spaniards who live in Flanders tell me that the commerce of Scotland is much more considerable now than formerly, and that it is continually increasing.

It is impossible to describe the immense quantity of fish. The old proverb says already 'piscinata Scotia'. Great quantities of salmon, herring, and a kind of dried fish, which they call stock fish, are exported. The quantity is so great that it suffices for Italy, France, Flanders, and England. They have so many wild fruits which they eat, that they do not know what to do with them. There are immense flocks of sheep, especially in the savage portions of Scotland. Hides are employed for many purposes. There are all kinds of garden fruits to be found which a cold country can produce. They are very good. Oranges, figs, and other fruits of the same kind are not to be found there. The corn is very good, but they do not produce as much as they might, because they do not cultivate the land. Their method is the following: they plough the land only once when it has grass on it, which is as high as a man, then they sow the corn, and cover it by means of a harrow, which makes the land even again. Nothing more is done till they cut the corn. I have seen the straw stand so high after harvest, that it reached to the girdle. Some kind of corn is sown about the feast of St John, and is cut in August.

The people are handsome. They like foreigners so much that they dispute with one another as to who shall have and treat a foreigner in his house. They are vain and ostentatious by nature. They spend all they have to keep up appearances. They are as well dressed as it is possible to be in such a country as that in which they live. They are courageous, strong, quick, and agile. They are envious to excess.

There are four duchies in the kingdom. Three of them are in the possession of the king; the fourth is held by the eldest brother of the king, who is duke of Ross and archbishop of St Andrews. There are fifteen earls, not counting the younger brother of the king, who holds two counties.

Nine other counties are in possession of the king. Some of the fifteen earls are great men. I saw two of them come and serve the king in the last war with more than 30,000 men, all picked soldiers and well armed. And yet they did not bring more than one-half of their men. Many others came with five or six thousand followers; some with more, and some with less. As I have already observed, this army does not cost the king a penny.

There are two principalities; one is the *principatus insularum* [Lordship of the Isles] and the other the *principatus Gallovidiae* [Lordship of Galloway]. Both are held by the king. There are five and thirty great barons in the kingdom, without counting the smaller ones.

There are two archbishoprics and eleven bishoprics, sixty-three monasteries, which they call abbeys, and many other religious houses, which are endowed with property and rents. The abbeys are very magnificent, the buildings fine, and the revenues great. All of them were founded by kings. There are seventy seaports. The harbours between the islands are not included in this number, though they are said to be very secure.

Sixty-four of the islands are inhabited. Some of them are 60 miles long, and as many miles in width. Besides, there are the Orcades towards Norway. It is said that they are very numerous.

On the islands there are many flocks, and great quantities of fish and of barley. The inhabitants are very warlike and agile. I saw them in the last war. They do not know what danger is. The present king keeps them in strict subjection. He is feared by the bad, and loved and revered by the good like a god. None of the former kings have succeeded in bringing the people into such subjection as the present king. He went last summer to many of the islands, and presided at the courts of law.

The prelates are very much revered; they have the larger share in the government. Spiritual as well as secular lords, if they have a title or a dignity, belong to the General Council. It meets four times a year in order to administer justice. It is a very good institution. All causes are decided after debating them. At the same time the king receives his revenues derived from the administration of the law. Both spiritual and secular lords have a certain number of followers, recorded in the books of the king, who are entitled to have their meals in the palace when they come to court. They have no other advantages. The king selects some of them for his Privy Council, and they always remain at court. They receive, nevertheless, no salary, except for other offices, which they may happen to hold. But they and their servants eat in the palace. The reason why they do so is, that the king may be always accompanied by them. It causes great expense.

The kings live little in cities and towns. They pass their time generally in castles and abbeys, where they find lodgings for all their officers. They do not remain long in one place. The reason thereof is twofold. In the first place, they move often about, in order to visit their kingdom, to administer justice, and to establish order where it is wanted. The second reason is, that they have rents in kind in every province, and wish to consume them. While travelling, neither the king nor any of his officers have any expenses, nor do they carry provisions with them. They go from house to house, to lords, bishops, and abbots, where they receive all that is necessary. The greatest favour the king can do to his subjects is to go to their houses.

The women are courteous in the extreme. I mention this because they are really honest, though very bold. They are absolute mistresses of their houses, and even of their husbands, in all things concerning the administration of their property, income as well as expenditure. They are very graceful and handsome women. They dress much better than here [England], and especially as regards the head-dress, which is, I think, the handsomest in the world.

The towns and villages are populous. The houses are good, all built of hewn stone, and provided with excellent doors, glass windows, and a great number of chimneys. All the furniture that is used in Italy, Spain, and France, is to be found in their dwellings. It has not been brought in modern times only, but inherited from preceding ages.

The queens possess, besides their baronies and castles, four country seats, situated in the best portions of the kingdom, each of which is worth about fifteen thousand ducats. The king fitted them up anew only three years ago. There is not more than one fortified town in Scotland, because the kings do not allow their subjects to fortify them. The town is a very considerable borough and well armed. The whole soil of Scotland belongs to the king, the landholders being his vassals, or his tenants for life, or for a term of years. They are obliged to serve him forty days, at their own expense, every time he calls them out. They are very good soldiers. The king can assemble, within thirty days, 120,000 horse. The soldiers from the islands are not counted in this number. The islands are half a league, one, two, three, or four leagues distant from the main land. The inhabitants speak the language, and have the habits of the Irish. But there is a good deal of French education in Scotland and many speak the French language. For all the young gentlemen who have no property go to France, and are well received there, and therefore the French are liked. Two or three times I have seen, not the whole army, but one-third of it assembled, and counted more than twelve thousand great and small tents. There is much emulation among them as to who shall be best equipped, and they are very ostentatious, and pride themselves very much in this respect. They have old and heavy artillery of iron. Besides this, they possess modern French guns of metal, which are very good. King Louis gave them to the father of the present king in payment of what was due to him as co-heir of his sister, the Queen of Scotland. This is all I am able to tell your Highness. Now I shall describe where Scotland is situated, and by what countries she is surrounded. She borders on England by land, and by sea on Brittany, France, Flanders, Germany, Denmark, Norway, and Ireland. She is surrounded by these countries. Scotland is powerful enough to defend herself against her neighbours should any one of them attack her without fear of God. No king can damage her without suffering greater damages from her, that is to say, in a war on land; for they know that on sea there are many kings more powerful than they are, although they possess many fine vessels. On land they think themselves the most powerful kingdom that exists; for they say the King of Scots has always a hundred thousand men ready to fight, and they are always paid. Towards the west there is no land between Scotland and Spain. Scotland is nearer to Spain than London, and the voyage is not dangerous. Scotland has succoured most of her neighbours. With respect to France and Flanders this is notorious. The Dukes of Burgundy wear the 'tan of St Andrew,' in memory of the succour which Scotland sent to Duke [*blank*]. Saint Andrew is the patron saint of Scotland. On the other hand, Scotland has never wanted foreign assistance. There is as great a difference between the Scotland of old time and the Scotland of to-day as there is between bad and good, as I have already written.

SOURCE: Hume Brown, P (ed) 1891 *Early Travellers in Scotland*. Edinburgh, 39–49.

Plan of Linlithgow Palace and Illustration of its East Range

These floor plans and view illustrate the development of the palace from James I's beginnings with a blank canvas and his erection of the eastern wing and entrance through to James IV's and James V's completion of the quadrangle. The latter king's queen, Marie de Guise, is said to have compared the palace favourably to any such chateau in France.

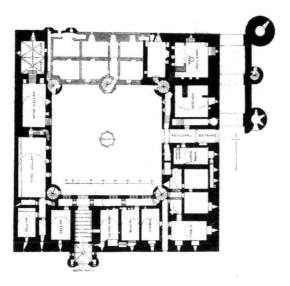

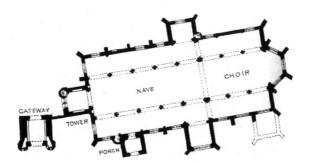

Linlithgow Palace and Gateway, with St Michael's Church (ground floor plan)

Linlithgow Palace: original entrance (east range).

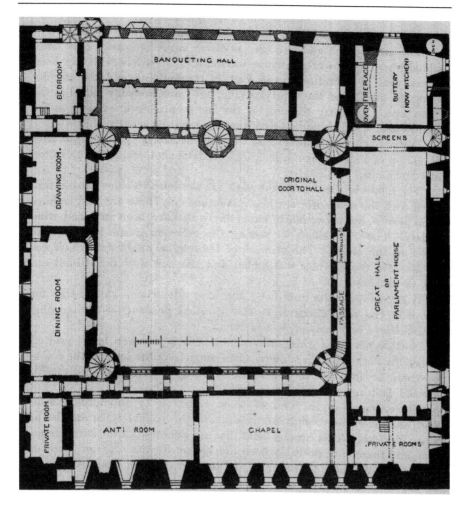

Linlithgow Palace: plan of first floor

SOURCE: MacGibbon, D and Ross, T 1887 *The Castellated and Domestic Architecture of Scotland*, i, 480, 484, 488.

The King's Works in the Fifteenth Century

These building materials and costs for Linlithgow Palace for the last year of the reign of James IV in 1513 (when the palace quadrangle neared completion) are detailed in the Exchequer Rolls of Scotland *and the* Accounts of the Lord High Treasurer of Scotland, *collated and published in the nineteenth century with the original manuscripts held by the National Archives of Scotland. The first five items are given in the original Scots to provide a flavour of the language in which the accounts were written. A translation of the whole text follows.*

The Werkis of Linlithqw

A.D. 1513

Item, to James Carvour, fra Pasche evin the 26 day of Marche exclusive to the Setterday the last day of Aprile inclusive, it beand in the haile 5 wolkis, he takand in the wolk for himself 12s, and for his servand 9s, makand in the 5 wolkis the soume of £5 5s.

Item, to Gilyem, Franchman, that maid the organis, for his laubouris tharon, at the kingis command, in ten licht Franche crownis, £7.

Item, to the sclatter tyrvand, thekand and correckand the chapel in Lithqw, for ilk rude, feit be Stevin Balty, 28s, quhilk met and mesurit contenis 6 rudis 1 ell; summa £8 14s 8d.

Item, for 6 puncionis to be pinnis to the said sclatter for the chapel, 7s.

Item, for fog brocht fra the hanyng to the chapel, 10s.

* * * * *

The Works of Linlithgow

Item, to James Carver, from Saturday 26 March (exclusive) until Saturday 30 April (inclusive), it being five whole weeks, he receiving 12s each week for himself and 9s for his servant, making in the five weeks the sum of £5 5s.

Item to Guillaume (Frenchman), who made the organs at the king's command, for his work thereupon, ten light French crowns [a kind of coin], £7.

Item to the slater for stripping, covering [literally thatching but see the reference to slates below] and mending the chapel [roof] of Linlithgow [Palace], 28s for each rood [36 square ells] agreed by Steven Balty, which when measured contains 6 roods, 1 ell [an ell is 37 inches], the total is £8 14s 8d.

Item for 6 wooden pegs for the said slater for the chapel, 7s.

Item for grass brought from the haining [enclosed woodland] to the chapel, 10s.

Item for 360 laths at 12d for 100, the total is 9s 6d.

Item for 8 great clasps delivered to Guillaume for fixing the organs to the wall, which were three quarters of length and weighed 2 stone at 5s 10d per stone, the total is 14s 7d.

Item to Guillaume, 200 flooring nails, 4d.

Item to him, 200 window nails, 4d.

Item, to him, 4 loads of coal, 2s.

Item, for 300 slates at 10s per hundred, the total is 30s.

Item, for carriage of them to Linlithgow, 6s.

Item for furnishing a door to David Lindsay in the north tower, which had 2 new bands and 2 hooks [i.e. 2 complete hinges] and nails to fix them, a lock with a key and for lead to mount the hinges in the wall, 6s.

Item, for nails for the chapel and larder doors, 8d.

Item, to 2 workmen for cleaning the larder, 4s.

Item, for clearing the over larder and setting floorboards in it to be a room, 4s.

Item, for building a lean-to on the east side of the palace, 5s.

Item, for a great lock for the foregate, for 2 great clasps and for mending the slot, 2s.

Item, for sawing 2 small joists and one spar, 16d.

Item, for sawing 6 'Estland' [Baltic] boards, 4s.

Item, for carrying up 36 'Estland' boards from Blackness, 6s.

Item, to Thomas Peebles, glazier, for 8 square feet of newly-made glass for the queen's oratory, measured by James Dog, at 14d per square foot, in total is 9s 11d.

Item for 7 stone of glass bands for the palace, at 6s 8d per stone, in total is 46s 8d.

Item to Steven Balty, mason, and his servant, from 15 May (inclusive) to 25 June (exclusive), being 6 weeks, he being paid 20s each week for himself and his servant, in total is £6.

Item, to 11 workmen who served for those 6 weeks, 36s.

Item, for 2 chalders [a dry volume measure of over 2,300 litres] of lime, 16s.

Item, for sand to mix the lime with, 4s.

Item to clear an opening of half a rood in the quarry, 40s.

Item, to the quarrier who quarried the stone for 4 days, 5s 4d.

Item, for 48 cartloads of stone, 32s.

Item, for half a chalder of lime, 4s.

Item, for sand, 2s.

Item, to the slater that roofed the eastern tower of the church with this lime and sand, 36s.

Item, to James Carver, 200 ceiling nails, 12d.

Item to Guillaume, for 2 loads of iron for the organs, 6 quarters in length, with 2 iron pins weighing 2 stones, 12s.

Item, for sawing the 'Estland' boards, 5s.

Item to Steven Balty and his servant, from 25 June (inclusive) to 6 August (exclusive), being 6 weeks, at 20s per week, the total is £6.

Item, accounted with Steven Balty and paid to him, from 12 July (inclusive) to 13 December (exclusive), for all necessary materials for Linlithgow as follows:

First, for the park gate, 4 great bands, 4 hooks, a staple and great nails for the bands weighing 2 stones, at 5s 4d for each stone, in total is 10s 8d.

Item, 3 bands and 3 hooks with nails for the prince's cellar door, 6s 8d.

Item, for a lock for the said door, 2s.

Item, for a lock for the spicehouse door, 4s.

Item, for a lock for the park door, 16d.

Item, for a lock for the particular house door where the timber lay, 2s.

Item, for 2 hooks for the chapel door weighing ½ a stone, 3s 4d.

Item, for a lock for the wardrobe door, 2s.

Item, for the carriage of 100 rafters from Blackness to Linlithgow, 6s.

Item, delivered to the wrights, 600 door nails at 12d per hundred, in total is 6s.

Item, 50 flooring nails, 10d.

Item, to the smith, Alexander Riddoch, for 3 stones of iron bands and hooks for the masons' lodge and the other office house, at 6s 6d per stone, the total is 19s 6d.

Item, for a lock for the queen's pantry door, 2s.

Item, to carry the timber out of the sledge that came up from the *Margaret* [a ship], 16d.

Item, for the carriage of 9 pieces of timber, 12 deal boards, 4 carts at 2s per cart, in total is 8s.

Item, for the carriage of 60 pieces of timber from Blackness to Linlithgow in 12 carts, at 2s per cart; the total is 24s.

Item, for storing the timber, 2s.

Item, to the sawyers sawing timber for Master John and for the lodge, and for the sawing of 7 deal boards, 14s.

Item, for 2,000 slates at £3 10s per 1,000, in total is £7.

Item, for the carriage of them to Linlithgow in 13 carts, 29s.

Item, for sawing of a rood of lath for the lodge, 9s.

Item, for 1,000 lath boards, 8s.

Item, for 50 slating nails, 12d.

Item, to the slater for roofing one rood, 28s.

Item, for 2 carts that went to the Torwood to fetch 4 great trees, at 7s for each cart, in total is 14s.

Item, to 2 workmen for cleaning of the closets, 8s.

Item, for 6 cartloads of stones, 4s.

Item, delivered to the wrights, between 13 September and 2 October, 600 door nails at 15s per hundred, in total is 7s 6d.

Item, 50 flooring nails, 15d.

Item, taken from the smith, 4 hooks for the lodge door, 12 for the windows, 2 for the furniture, 2 for the kitchen window, and 10 pairs of bands to go with them and nails for the bands, which amounts to 3 stones of made work, in total is 16s 6d.

Item, for a lock for James Carter, 2s.

Item, accounted with Steven Balty, mason, from 31 October to 19 December, being 7 weeks, he taking 14s each week for himself and his apprentice and 7s for his servant, which is 21s each week, in total is £7 7s.

Item, for a boat to pass up the water with 36 'Estland' boards to Linlithgow, 8s.

Item, for the said boat to go for hides to Leith, 7s.

Item, to Steven Balty for stuff bought by him for the wrights and masons, furnishing and all other necessaries in Linlithgow during the said time of 7 weeks, after his account made thereupon, by the king's command, £15 15s.

Item, to James Carver for 7 weeks immediately after Whitsun, he working at Linlithgow, at the king's command, £12 16s 4d.

Summa of the werkis of Lithgw £109 2d.

SOURCE: Dickson, T (ed) 1877–1902 *Accounts of the Lord High Treasurer.* Edinburgh, iv, 523–5.

Baronial Architecture – Crichton Castle

These two views depict Crichton Castle in East Lothian and reflect the rise in fortunes of the Crichton family in the service of the crown in the fifteenth century, especially during the reigns of James II and James III. As new Lords of Parliament by the 1450s, the Crichtons were able to invest in the fashionable architectural statements of the age and developed their formerly simple and highly defensible tower house to reflect palatial and decorative Renaissance tastes, particularly through court-yard embellishments and the addition of a Great Hall.

Crichton Castle: east side of the courtyard

SOURCE: Billings, RW 1908 *The Baronial and Ecclesiastical Antiquities of Scotland*. Edinburgh, i, 106–8.

Ecclesiastical Architecture – Corstorphine Church

This view depicts Corstorphine Church just outside Edinburgh. This church is illustrative of developments in lay patronage of ecclesiastical architecture in the fifteenth century. The noble family of Forrester – who rose to be financial officers for the dukes of Albany and James I and continued in royal service into the reign of James IV – raised Corstorphine Parish Church into a collegiate church in 1429, matching similar foundations by other up-and-coming noble families elsewhere at this time (like the Sinclairs at Rosslyn or the Setons at Seton). A collegiate church – consisting of a college (group) of clergy – was dedicated to undertaking perpetual ceremonial masses for the memory of their patrons, typically before the tombs of these wealthy noble individuals who would be interred at the high altar or in a family aisle.

SOURCE: Billings, RW 1908 *The Baronial and Ecclesiastical Antiquities of Scotland*. Edinburgh, i, 84–6.

Medieval Literature

DOCUMENT 56

John Barbour's *The Bruce*, 1371x5

John Barbour (c.1320–95) was archdeacon of Aberdeen and author of a number of works current at the Stewart court from the last quarter of the fourteenth century. The Bruce is the only one of these works to survive, an epic of some 13,000 lines, most of which covers the story of Robert Bruce from 1286 through to his victory at Bannockburn in 1314. Written (or rather compiled from a number of earlier sources now lost and then embellished) c.1371–75 in vernacular verse, this work was designed to be read out at court and to inspire chivalric, and perhaps patriotic, feeling in its audience. However, the poem may also have been written to inspire the nobles and royal (Stewart) house of the 1370s to co-operate with each other rather than fight and plot politically amongst themselves: Barbour sought to do this by holding up the ideal figures of King Robert I and his loyal knights James Douglas and Thomas Randolph. The Stewart kings certainly paid Barbour a generous pension and may also have viewed his work as a suitable riposte to the ideas of David II (1329–71) of introducing an English prince to the Scottish succession, ahead of the Stewarts. In this extract, Barbour describes Bruce's preparations for battle at Bannockburn, readying to exploit the terrain; the text also speaks to the Scots' tradition of fighting pitched battles on foot, rather than on horse, a tactic which may have cost them dear at such battles as Poitiers (1356) and Verneuil (1424), both fought in France.

The worthi king, quhen he has sene	
Hys ost assemblit all bedene;	bedene: forthwith
And saw thaim wilfull to fulfill	
His liking, with gud hart and will;	
And to maynteyne weill thar franchiss,	franchiss: freedom
He wes rejoysit mony wyss.	
And callyt all his consaile privé,	
And said thaim: 'Lordis, now ye se	
That Inglismen with mekill mycht	
Has all disponyt thaim for the fecht,	disponyt: prepared
For thai yone castell wald reskew.	
Therefor is gud we ordane now	
How we may let thaim of thair purpos;	let: hinder
And sa to thaim the wayis closs,	
That thai pass nocht, but gret letting.	but gret letting: without great

We haiff her with us, at bidding   hinderance
Weill thretty thousand men, and ma.
Mak we four batailis of tha,
And ordane us on sic maner,
That when our fayis cummys ner,   fayis: foes
We to the New Park lad our way;
For that behovys thaim nede away.
Bot giff that thai will benewth us ga,
And our the morraiss passand sa,
We sall be at avantage thar.
And we think that rycht spedfull war
To gang on fute to this fechting,
Armyt bot in litill armyng;
For schup we us on hors to fycht,   schup: risk
Sen our fayis ar mar of mycht,
And better horsyt than ar we,
And gyff we fecht on fute, perfay,
At a vantage we sall be ay;
For in the park, amang the treys,
The horsemen cumbryt beis always.
And the sykis als sa, that ar thar doun,   sykis: ditches/streams
Sall put thaim to confusione.'
All thai consentyt till that saw;
And than in till a litill thraw   litill thraw: short time
Thar four bataillis ordanyt thai.

SOURCE: Burns, W 1874 *The Scottish War of Independence*. Glasgow, ii, 311–12.

Walter Bower's *Scotichronicon* on the Battle of Falkirk, 1298

Bower was abbot of the Augustinian abbey of Inchcolm in the Forth and a tax collector for James I (1406–37). He wrote his great chronicle between 1440 and his death in 1449, at a time of civil strife during the minority of James II (1437–60): for earlier events he used the fourteenth-century chronicle of John of Fordun.

In the year 1298 the said king of England, grieving at the losses and difficulties inflicted on him and his people by William Wallace in numerous ways, gathered a large army and entered the country of Scotland with hostile intent, having with him certain of the nobles of Scotland to help him. Meeting him, the said William with the rest of the magnates of the said kingdom engaged in an arduous battle near Falkirk on July on the feast of St Mary Magdalene, not without severe losses among both the leading men and those of the middle rank of the Scottish nation, and was put to flight. For an account of the malicious outlook which they had adopted, arising from the stream of jealousy which the Comyns directed towards the said William, they abandoned the field along with their accomplices and escaped uninjured. When their malice became known, the aforesaid William, desiring to save his men and himself, hurried to flee by another road.

Pursuing them on the other side, Robert de Bruce, when a steep and impassibly deep valley between the troops of the two armies came into view, is said to have called out loudly to William, asking him who it was that drove him to such arrogance as to seek so rashly to fight in opposition to the exalted power of the king of England and of the more powerful section of Scotland. It is said that William replied like this to him: 'Robert, Robert, it is your inactivity and womanish cowardice that spur me to set authority free in your native land. But it is an effeminate man even now, ready as he is to advance from bed to battle, from the shadow into the sunlight, with a pampered body accustomed to a soft life feebly taking up the weight of battle for the liberation of his own country, the burden of the breastplate – it is he who has made me so presumptuous perhaps even foolish, and has compelled me to attempt or seize these tasks.' With these words William himself looked to a speedy flight, and with his men sought safety.

On account of all this Robert himself was like one awakening from a deep sleep; the power of Wallace's words so entered his heart that he had no longer any thought of favouring the view of the English. Hence, as he became every day braver than he had been, he kept all these words uttered by his faithful friend, considering them to his heart. In this the words written by Seneca prevailed: 'The finest characteristic of a noble mind is that it is easily urged towards honourable ends. Things that are worthless delight no man of lofty disposition. Happy is the man who has turned his mind to better things on the advice of another. He places himself outside the terms of chance, he will attempt what is favourable, he will crush what is unfavourable, and will despise other things which are held in admiration'.

SOURCE: Watt, DER *et al* (ed) 1987–99 *Scotichronicon – Walter Bower*. Aberdeen, vi, 95–7.

Blind Hary's *The Wallace*

Hary, a court poet (though probably only 'blind' in the great Homeric tradition of epic poets), wrote his vernacular poem at the behest of knights in the service of Alexander Stewart the duke of Albany and earl of March c.1474–78. Albany's following in the Borders was a party which opposed the policy of the then King James III of marriage alliance and peace with England: thus there were meant to be clear allegorical lessons in Hary's poem, comparing Wallace with Albany and Bruce with James III, with Wallace advising Bruce to fight the English as the true and patriotic path. Hary's work went on to appear in many published editions into the nineteenth century, making it second only to the Bible in its popularity in Scottish households.

On Magdaleyn day thir folk to ded was dycht.	
Xxxty thousand off Inglismen for trew	Xxx: thirty
The worthy Scottis apon that day thai slew,	
Quhat be Stwart and syn by wicht Wallace.	wicht: strong
For all his prys king Eduuard rewyt that race.	
To the Tor wod he bad the ost suld ryd.	Tor wod: Torwood; ost:
Kerle and he past upon Caroun syd,	host, armed company
Behaldand our apon the south party.	
Bruce formast com and can on Wallace cry,	formast: walking in front
'Quhat art thou thar?' 'A man,' Wallace can say.	
The Bruce answered, 'That has thou prewyt to-day.	prewyt: proved
Abyd,' he said, 'thou nedis nocht now to fle.'	
Wallace answered, 'I eschew nocht for the	eschew nocht for the: I do
Bot that power, has this awn ner Fordon.	not fear thee
Amendis off this, will god, we sall haiff son.'	
'Language off the,' the Bruce said, 'I desyr.'	Language off the: to talk to
'Say furth,' quod he; 'thou may for litill hyr.	you; hyr: hear
Ryd fra that ost and gar thaim bid with Beik.	gar: make
I wald fayn her quhat thou likes to speik.'	fayn: gladly
The ost baid styll, the Bruce passyt thaim fra.	
He tuk with him bot a Scot that hecht Ra.	
Quhen that the Bruce out off that heryng wer,	
He turned in and this question can sper,	
'Quhy wyrkis thou thus and mycht in gud pes be?'	pes: peace

Than Wallace said, 'Bot in defawt of the,   in defawt of the: because of
Throuch thi falsheid thin awn wyt has myskend.   your shortcomings
I cleym no rycht bot wald this land defend,
At thou wyndoys throu thi fals cruell deid.
Thou has tynt two, had beyn worth fer mair meid   tynt: lost
On this ilk day with a gud king to found,
Na v mylyon off fynest gold so round   v: five; Wallace's fallen
That evir was wrocht in werk or ymage brycht!   knights are worth their
I trow in warld was nocht a bettir knycht   weight in gold
Than was the gud Graym off trewth and hardement.'
Teris tharwith fra Wallace eyn doun went.   Teris: tears; eyn: eyes
Bruce said, 'Fer ma on this day we haiff losyt.'   Fer ma: far more
Wallace answerd, 'Allace, thai war ewill cosyt,
Through thi tresson, that suld be our rycht king,
That wilfully dystroyis thin awn off-spryng.'
The Bruce askyt, 'Will thou do my dewys?'   my dewys: as I suggest
Wallace said, 'Nay thow leyffis in sic wys
Thow wald me mak at Eduuardis will to be.
Yeit had I levir to-morn be hyngyt hye!'   had I levir: I would rather
'Yeit sall I say as I wald consaill geyff,   if you do as I advise
Than as a lord thou mycht at liking leiff,
At thin awn will in Scotland for to Ryng   Ryng: reign
And be in pece and hald off Eduuard king.'
'Off that fals king I nevir wage to tak
Bot contrar him with my power to mak.
I cleym no thing as be titill off rycht,
Thocht I mycht reiff, sen god has lent me mycht,   Thocht I mycht reiff:
Fra the thi crowne off this regioun to wer,   though I might be torn in
Bot I will nocht sic a charge on me ber.   two
Gret god wait best quhat wer I tak on hand   wait: knows
For till kep fre that thou art gaynstandand.   to keep free what you betray,
It mycht beyn said off lang gone her off forn,   reject; forn: formerly
In cursyt tym thou was for Scotland born.
Schamys thou nocht that thou nevir yeit did gud,
Thou renygat devorar off thi blud?   renygat devorar: renegade
I vow to God, ma I thi maister be   devourer
In ony field, thou sall fer werthar de   werthar: deservedly
Than sall a Turk, for thi fals cruell wer.
Pagans till us dois nocht so mekill der.'
Than lewch the Bruce at Wallace ernystfulnas   lewch: laughed
And said, 'Thou seis at thus standis the cas,
This day thou art with our power our-set.
Agayn yon king warrand thou may nocht get.'
Than Wallace said, 'We are be mekill thing

Starkar this day in-contrar off yon king,   Starkar: stronger
Than at Beggar, quhar he left mony off his
And als the feild. So sall he do with this
Or de thar-for, for all his mekill mycht.
We haiff nocht losyt in this feild bot a knycht,
And Scotland now in sic perell is stad
To leyff it thus my selff mycht be full mad.'
'Wallace,' he said, 'it prochys ner the nycht.   prochys: approaches
Wald thou to-morn, quhen at the day is lycht,
Or nyn off bell, meit me at this chapel
Be Dunypas? I wald haiff your consell.'
Wallace said, 'Nay, or that Ilk tyme be went,
War all the men hyn till the orient
In-till a will with Eduuard, quha had sworn,
We sall bargane be ix houris to-morn;
And for his wrang reyff othir he sall think scham,
Or de tharfor, or fle in Ingland haym.
Bot and thou will, son be the hour off thre
At that Ilk tryst, will God, thou sall me se.
Quhill I may les this Realm sall nocht forfar.'
Bruce promest hym with xii Scottis to be thar,
And Wallace said, 'Stud thou rychtwys to me,
Cowntir-palys I suld nocht be to the.
I sall bring x, and for thi nowmer ma   x: 10
I gyff no force thocht thou be freynd or fa.'
Thus thai departyt. The Bruce past his way,
Till Lithqwo raid quhar that king Edduard lay,   Linlithgow
The feild had left and lugyt be-south the toun,   lugyt: lodged
To souper set as Bruce at the palyoun   souper: supper; palyoun:
So entryt In and saw vacand his seit.   pavilion
No wattir he tuk bot maid him to the meit.
Fastand he was and had beyn in gret dreid.
Bludyt was all his wapynnys and his weid.   wapynnys: weapons
Sotheroun lordys scornyt him in termys rud.
Ane said, 'Behald, yon Scot ettis his awn blud.'
The king thocht Ill thai maid sic derisioun.
He bad haiff watter to Bruce off Huntyntoun.
Thai bad hym wesche. He said that wald he nocht:
'This blud is myn. That hurtis most my thocht.'
Sadly the Bruce than in his mind remordyt   remordyt: felt remorse
Thai wordis suth Wallace had him recordyt.
Than rewyt he sar, fra resoun had him knawin
At blud and land suld all lik beyn his awin.
With thaim he was lang or he couth get away,

Bot contrar Scottis he faucht nocht fra that day.
Lat I the Bruce sayr movyt in his entent.

SOURCE: McDiarmid, MP (ed) 1969 *Hary's Wallace*. Edinburgh, Scottish Text Society, ii, 55–7.

Robert Henryson, 'The Wolf and the Lamb'

This vernacular poem by Robert Henryson (c.1430–1500) is an allegory for crown-magnate relations and the provision of justice. It was written as poetical advice to James III who was often criticised in parliament for his neglect of justice circuits (ayres) and for his selling of pardons (remissions) for homicide.

Ane cruell wolff, richt rauenous and fell,   fell: fierce
Vpon ane tyme past to ane reueir
Descending from ane rotche vnto ane well;
To slaik his thirst, drank of the watter cleir.
Swa vpon cace ane selie lamb come neir,   selie: weak, defenceless
Bot of his fa the volff na thing he wist,   he did not know of the
And in the streme laipit to cuill his thirst.   wolf's presence

Thus drank thay baith, bot not of ane intent:
The volfis thocht wes all on wickitnes;
The selie lamb was meik and innocent:
Vpon the reuer in ane vther place
Beneth the volff he drank ane lytill space,
Quhill him thocht gude, presomyng thair nane ill.
The volff this saw, and rampand come him till,

With girnand teeth and angrie austre luke,   girnand: bared
Said to the lamb, 'Thow cative wretchit thing,   cative: feeble
How durst thow be sa bald to fyle this bruke   fyle: defile
Quhar i suld drink with thy foull slavering?
It wer almous the for to draw and hing,
That suld presume with thy foull lippis wyle
To glar my drink and this fair watter fyle'.

The selie lamb, quaikand for verray dreid,
On kneis fell and said, 'Schir, with your leif,
Suppois I dar not say thairoff ye leid,   leid: lied
Bot, be my saull, I wait ye can nocht preif   preif: prove
That I did ony thing that suld yow grief;
Ye wait alswa that your accusatioun
Failyeis fra treuth and contrair is to ressoun.

'Thocht I can nocht, nature will me defend,
And off the deid perfyte experience:
All heuie thing man off the self discend,
Bot giff sum thing on force mak resistence;
Than may the streme on na way mak ascence
Nor ryn bakwart; I drank beneth yow far:
Ergo, for me your bruke wes neuer the war.

Ergo [Lat.]: therefore

'Alswa my lippis, sen that I wes ane lam,
Tuitchit na thing that wes contagious,
Bot sowkit milk from pappis off my dam,
Richt naturall, sweit, and also delitious,'
'Weill,' quod the volff, 'thy language rigorus
Cummis the off kind; swa they father before
Held me at bait, baith with boist and schore.

sen: since

This language runs in your blood, your father did the same and escaped all blame

'He wraithit me, and then I culd him warne,
Within ane yeir, and I brukit my heid,
I suld be wrokkin on him or on his barne
For his exorbitant and frawart pleid:
Thow sall doubtless for his deidis be deid.'
'Schir, it is wrang that for the fatheris gilt
The saikles sone suld punist be or split.

wraithit: angered

wrokkin: avenged; barne: bairn

saikles: innocent

'Haiff ye not hard quhat Halie Scripture sayis,
Endytit with the mouth off God almycht?
Off his awin deidis ilk man sall beir the pais,
As pyne for sin, reward for werkis rycht;
For my trespass, quhy suld my sone haue plycht?
Quha did the mis, lat him sustene the pane.'
'Yaa!' quod the volff, 'yit pleyis thow agane?

Quha did the mis: whoever did the harm

'I let the wit, quhen that the father offendis,
I will cheris nane off his successioun,
And off his barnis I may weill tak amendis
Vnto the twentie degree descending doun.
Thy father thocht to mak ane strang poysoun,
And with his mouth in to my watter spew.'
'Schir,' quod the lamb, 'thay twa ar nouther trew.

I let the wit: I let you know

'The law sayis, and ye will vnderstand,
Thair suld na man, for wrang nor violence,
His aduersar punis at his awin hand
With-out proces off law and audience;
Quhilk suld haue leif to mak lawfull defence,
And thairupon summond peremtourly
For to propone, contrairie, or reply.

'Set me ane lauchfull court; I sall compeir
Befoir the lyoun, lord and leill Iustice,
And be my hand I oblis me rycht heir
That I sall byde ane vnsuspect assyis.
This is the law, this is the instant wyis;
Ye suld pretend thairfoir ane summondis mak
Aganis that day, to gif ressoun and tak.'

'Ha,' quod the volff, 'thou wald intruse ressoun
Quhair wrang and reif suld duell in propertie.
That is ane point and part of fals tressoun,
For to gar reuth remane with crueltie.
Be Goddis woundis, fals tratour, thow sall de
For thy trespass, and for they fatheris als.'
With that anone he hint him be the hals.

hint him be the hals:
    gripped him by the head

The selie lamb culd do na thing bot bleit:
Sone wes he hedit; the volff wald do na grace;
Syne drank his blude and off his flesche can eit
Quhill he wes full; syne went his way on pace.
Off his murther quhat sall we say, allace?
Wes not this reuth, wes not this grit pietie,
To gar this selie lamb but gilt thus de?

hedit: beheaded

Moralitas

The pure pepill, this lamb may signifie,
As maill men, merchandis, and all lauboureris,
Of quhome the lyfe is half ane purgatorie,
To wyn with lautie leuing, as efferis.
The wolf betakinnis fals extortioneris
And oppressouris of pure men, as we se,
Be violence, or craft in facultie.

Thre kind of wolfis in this warld now rings:
The first ar fals perverteris of the lawis,
Quhilk vnder poet termis falset mingis,   maintain their power by words
Lettand that all wer gospel that he schawis;   and swear it is the truth
Bot for ane bud the pure man he ouerthrawis, bud: bribe
Smoirand the richt, garrand the wrang proceid – Smoirand: smothering;
Of sic wolfis hellis fyre sall be thair meid.   garrand: helping

O man of law, let be they subteltie,   let be: abandon
With nice gimpis and fraudis intricait,   gimpis: subtlety
And think that God in his diuinitie   think: remember
The wrang, the richt, of all they werkis wait.
For prayer, price, for hie nor law estait,
Of fals querrellis se thow mak na defence:
Hald with the richt, hurt not they conscience.

Ane vther kind of wolfis rauenous
Ar mychtie men, haifand aneuch plenty,   haifand aneuch plenty:
Quhilkis ar sa gredie and sa couetous   having enough
Thay will not thoill in pece ane pureman be: thoill: allow, suffer
Suppois he and his houshald baith suld de
For falt of fude, thairof thay gif na rak,
Bot ouer his heid his mailing will thay tak.

O man but mercie, quhat is in thy thocht?
War than ane wolf, and those culd vnderstand!
Thow hes aneuch; the pure husband richt nocht, husband: farmer
Bot croip and crufe vpon ane clout of land.   croip and crufe: crops and
For Goddis aw, how durst thow tak on hand –   livestock
And throw in barn and byre sa bene and big – bene: in good condition
To put him fra his tak and gar him thig?   thig: beg

The third wolf ar men of heritage,   heritage: lands
As lordis that hes land be Goddis lane,
And settis to the mailleris ane village,   mailleris: tenants
And for ane tyme gressome payit and tane;   gressome: downpayment
Syne vexis him, or half his terme be gane,
With pykit querrellis for to mak him fane   pykit: picked (as in picking
To flit or pay his gressome new agane.   a fight)

His hors, his meir, he man len to the laird,   man: must
To drug and draw in cairt and carriage;
His seruand or his self may not be spaird
To swing and sweit withoutin meit or wage:
Thus how he standis in labour and bondage
That scantlie may he purches by his maill
To leue vpon dry breid and watter caill.

Hes thow not reuth to gar they tennentis sweit   reuth: pity
In to thy laubour, with faynt and hungrie wame,   wame: belly
And syne hes lytill gude to drink or eit
With his menye, at euin quhen he cummis hame?   menye: family
Thow suld be rad for richteous Goddis blame,   rad: afraid
For it cryis ane vengeance vnto the heuinnis hie
To gar ane pur man wirk but meit or fe.   but: without

O thow grit lord, that riches hes and rent,
Be nocht ane wolf, thus to deuoir the pure!   pure: poor
Think that na thing cruell nor violent
May in this warld perpetuallie indure.
This sall thow trow and sikkerlie assure: trow: believe; sikkerlie:
For till oppress, thow sall haif als grit pane   surely
As thow the pure with thy awin hand had slane.

God keip the lamb, quhilk is the innocent,   quhilk: which
From wolfis byit and men extortioneris;
God grant that wrangous men of fals intent
Be manifest, and punischit as effeiris;
And God, as thow all rychteous prayer heiris,
Most saif our king, and gif him hart and hand   Save our king and give him
All sic wolfis to banes of the land.   strength; banes: banish

SOURCE: Smith, GG (ed) 1906–14 *Poems of Robert Henryson*. Edinburgh, ii, 194–205.

'The Ballad of the Outlaw Murray'

This late-fifteenth- or sixteenth-century ballad – illustrative of the strong Border tradition of such song-verse – takes its inspiration probably from real-life incidents which saw James IV exercising justice ayres in the Borders against lawbreakers, for example in 1504 when the king conducted an ayre in concert with the English March Warden and did indeed impose summary justice on a number of outlaws. The outlaw of the ballad may be based on Sir John Murray, seventh laird of Falahill in Peebleshire (or one of his ancestors). Murray of Falahill did assign lands in Ettrick forest to Queen Margaret Tudor, wife of James IV, in 1508–09, and the king had given the forest to the queen as part of her dower. But Murray of Falahill was killed in a skirmish against the Kerr family in 1510, not by a Scott of Buccleuch as the ballad suggests. In many ways Murray is the Scottish version of the archetype Robin Hood forest outlaw figure of contemporary English song, verse and drama.

. . . Word is gane to our nobell king,
  In Edinburgh where that he lay,
  That there was an Outlaw in Etterick forest
  Counted him nought and all his courtrie gay.

'I mak a vowe,' then the goode king said,
  'Unto the man that dear bought me,
  I'se either be king of Etrick forest,
  Or king of Scotland that Outlaw's bee.'

Then spak the erle hight Hamilton,
  And to the noble king said he;
  'My sovereign prince, sum counsell tak,
  First of your nobles, syne of me.

'I redd you send yon bra Outlaw till
  And see gif your man cum will he;
  Desire him cum and be your man,
  And hald of you yon forest frie.

'And gif he refuses to do that,
We'll conquess both his lands and he,
Or else we'll throw his castell down,
And mak a widowe of his gaye ladie . . .

. . . 'The king has vowd to cast my castell down,
And mak a widow of my gay ladye;
He'll hang my merry men pair by pair
I[n] ony place where he may them see.'

'It stands me hard,' quoth Andrew Murray,
'Judge if it stands not hard with me,
To enter against a king with crown,
And put my lands in jeopardie.'

SOURCE: Sargent, HC and Kitteridge, GC (eds) 1905 *English and Scottish Popular Ballads*, London.

PART II

Early Modern Scotland

Flodden to the Marian Civil War: 1513–1573

DOCUMENT 61

The Reactions of Edinburgh to the Defeat at Flodden, 1513

The treaty of 'Perpetual Peace' and the marriage of James IV to Margaret Tudor – the marriage of 'the thistle and the rose' – was a triumph of rhetoric over reality Anglo-Scottish relations remained difficult and James remained committed to alliance with France. In pursuing this aim, his highly popular invasion of northern England ended in disaster at Flodden with the loss of his own life and many of his nobility. Edinburgh reacted with panic to the news of the defeat, fearing invasion and recognising that the city's defensive walls were outdated.

10 September, 1513.

. . . thair is ane greit rumour now laitlie rysin within this toun tuiching our Souverane Lord and his army . . .

All maner of personis nychtbouries within the samyn [burgh] haue reddye thair fensabill geir and wapponis for wier [fencible gear and weapons for war] and compeir [show themselves] thairwith . . . at the jowyng [pealing] of the commoun bell, for the keiping and defens of the town aganis thame that wald invaid the samyn.

And als chairgis that all wemen, and specialie vagabondis, that thai pas to thair labouris and be nocht sene upoun the gait clamorand and cryand, under the pane of banesing and that uther wemen of gude pas to the kirk and pray quhane tyme requiris for our souerane Lord and his armye . . .

SOURCE: Adam, R (ed) 1899 *Edinburgh Records: the burgh accounts*. Edinburgh, 1403–1528, 143–4.

Lawlessness in the Borders, 1518

This document illustrates the lawlessness and violence of the Borders in the early sixteenth century. In the course of the power struggle during the minority of James V, Alexander Hume, third Lord Hume was executed for treason. This led to local unrest in the east march, the local jurisdiction by which justice was supposed to be administered in the region. The acting warden of the march, Anthony d'Arces, Sieur de Labastie, held a justice court at Duns in Berwickshire before he met his end at the hands of the disgruntled Hume family.

He tuik ane feir that he spurit his horse and tuik the flight and fled towards the castell of Dunbar thinkand to win the samin because his horse was goode . . . he was bot an stranger and knew well nocht the gait and rane his horse in ane mose [bog] quhair he could nocht gett out quhill his enemeis come upoun him and thair murdreist him . . . It was said his hair was lang lyke wemens and plat in ane heid lace, the quhilk David Home of Wedderburne knitt on his sadill bow.

SOURCE: Lindsay of Pitscottie, R 1899–1911 *Historie and cronicles of Scotland.* Edinburgh, i, 300–1.

The Funeral of James V (1542) and an Assessment of his Reign

A loyal Catholic and servant of Mary Queen of Scots, John Lesley, bishop of Ross worked (and conspired) to bring about her restoration to the throne of Scotland following her deposition in 1567. His History of Scotland was written to signal his devotion to his queen, and this extract gives an obsequious assessment of the reign of Mary's father, James V.

His burial with publicke processioune was brocht frome Falkland till Edinburgh, quhair quhat evir culd be devysed in solemne pompe, or honourable decore, or duilful dolour and dule [grief] . . . was done, fulfillit with al dew ceremonies and all diligance, Torches lychtet, places spred with Tapestrie, with notable claith, and weil paincted, lamentable trumpetis, qwissels of dule [bagpipes] . . . [and] in the samyn sepulchre quhair Magdalen his sueit wyfe was buriit, was he layd. The people all in dule and lamentatioune . . .

Gif his claithis was onything ornat, he stidiet [strove] never to follow the fassoune of the court or brauitie of women. From pryd he was far . . . He was a manteiner of Justice, an executor of the lawis, a defender of the Innocent and the pure . . . Quhairthrouch he was namet commounlie be his speciall Nobilitie the pure manis king . . . [and] quhen he Diet, his Realme he left ryche, the Tresure nocht tume [empty] and bair of money.

SOURCE: Lesley, J 1888–95 *Historie of Scotland*. Edinburgh, ii, 259–60, 261–2.

DOCUMENT 64

The Scots' Denunciation of the Treaties of Greenwich, 1543

The Treaties of Greenwich of July 1543 provided for Anglo-Scottish peace and the betrothal of Prince Edward, heir of Henry VIII, to the infant Mary Queen of Scots. Less than six months later they were renounced by the Scots, prompting the war between the two kingdoms known as the 'Rough Wooing'.

The quhilk day anentis [concerning] the article proponit tuiching the pece [peace] and contract of mariage laitlie tane and maid betuix the ambassadoris of our soverane lady the quenis grace and the commissaris of the king of Ingland betuix our said soverane lady and Edward prince of Ingland, sone and apperand air to the king of Ingland . . . the said king of ingland hes violate and brokin the said pece and tharfor becaus the said contract of marriage was grantit for the said peice to have bene observit and keipit betuix the twa realmes . . . My lord governour and thre [three] estaitis in parliament forsaid has declarit and declaris the saidis contractis to be expirit in thame selfis and nocht to be keipit in tyme cuming for the part of Scotland be law, equite and just resoun.

SOURCE: 1814–75 *Acts of the Parliaments of Scotland*. Edinburgh, ii, 431.

The Hertford Invasion, 1544

Edward Seymour, earl of Hertford was appointed lieutenant-general in the north to command the English response to the Scottish renunciation of the Treaties of Greenwich. He pillaged Edinburgh, although he found no resistance from the townspeople. The consequence was only to push Scotland further into the arms of France.

A) ORDERS OF THE ENGLISH PRIVY COUNCIL TO THE EARL OF HERTFORD, 10 APRIL 1544

Considering the King's purpose to invade France this summer in person, the principal cause of his sending the army into Scotland was to devastate the country, so that neither they nor any sent thither out of France or Denmark might invade this realm . . . burn Edinborough towne, so rased and defaced when you have sacked and gotten what ye can of it, as there remayn forever a perpetual memory of the vengeaunce of God lightened upon [them] for their falsehood and disloyalty . . . beate down and over throwe the castle, sack Holyrood house and as many townes and villages about Edinborough ye may conveniently, sack Lythe [Leith] and burn and subverte it and the rest, putting man, woman and childe to fire and sword where resistance is made . . .

B) THE ENGLISH BOAST THAT THEIR OBJECTIVES FOR EDINBURGH WERE ACHIEVED, MAY 1544

. . . neither within the walls nor in the suburbs was left one house unburnt: besides the innumerable booty, spoil and pillage that our soldiers brought from thence . . . we burnt the Abbey called Holy Rood House, and the Palace adjoining the same . . . 4,000 light horsemen from the Borders . . . devastating the country within seven miles every way of Edinburgh, they left neither pile, village, nor house standing unburnt, nor stacks of corn; besides great numbers of cattle, which they brought daily into the army . . .

SOURCE: a) Brewer, JS (ed) 1864–1932 *Letters and Papers, foreign and domestic, of the reign of Henry VIII.* London, xix, pt 1, no. 314; b) Secombe, T (ed) 1903 *Tudor Tracts 1532–1588.* London, 43.

DOCUMENT 66

Eyewitness Account of the Battle of Pinkie, 1547

Somerset, by this time Lord Protector of England in the minority of Edward VI, orchestrated an invasion of Scotland in 1547, during which the Scots were defeated at the Battle of Pinkie. The defeat again highlighted the shortcomings of the Scottish army, shortcomings that the English officer and eyewitness William Patten was well placed to chronicle.

Between the two hillocks betwixt us and the Church, they mustered somewhat brim [exposed] in our eyes: at whom as they stayed there awhile, our galley shot off, and slew the Master of Graham with five and twenty near by him: and therewith so scared the four thousand Irish [Gaelic] archers brought by the Earl of Argyle; that where, as it was said, they should have been a wing to the Foreward, they could never after be made to come forward. Hereupon their army did hastily remove . . . toward Fawside Brae . . .

. . . But what after I learned, specially touching their order, their armour, and their manner of fight . . . I have thought necessary here to utter. Hackbutters [hackbut = handgun] have they few or none: and they appoint their fight most commonly always foot. They came to the field, all well furnished with jack [light iron jackets] and skull [helmet], dagger, buckler and swords all notably broad and thin, of exceeding good temper and universally so made to slice, that as I never saw any so good, so I think it hard to devise the better . . .

Herewith waxed it very hot, on both sides, with pitiful cries, horrible roar, and terrible thundering of guns besides. The day darkened above head, with smoke of shot . . . The danger of death on every side . . . The bullets, pellets, and arrows flying each [everywhere] were so thick, and so uncertainly lighting, that nowhere was there any surety of safety . . . The whole face of the field, on both sides . . . both to the eye and the ear, so heavy, so deadly, lamentable, outrageous, terribly confused, and so quite against the quiet nature of man . . .

SOURCE: Secombe, T (ed) 1903 *Tudor Tracts 1532–1588*. London, 108, 111–13.

Bishop Lesley's Epitaph for Mary of Guise

Bishop Lesley's devotion to Mary Queen of Scots was again revealed in his account of her mother, Mary of Guise, who had served from 1554 as regent of Scotland in her daughter's absence and had died in 1560. The devotion that Mary of Guise displayed towards her Catholic faith and the interests of her French family made her a controversial figure, but Lesley's description of her qualities should not be seen as a baseless exaggeration: even Protestant historians grudgingly admitted her talent for politics.

. . . quhen scho [she] was quene regent, and evin than quhen scho was Governour, and rulet the Realme, scho was than, baith of sick [such] humanitie and prudencie, that her wil and maneris with gud will, willinglie scho appliet to all honest maneris of al Scotis, commendable, and probable. Throw use, and experience scho could meikle of our effairis And was verie expert . . . sa did scho Justice with all diligence al her dayes . . . in her selfe the Image of her housband Because he studiet sa mekle til equitie and sa mekle to vertue gave his lyfe. Scho lykwyse in vertues and monie offices of humanitie, far overcam monie utheris women . . .

SOURCE: Lesley, J 1888–95 *Historie of Scotland*. Edinburgh, ii, 441.

Treaty of Edinburgh, 1560

In 1560 an occupying French force supported the authority of the queen regent, Mary of Guise, while an English fleet arrived in support of the emerging Reformation. The death of the queen regent in June acted as an unexpected catalyst to break the deadlock, and on 6 July 1560 the representatives of the French and the English met at Edinburgh to agree that the military forces of both sides, both on land and sea, would withdraw from the kingdom of Scotland. Soon afterwards the 'Reformation Parliament', although unsanctioned by Mary Queen of Scots, met to effect a Protestant settlement.

Since the realms of England and Ireland belong of right to the said most serene lady and princess Elizabeth and no other is therefore allowed to call, write, name or entitle himself or have himself called, written, named or entitled King or Queen of England or Ireland, it is therefore decided, concluded and agreed that the most Christian King [Francis] and Queen Mary . . . shall henceforth abstain from using or bearing the said title and arms of the kingdom of England and Ireland . . .

. . . hereafter their Majesties shall not introduce into this kingdom any soldiers out of France, or any other nations whatsoever, unless in the event of a foreign army's attempting to invade and possess this kingdom, in which case the king and queen shall make provision by and with the counsel and advice of the three estates of this nation . . .

SOURCE: Donaldson, G (ed) 1970 *Scottish Historical Documents*. Edinburgh, 120–4.

John Knox's Account of the Return of Mary Queen of Scots from France, 1561

Mary spent almost all of her life in France before the death of her husband, Francis II, left her with no option but to return to the kingdom that she had never ruled in person and barely knew. John Knox's account, written in 1566, gives an indication of the welcome that the queen received upon her return to Scotland, and the reactions of Protestants to her intention to continue to practise her Catholic faith, a faith that was illegal for any of her subjects to practise.

The 19th day of August, 1561, betwixt seven and eight hours before noon, arrived Mary queen of Scotland, then widow, with two gallies out of France . . . The very face of the heaven, at the time of her arrival, did manifestly speak what comfort was brought into this country with her, *to wit*, sorrow, dolor, darkness, and all impiety; for the memory of man, that day of the year was never seen a more dolorous face of the heaven, than was at her arrival, which two days after did so continue: for, besides the surface wet, and corruption of the air, the mist was so thick and dark, that scarce might any man espy another . . . the sun was not seen to shine two days before, not two days after. That forewarning gave God unto us but alas the most part were blind. At the sound of the cannons, which the gallies shot, the multitude being advertised, happy was he or she that first must have the presence of the queen; the protestants were not the slowest, and therein they were not to be blamed . . .

Fires of joy were set forth at night, and a company of most honest men with instruments of music, and with musicians, gave their salutations at her chamber window: the melody, as she alledged, liked her well; and she willed the same to be continued some nights after with great diligence. The lords repaired to her from all quarters, and so nothing understood but mirth and quietness, till the next Sunday, which was the 24th of August: when that preparations began to be made for that idol of the mass to be said in the chapel; which perceived, the hearts of all the godly began to be emboldened, and men began to openly speak, 'Shall that idol be suffered again to take place within this realm? It shall not.' The lord Lindsay, then but master, with the gentlemen of Fife, and others, plainly cried in the closs or yard, 'The idolatrous priests should die the death, according to God's law.' . . . The door was kept that none should have entry to trouble the priest . . . And so the godly departed with grief of heart, and after noon repaired to the abbey in great companies, and gave plain signification, that they could not abide that the land, which God by his power had purged from idolatry, should in their eyes be polluted again.

SOURCE: John Knox, *History of the Reformation,* in Fyfe, JG (ed) 1928 *Scottish Diaries and Memoires 1550–1746.* Stirling, 18–20.

Accounts of Two Murders, 1566–67

In 1566 (while heavily pregnant with the future James VI) and in 1567 Mary had to endure the murder of two men who were close to her, both acts committed by members of her nobility. In both cases, some of the blame for the deeds was laid at Mary's own door. In the case of David Riccio it was alleged that she had become too dependent on a lowborn musician as her counsellor, when she should have paid more attention to her nobility. In the case of her husband, Darnley, who had fallen out of her favour, it was alleged that she and her new favourite, the earl of Bothwell (whom she married shortly afterwards), were instrumental in the conspiracy. Shortly afterwards Mary was forced to abdicate in favour of her infant son, who was delivered into the care and control of her Protestant half-brother, the earl of Moray.

A) THE MURDER OF DAVID RICCIO, MARCH 1566

the quenis grace, the countes of Ergyle, and the said David being talkand togidder at the quenis burde [table], quhair her majestie haid sowpit [supped] in her cabonate . . . he fled to hir for his refuge, yit thai unmercifully had him to that chamber quhair hir majestie eittis, and thair crewellie and maist shamefully slew and murderit him with quhingaris [daggers]; it is said he had twa and fyftie strakis in his bodie . . .

B) THE MURDER OF LORD DARNLEY AT KIRK O' FIELD, FEBRUARY 1567

At nicht the quein passit to hir bed to the abbey and the king to his bed in the kirk of feild and at the hour of twa eftir midnycht certane conspiratours or traittouris come into his chalmer he beand in his bed and tuik him furth and maist traittorouslie and cruellie thair thay wirrit [strangled] him to the deid witht his awin paige witht him.

SOURCE: a) 1833 *Diurnal of remarkable occurrents that have passed within the country of Scotland.* Edinburgh, 89–90; b) Lindsay of Pitscottie, R 1899–1911 *Historie and cronicles of Scotland.* Edinburgh, ii, 191.

The Reign of James VI: 1573–1625

DOCUMENT 71

Spottiswoode on Presbyterianism, 1575

The historian John Spottiswoode (1565–1639), son of a Protestant reformer and later archbishop of St Andrews, narrates the developing conflict as the Reformed Church of Scotland was torn between presbyterianism and episcopalianism, and identifies Andrew Melville (1545–1622) as the principal troublemaker of the presbyterian party.

In the Church this year began the innovations to break forth that to this day have kept it in a continual unquietness. Mr Andrew Melvill, who was lately come from Geneva, a man learned (chiefly in the tongues), but hot and eager upon any thing he went about, labouring with a burning desire to bring into this Church the Presbyteriall discipline of Geneva; and having insinuated himself into the favour of divers preachers, he stirred up John Dury, one of the ministers of Edinburgh, in an Assembly which was then convened, to propound a question touching the lawfulness of the episcopal function, and the authority of chapters in their election.

SOURCE: Dickinson, WC 1954 *A Source Book of Scottish History*. London, iii, 16–17.

Second Book of Discipline, 1578

Andrew Melville was one of over thirty members of a committee charged with the task of producing a Second Book of Discipline, *as the Reformed Church sought to consolidate and strengthen its position on the separation of the ecclesiastical and civil spheres, of church and state. Although the document is consonant with Melville's ideas on presbyterian purity, he should not be seen as a dominant influence in its creation.*

The kirke . . . hes a certane power grantit be God, according to the quhilk it uses a proper jurisdiction and government, exerciseit to the confort of the haill kirk. This power ecclesiasticall is an authoritie granted be God the Father, throw the Mediator Jesus Christ, unto his kirk gatherit, and having the ground in the Word of God; to be put in execution be them, unto quhom the spirituall government of the kirk be lawfull calling is committit.

The policie of the kirk flowing from this power is an order or forme of spirituall government, quhilk is exercisit be the members appoyntit thereto be the Word of God; and therefore is gevin immediatly to the office-beararis, be whom it is exercisit to the will of the haill bodie . . .

This power and policie ecclesiasticall is different and distinct in the awin nature from that power and policie quhilk is callit the civill power, and appertenis to the civill government of the commonwelth; albeit they be both of God, and tend to one end, if they be rightlie usit, to wit, to advance the glorie of God and to have godlie and gud subjectis.

For this power ecclesiasticall flowes immediatlie from God, and the Mediator Jesus Christ, and is spirituall, not having a temporall heid on earth, bot onlie Christ, the onlie spirituall King and Governour of his kirk.

Therefore this power and policie of the kirk sould leane upon the Word immediatlie, as the onlie ground thereof, and sould be tane from the pure fountaines of the Scriptures, the kirk hearing the voyce of Christ, the onlie spirituall King, and being rewlit be his lawes.

It is proper to kings, princes and magistrates, to be callit lordis, and dominators over their subjectis, whom they govern civilly; bot it is proper to Christ onlie to be callit Lord and Master in the spirituall government of the kirk: and all uthers that bearis office therein aucht not to usurp dominion therein, nor be callit lordis, bot onlie ministeris, disciples and servantis. For it is Christis proper office to command and rewll his kirk universall, and every particular kirk, throw his Spirit and Word, be the ministrie of men.

Notwithstanding, as the ministeris and uthers of the ecclesiasticall estait ar subject to the magistrat civill, so aught the person of the magistrat be subject to the kirk spiritually and in ecclesiasticall government. And the exercise of both these jurisdictiones cannot stand in one person ordinarlie. The civill power is callit the Power of the Sword, and the uther the Power of the Keyes.

The civill power sould command the spiritual to exercise and doe their office according to the Word of God: the spiritual rewlaris sould require the Christian magistrate to minister justice and punish vyce, and to maintaine the libertie and quietness of the kirk within their boundis.

. . . The ministeris exerce not the civill jurisdictioun, bot teach the magistrat how it sould be exercit according to the Word.

. . . Finally, as ministeris are subject to the judgement and punishment of the magistrat in externall things, if they offend; so aucht the magistratis to submit themselfis to the discipline of the kirk gif they transgresse in matteris of conscience and religioun.

SOURCE: Dickinson, WC 1954 *A Source Book of Scottish History*. London, iii, 22–3.

Act Establishing Presbyterian Government, 1592

The struggle between presbyterianism and episcopalianism intensified as James VI reached maturity. The 'Black Acts' of 1584 had set back the presbyterian cause by asserting the supremacy of the crown and the authority of the bishops. The 'Golden Act' of 1592 signified the recovery of presbyterian strength, although it did not overthrow the power of the crown or of the bishops. Most significantly, the right to name the place and time of general assemblies was vested with the king.

Oure soverane lord and estaittis of this present parliament, following the lovable and gude example of thair predicessouris, hes ratifiet and apprevit and be the tennour of this present act ratifies and apprevis all liberties, privileges, immunities and freedoms quhatsumevir gevin and grantit be his hienes, his regentis in his name or ony of his predicessouris, to the trew and haly kirk presentlie establishit within this realme . . .

And siclyk ratifies and apprevis the general assemblies appoyntit be the said kirk, and declairis that it salbe lauchfull to the kirk and ministrie everilk yeir at the leist and ofter *pro re nata* [for matters arising] as occasioun and necessitie sall require to hald and keip generall assemblies providing that the kingis majestie or his commissioner with thame to be appoyntit be his hienes be present at ilk generall assemblie befoir the dissolving thairof nominat and appoint tyme and place quhen and quhair the nixt general assemblie salbe haldin. And in cais nather his majestie nor his said commissioner beis present for the tyme in that toun quhair the said generall assemblie beis haldin, than and in that cais it salbe lesum to the said generall assemblie be thame selffis to nominat and apoynt tyme and place quhair the nixt generall assemblie of the kirk salbe keipit and haldin as they haif bene in use to do thir tymes bypast.

And als ratifies and apprevis the sinodall and provinciall assemblies to be haldin be the said kirk and ministrie twyis ilk yeir as thay haif bene and ar presentlie in use to do within every province of this realme. And ratifies and apprevis the presbiteries and particulare sessionis appointit be the same kirk with the haill jurisdictioun and discipline of the same kirk aggreit upoun be his majestie in conference had be his hienes with certain of the ministrie convenit to that effect . . .

And because thair ar divers actis of parliament maid in favouris of the papistical kirk . . . not abrogat nor annullit: thairfoir his hienes and estaittis foirsaidis hes abrogat, cassit and annullit etc. all actis of parliament maid be ony of his hienes predecessouris for mantenance of supersitioun and idolatrie with all and quhatsumevir actis, lawes and statutes maid at ony tyme befoir the day and dait heirof aganis the libertie of the trew kirk, jurisdictioun and discipline thairof as the samyn is usit and exerceisit within this realme . . .

Item the kingis majestie and estaittis foirsaidis declairis that the secund act of the parliament haldin at Edinburgh the xxii day of May, the yeir of God [1584] sall na wayes be prejudiciall nor dirogat any thing to the privilege that God hes gevin to the spirituall office beraris in the kirk concerning headis of religioun, materis of heresie, excommunicatioun, collatioun or deprivatioun of ministeris or ony sic essentiall censouris specially groundit and havand warrand of the Word of God. Item . . . annullis the xx act of the same parliament [at Edinburgh 1584] granting commissioun to bishoppis and utheris juges constitute in ecclesiastical caussis to resave his hienes presentatioun to benefices, to give collatioun thairupon and to put ordour in all caussis ecclesiasticall . . . and thairfoir ordains all presentationis to benefices to be direct to the particular presbiteries in all tyme cuming, with full power to thame to giff collationis thairupoun and to put ordour to all materis and caussis ecclesiasticall within thair boundis . . .

SOURCE: Dickinson, WC 1954 *A Source Book of Scottish History*. London, iii, 48–9.

The Resurgence of the Bishops

As a powerful adult monarch, and as king of England and Ireland as well as Scotland, James VI was keen to restore and extend the power of bishops, and through them the power of the crown, over the Scottish Church. He used his power to decide the time and place of general assemblies, and constrained Andrew Melville to remain in exile in England as he sought to have bishops recognised as moderators, first of presbyteries, and then of synods; and for their power to be extended to cases of excommunication and the deposition of ministers.

A) THE PRIVY COUNCIL ON THE ROLE OF BISHOPS, 1607

Forsamekle as, at the Assemblie of the Kirk keipit and haldin at the burgh of Linlithqu in the moneth of [December] last bypast, and assisted with a verie frequent number of the Nobilitie, Counsale, and Estaittis of this kingdome, it wes ordanit that the moderatour of every synode sould be nominat and chosin out of the Moderatouris of the prisbitereis quhair[of] the synode consisted, and gif thair be a Bischop within the synode that the Bischop salbe Moderatour of the synode, as in ane Act of the said Assemblie maid to this effect at lenth is contenit: and seing the Synode of Fyff is appointed to be haldin at the burgh of Dysart upoun the nynt day of Junii instant, necessar it is that the Archibischop of Sanctandrois, who is ane of the number of that Synode, be nominat, electit, and chosin Moderatour of the said Synode, conforme to the said Act of Linlithqu: Thairfoire the Lordis of Secrite Counsale ordanis letters to be direct chairgeing the bretherine of the ministerie of the said Synode to ressave and admit the said Archibischop of St Androis as Moderatour of the said Synode within three houris nixt efter the chairge, undir the pane of rebellioun, etc; as alsua chairgeing the said Archibischop to accept that chairge upoun him . . .

B) GLASGOW ASSEMBLY ACTS, 1610

It is thought expedient that the Bischops salbe Moderatours in every Diocesian Synod, and the Synods salbe haldin twyse in the yeir of the kirks of every Dyocie . . . No sentence of excommunicatioun or absolutioun therfra [may] be pronouncit against or in favours of any person without the knowledge and approbation of the Bischop of the Dyocie . . . In depositioun of Ministers, the Bischop associating to himselfe the Ministrie of these bounds quher the delinquent served, he is then to take tryall of his fault, and upon just cause found, to depryve him . . . The Bischops salbe subject in all things concerning thair lyfe, conversatioun, office, and benefice, to the censures of the Generall Assemblie; and being found culpable, with his Majesties advyce and consent, to be deprivit.

SOURCE: Dickinson, WC 1954 *A Source Book of Scottish History*. London, iii, 56–7, 60–1.

The Five Articles of Perth, 1618

Following his visit to Scotland in the summer of 1617, James VI demanded further changes to the church, which included the restoration of traditional Christian ceremonies and, most controversially, the demand that worshippers kneel to receive communion. The articles were rejected by a general assembly at St Andrews in November 1617, but were accepted by a more compliant general assembly held at Perth in August 1618.

James by the grace of God, etc.

Forsameikle as in the Generall Assemblie of the Kirk, holden latelie at our burgh of Perth, in the moneth of August last bypast, which was countenanced by the presence and assistance of certane commissioners for us, and of diverse noblemen, barons, and commissioners from the cheefe and principall burrowes of this our kingdome, there were certane godlie and good acts made and sett doun, concerning the glorie of God and governement of his church, agreeable to that decent and comelie order which was observed in the primitive kirk, when the same was in the greatest puritie and perfection; as namelie,

An act ordaining, that everie minister sall have the commemoration of the inestimable benefites received from God by and through our Lord and Saviour Jesus Christ his Birth, Passion, Resurrection, Ascension, and sending doun of the Holie Ghost, upon the days appointed for that use; and that they sall make choice of severall and pertinent texts of Scripture, and frame their doctrine and exhortation thereto, and rebuke all superstitious observation and licentious profanation of the said dayes:

An act anent the administration of baptisme in privat houses, when the necessitie sall require:

An act anent the catechising of young children of eight yeers of age, and presenting them to the bishop to lay hands upon them, and blesse them, with prayer for increase of their knowledge, and continuance of God's heavenlie graces with them:

An act anent the administration and giving of the Holie Communion in private houses to sicke and infirme persons:

An act, that the blessed sacrament of the Holie Communion of the bodie and blood of our Lord and Saviour Jesus Christ be celebrate to the people humblie and reverentlie kneeling upon their knees:

[And other acts cited]

Which acts being seene and considered by us, and we finding that the same has beene verie wiselie, gravelie, and with good deliberation, made and sett doun for the weill of the kirk: Therefore we, out of our true respect to the honour of God, and to have him honoured by all our people, has by our authoritie royall, with the advice of the Lords of our Privie Counsell, ratified, allowed, approven, and confirmed, and by the tenor of this our present act ratifies, allowes, approves, and confirmes the acts particularlie above writtin, in all and sundrie points, clauses, heads, articles, and conditions thereof; and ordains the same to have the force and strength of lawes in all time coming, and to have effect and execution in all places of this our kingdome. And in speciall, that there sall be a cessation and abstinence from all kinde of labour and handie-worke upon the five dayes above written, which are appointed to be dedicate to God's service, to the effect our subjects may the better attend the holie exercises which are to be keeped in the kirks at these times . . . Certefying [*that all those who do not observe the acts and who do not abstain from labour upon the five days mentioned*] sall be repute, holden, and esteemed as seditious, factious, and unquyett persons, disturbers of the peace and quyet of the kirk, contemners of our just and royall commandement, and sall be punished therefore in their persons and goods with all rigour and extremitie to the terrour of others, at the arbitriment of the Lords of our Privie Counsel . . .

Given under our signet, at Halyrudehouse, the 21st day of October, and of our raigne the 16 and 52 yeers, 1618.

SOURCE: Dickinson, WC 1954 *A Source Book of Scottish History*. London, iii, 63–5.

The Abolition of Norse Law in Orkney and Shetland, 1611

Although it had long been intended that Orkney and Shetland would retain their own laws, the abuses of the Stewart magnates made this unworkable. Patrick Stewart, second earl of Orkney (c.1566–1615) lived an extravagant lifestyle and embroiled himself in debt, and in rebellion against the king, for which he was executed in 1615.

Forsamekle as the kingis majestie and his predicessouris of famous memorie with the consent and auctorotie of thair esteatis of parliament hes statute and ordanit that all and sindrie the subjectis of this kingdome sould lieve and be governit under the lawis and statutes of this realme allanarlie [only] and be no law of foreyne cuntreyis, as in the actis maid thairanent at lenth is contenit, nochtwithstanding it is of treuthe that some personis beiring power of magistracie within the boundis of Orknay and Yetland hes thir divers yeiris bigane maist unlauchfullie tane upoun thame for thair awne privat gayne and commoditie to judge the inhabitantis of the saidis cuntreyis be foreyne lawis, making choise sometimes of foreyne lawis and sometymes of the proper lawis of this kingdome as thay find mater of gayne and commoditie, in heich contempt of our soverane lord and to the grite hurte and prejudice of his majesteis subjectis: Thairfoir the lordis of secreit counsaile hes dischargeit and be the tennour heirof dischargeis the saidis foreyne lawis, ordaining the same to be no forder usit within the saidis cuntreyis of Orknay and Yetland at ony tyme heirefter, and that letters of publicatioun be direct heirupoun commanding and inhibiting all and sindrie personis beiring office of magistracie and judicatorie within the same that nane of thame presome nor tak upoun hand at ony tyme heirefter to judge or censure the inhabitantis within the saidis boundis be foreyne lawis nor to proceid in ony actioun or caus criminal or civile according to foreyne lawis, bot to use the proper lawis of this kingdome to his majesteis subjectis in all thair actionis and caussis as thay and ilk ane of thame will answer upoun the contrarie at thair heichest perrell.

SOURCE: Dickinson, WC 1954 *A Source Book of Scottish History*. London, iii, 273–4.

Act of Parliament on Taxation, 1599

This act of parliament illustrates the sensitivity and diplomacy required in handling the issue of taxation.

The Kingis Majestie haifing exponit and declairit to his nobilitie and estaittis how that the necessar charges of his honourable effairis and adois daylie incresse, and that his majesties rentis and casualities ar not able to interteny his present estait in that honour and royall port quhilk his place and apperance dois require, and how that beside and attour the intertinement of thair majesties houssis and bairnis his hienes palaceis and castellis ar altogidder ruinous and at the point of decay, his munitioun and ordinance unmountit without provisioun of pulder [powder] and bullet, his majesties movabillis waisted worne and consumit, Besydis divers utheris his majesties extraordiner charges in his maist wechtie effairis at mair lenth declairit befoir the saidis estaittis, Quhilkis the offices of thesaurie comptrollarie and collectorie ar nocht able to defray; And how that the default of moyane hes bene ane greit lat and impediment to his majestie in the dew prosequutioun and punischement of the avowit contempt rebellioun and disobedience sa publict and complenit upoun all in the land: Consideddring lykewayes how grevous the burden of taxationis hes bene to his majesties subjectis and how litill profitable ather to the supplie of the foirsaidis defectis or ony uther his majesties necessary serviceis; Quharupoun his majestie is resolvit in his tyme never to impone ony taxatioun heirefter upoun his pepill bot rather to expect at thair handis sum favourable relief of thair benevolence without ony grudge. The saidis estaittis haifing hard and being surelie informit of his majesties gracious resolution foirsaid, thay haif all aggreit in ane voice that his majesties honorable necessities salbe suppliet be ilkane of thame at thair uttermost powar. Bot becaus of the schortnes of the tyme and thair langsum tarying, besydis the few nowmer of the estaittis presentlie convenit, the supplie of his majesties necessitie and maist feit moyane for prosequuting of the best remeid therof is be all thair consentis remittit to ane mair frequent conventioun to be apointit at his majesties guid plesur sa convenientlie as it may be. At the quhilk tyme the estaittis presentlie convenit hes faithfullie promeist to hald hand and concur to sie the necessitie of his majesties effairis suppliet be sic meanis as may be best fund out to his hienes greittest weill and smallest grief to his subiectis.

SOURCE: Dickinson, WC 1954 *A Source Book of Scottish History*. London, iii, 290–1.

Election of Lords of the Articles, 1617 and 1621

The Lords of the Articles, or Committee of the Articles, was a standing committee of parliament consisting of eight churchmen, eight noblemen, eight representatives of the shires, and eight of the burghs, as well as the officers of state. Its function was the drafting of legislation, and it was an important mechanism of James VI's control of Scotland after his relocation to Westminster. Two elections to the committee are recorded in these documents by the presbyterian historian and critic of the king, David Calderwood.

A) 1617

The tyme being thus spent til foure of the afternoone, they proceedit to the choosing of the Lords of the Articles. The noblemen, speciallie suche as feared a prejudice to their estate, and namelie touching the dissolution of the erectiones and of the right they had to the tythes, were not content that they sould be chosen as the king and the bishops would have them. The king purposed once to dissolve the parliament and the lords were readie to depart. At last they were chosen, but not altogether to the king and the bishops' contentment. But the king would in noe case suffer the Laird of Dunipace to be one of the number becaus he had found him his opposite at the assize of Linlithgow, where the ministers were convict of treasone [in 1606]. The king and the estates came out of the Tolbuith after ten houres at night, and went doun to the palace in great confusion, some ryding in their robes, others walking on foote and the honours not caried as before. The Lords of the Articles satt everie day, except the Lord's day, and the king himself was ever present.

B) 1621

The Grand Commissioner, the noblemen and the prelates, the chancelour, the thesaurer, the secretarie, and clerk of register went into the Inner-House to choose the Lords of the Articles. The choise was not made of persons most indifferent, of best judgement, and noe ways partiallie affected to anie partie, as beseemeth free parliaments and counsels. The bishops choosed eight of the nobilitie, Anguse, Mortoun, Niddisdaill, Wigtoun, Roxburgh, Balcleugh, Scoone, Carnegie. These choosed eighte bishops, St Androes, Glasco, Dunkeld, Aberdeen, Brechine, Dumblaine, Argile, Orkney, and these together choosed eight barons and eight burgesses ... The officers of estate, the chancellour, the thesaurer, privie seale, justice clerk, the king's advocate, and the clerk of register, men readie to serve the king's humour for the benefite they had by their offices and hopes of greatter preferments, satt and voted with them, howbeit not chosen.

SOURCE: Dickinson, WC 1954 *A Source Book of Scottish History*. London, iii, 236–7.

DOCUMENT 79

Basilikon Doron

James VI wrote Basilikon Doron *in 1598 to give his eldest son and heir Henry advice on ruling a kingdom. Henry predeceased his father and when James VI died in 1625 his second son succeeded him as Charles I. Only a few copies of this first edition are known to have been published, suggesting that the text was first intended to remain within the court before its wider publication.*

A) INTRODUCTORY SONNET

God gives not Kings the style of Gods in vaine,
For on his throne his Scepter do they swey:
And as their subjects ought them to obey,
So Kings should feare and serve their God againe.
If then ye would enjoy a happie raigne,
Observe the Statutes of your Heavenly King;
And from his Lawe make all your Lawes to spring:
Since his Lieutenant heare ye should remaine.
Reward the just, be steadfast, true, and plaine:
Represse the proud, mainting ay the right,
Walke alwaies so, as ever in his sight
Who guardes the godly, plaging the prophaine,
      And so ye shall in princely vertues shine.
      Resembling right your mighty King divine.

B) PREFATORY LETTER FROM THE KING TO HIS SON

To Henrie My Dearest Sonne and Natural Successour
. . . Since I the author thereof as your naturall Father, must be carefull for your godlie and vertuous education as my eldest Sonne, and the first fruites of Gods blessing towards me in my posteritie: And (as a King) must timouslie prouide for your training up in all the poyntes of a Kinges office . . .

I have therefore, (for the greater ease to your memorie, and that ye may at the first, cast up any part that ye have to doe with) devided this whole booke in three partes. The first teacheth you your duty towards God as a Christian: the next your duetie in your office as a King: And the third teacheth you how to behave your selfe in indifferent things, which of themselves are neither right nor wrong, but according as they are rightly or wrongly used: & yet will serve (according to your behaviour therein) to augment or impair your fame and authoritie at the hands of your people.

Receive and welcome this booke then, as a faithfull praeceptour and counsellor unto you: which (because my affaires will not permit me ever to be present with you) I ordaine to be a resident faithfull admonisher of you. And because the houre of death is uncertaine to me (as unto all flesh) I leave it as my Testament, & latter wil unto you.

I charge you (as ever ye think to deserve my fatherly blessing) to follow and put in practise (as farre as lyeth in you) the precepts hereafter following: and if ye follow the contrair course, I take the greate God to recorde, that this booke shall one day be a witnes betwixt me and you, and shall procure to bee ratified in heaven, the curse that in that case here I give you; for I protest before that great God, I had rather be not a Father and child-lesse, nor a Father of wicked children. But (hoping, yea, even promising unto my selfe, that God who in his greate blessing sent you unto mee, shall in the same blessing as he hath given me a Sonne, so make him a good and a godlie sonne, not repenting him of his mercy shewen unto me) I end this preface with my earnest prayer to God to worke effectually into you, the fruits of that blessing which here from my hearte, I bestow upon you.

SOURCE: James VI, 1599 *Basilikon Doron*. Edinburgh.

Speech of James VI and I to the English Parliament, 1607

James's speech was an impassioned and eloquent plea for closer union between England and Scotland, at a point when the ramifications of the Union of the Crowns were still being worked out. While English MPs could not agree with the king's proposals, this document illuminates how the Scots and the English understood (and misunderstood) one another. The king highlighted a number of anxieties about the prospect of Anglo-Scottish Union that dogged not only his own plan but successive discussions of this possibility through to 1707. Also in this speech, he made his famous statement that he could govern Scotland by his pen.

For the supposed inconveniences rising from Scotland, they are three. First, that there is an evill affection in the Scottish Nation to the Union. Next, the Union is incompatible betweene two such Nations. Thirdly, that the gaine is small or none. If this be so, to what end doe we talke of an Union? For proofe of the first point, there is alledged an aversenesse in the Scottish Nation expressed in the Instrument, both in the preface and body of their Act; In the preface, where they declare, that they will remaine an absolute and free Monarchie; And in the body of the Acte, where they make an exception of the ancient fundamentall Lawes of that kingdome. And first

for the generall of their aversenesse, All the maine current in your Lower-house ranne this whole Session of Parliament with that opinion, That Scotland was so greedy of this Union, and apprehended that they should receive so much benefit by it, as they cared not for the strictnesse of any conditions, so they might attaine to the substance: And yet you now say, they are backwards and averse from the Union. This is a direct contradiction . . .

And first I confesse, that the English Parliaments are so long, and the Scottish so short, that a meane betweene them would do well: For the shortnesse of their continuing together, was their cause of their hastie mistaking, by setting these wordes of exception of fundamentall Lawes in the body of the Acte, which they onely did in pressing to imitate word by word the English Instrument, wherein the same words be conteined in your Preface.

And as to their meaning and interpretation of that word, I will not onely deliver it unto you out of mine owne conceipt, but as it was delivered unto mee by the best Lawyers of Scotland, who were at the making thereof in Scotland, and were Commissioners here for performance of the same.

Their meaning in the word of Fundamentall Lawes, you shall perceive more fully hereafter, when I handle the objection of the difference of Lawes: For they intend thereby onely those Lawes whereby confusion is avoyded, and their Kings descent mainteined, and the heritage of the succession and Monarchie, which hath bene a kingdome, to which I am in descent, 300 yeeres before CHRIST; Not meaning it, as you doe, of their Common Law, for they have none, but that which is called Ius Regis: and their desire of continuing a free Monarchie, was onely meant, That al such Priviledges (whereof I spake before) should not bee so confounded, as for want either of Magistrate, Law, or order, they might fall in such a confusion, as to become like a naked Province, without Law or libertie under this kingdome. I hope you meane not I should set Garrisons over them, as the Spaniards doe over Sicily and Naples, or governe them by Commissioners, which are seldome found succeedingly all wise and honest men.

This I must say for Scotland, and I may truly truely vaunt it; Here I sit and gouerne it with my Pen, I write and it is done, and by a Clearke of the Councell I governe Scotland now, which others could not doe by the sword. And for their aversenesse in their heart against the Union, It is true indeede, I protest they did never crave this Union of men, nor sought it either in private, or the State by letters, nor ever once did any of that Nation presse me forward or wish me to accelerate that businesse. But on the other part, they offerd alwayes to obey when it should come to them, and all honest men that desire my greatnesse have beene thus minded, for the personall reverence and regard they beare unto my Person, and any of my reasonable and just desires.

I know there are many *Piggots* amongst them, I meane a number of seditious and discontented particular persons, as must be in all Common-wealths, that where they dare, may peradventure talke lewdly enough: but no Scottishman ever speake dishonourably of England in Parliament. For here must I note unto you the difference of the two Parliaments in these two Kingdomes; for there they must not speake without the Chancellors leave, and if any man doe propound or utter any seditious or uncomely speeches, he is straight interrupted and silenced by the Chancellors authoritie: where as here, the libertie for any man to speake what hee list, and as long as he list, was the onely cause hee was not interrupted. It hath beene objected, that there is a great Antipathy of the Lawes and Customes of these two Nations. It is much mistaken . . .

It hath likewise been objected as an other impediment, that in the Parliament of Scotland the King hath not a negative voice, but must passe all the Lawes agreed on by the Lords and Commons. Of this I can best resolve you: for I am the eldest Parliament man in Scotland, and have sit in more Parliaments than any of my Predecessors. I can assure you, that the forme of Parliament there, is nothing inclined to popularitie . . . If any man in Parliament speake of any other matter then is in this forme first allowed by me, The Chancellor tells him there is no such Bill allowed by the King . . .

The last impediment is the French liberties: which is thought so great, as except the Scots forsake France, England cannot bee united to them. If the Scottish Nation would be so unwilling to leave them as is said, it would not lye in their hands. For the League was never made betweene the people, as is mistaken, but betwixt the Princes onely and their Crownes . . .

And as for the last point of this subdivision concerning the gaine that England may make by this Union, I thinke no wise nor honest man will aske any such question. For who is so ignorant, that doeth not know the gaine will bee great? Doe you not gaine by the Union of Wales? And is not Scotland greater than Wales? Shall not your Dominions bee encreased of Landes, Seas, and persons added to your greatnesse? And are not your Landes and Seas adjoyning? . . . You shall have them that were your enemies to molest you, a sure backe to defend you: their bodies shall be your aides, and they must be partners in all your quarels: Two snow-balls put together, make one the greater: Two houses joyned, make the one larger: two Castle walles made in one, makes one as thicke and strong as both.

SOURCE: James VI and I 1607 *His Maiesties speech to both the houses of Parliament . . . the last day of March 1607*. London.

Charles I, The Covenants and Cromwell: 1625–1660

DOCUMENT 81

Henry Guthrie on the Opponents of Charles I's Religious Policies

Henry Guthrie is a representative example of a man swept in different directions by the upheavals of the mid-seventeenth century. In 1637 he opposed Charles I's liturgical innovations, and he subscribed to the National Covenant in 1638. He made enemies among radical presbyterians, however, because he believed that they leaned too closely to congregational independence, while he was committed to a presbyterian church system organised on local, regional and national lines. By the Restoration period, however, he had come to believe that bishops were necessary to maintain order in the church, and he became bishop of Dunkeld in 1665.

When, by the death of that renowned king James VI, Charles I came to sit upon the throne, they [those opposed to James VI's religious policies] resolved upon application to his majesty for remedy . . . but . . . they found nothing was to be expected that way, but that King Charles was resolved to maintain the government which his royal father had established . . . In their carriage nothing appeared whereby men could conjecture that which afterwards came to pass; for their deportment favoured of gravity and meekness, neither acted they anything which was much taken notice of . . . In the meantime they laboured to increase the number of their proselytes [converts] every where, and that not without success, especially in Fife, and in the western parts.

But [what] advanced them more was the turning of certain noblemen to their side; for besides that the generality of the nobility was malcontented, there were by this time observed to be avowed owners [supporters] of their interest, in Fife the earl of Rothes and Lord Lindsay, in Lothian the earls of Lothian and Balmerino, and in the west the earls of Cassils and Eglinton, and Lord Loudon, which accession rendered them very considerable . . .

When the king came to Scotland in the year 1633, to hold his first parliament, they resolved upon a petition . . . for redress of all their grievances; and the same being subscribed with their hands, was committed to the earl of Rothes . . . Rothes . . . imparted the business to the king; but his majesty . . . [said] 'No more of this, my lord, I command you;' which Rothes having at his return communicated to the rest, they concluded to suppress the petition, and so nothing more was heard anent it, until the next year . . .

[In 1634 Lord Balmerino was found to have a copy of the petition.]

Whereupon . . . Balmerino [was] sent prisoner to the castle of Edinburgh; and after many appearances before the [privy] council . . . was at last . . . by an assize [jury] of his peers condemned to die; yet did the gracious king reprieve him, and ere long gave him a remission . . .

This risk which Balmerino had run, sunk deep in their hearts who were of his party, and exasperated them against the bishops more than before, so that they spared not thereafter (whensoever they found opportunity) to undermine their [the bishops] reputation, taxing them of worldliness, and that their care was only to make up estates for their children, but no ways to procure the good of the church; defaming them, that they thought it not enough to trample upon the church, but strove also to domineer over the state; yea, they accused them of unsoundness also, that they were friends to Popery, and had it in their thoughts to bring in the [Catholic] Mass . . .

[Charles I] conferred the office of chancellor upon the archbishop of St Andrews; which disappointment irritated [Lord] Lorn [later marquis of Argyll] against the bishops, whom he blamed for the same . . .

John earl of Traquair, high treasurer (under profession of friendship enough to the bishops) had under-hand dealing with their adversaries; for he conceived a jealousy (and many thought not without cause) that the bishops intended his fall, to the end Mr John Maxwell, bishop of Ross, might be made treasurer; and therefore in a covered way he did what he could to supplant them . . .

It had been King James's custom, when a bishopric fell void, to appoint the archbishop of St Andrews to convene the rest, and name three or four well qualified, so that there could not be an error in the choice, and then out of that list that king pitched upon one . . .

But King Charles followed another way, and without any consultation had with the bishops, preferred men by moyen at court . . . Now among these late bishops whom King Charles preferred, none were generally esteemed gifted for the office, except Bishop Maxwell of whom it cannot be denied [that] he was a man of great parts; but the mischief was, they were accompanied with unbounded ambition; for it did not content him to be a lord of the secret council (as were the rest) but he behoved also to be a lord of the exchequer, and a lord of the session extraordinary, and at last to be lord high-treasurer, which proved fatal to them all.

Thus the young bishops, not having been beholden to the old bishops for their preferment, for that cause they depended not upon them, but kept a fellowship among themselves apart; and happening to gain an intimacy with the archbishop of Canterbury caused him to procure from the king power to [themselves] to prescribe things to the old bishops; which they did not well relish.

SOURCE: Guthrie, H 1748 *Memoirs of Henry Guthry, late bishop of Dunkeld.* Glasgow.

The National Covenant, 1638

In response to the attempts of Charles I to extend liturgical innovations to the church, presbyterian Covenanters coalesced and bound themselves by oath to maintain the cause of their religion, a practice that had begun among Scottish reformers in the 1550s, but culminated with the National Covenant. The document opens by claiming that it is a renewal of the so-called Negative Confession of 1581, a document which was initially intended to reduce Catholic influence on the young James VI, and which only later came to be seen as a significant document in defining and consolidating presbyterianism. The Confession itself is transcribed, and then relevant acts of parliament cited in detail. The paragraph structure of this document has been altered to aid comprehension.

In obedience to the Commandment of God, conform to the practice of the godly in former times, and according to the laudable example of our Worthy and Religious Progenitors, . . . warranted also by act of Council [in 1590], commanding a general band to be made . . . for two causes.

One was, For defending the true Religion, as it was then reformed, and is expressed in the Confession of Faith [the Negative Confession] above written . . . which had been for many years with a blessing from Heaven preached, and professed in this Kirk and Kingdom, as God's undoubted truth, grounded only upon his written Word.

The other cause was, for maintaining the Kings Majesty, His Person, and Estate, the true worship of God and the Kings authority, being so straitly joined, as that they had the same friends, and common enemies, and did stand and fall together.

And finally, being convinced in our minds . . . that the present and succeeding generations in this land, are bound to keep the foresaid national oath and subscription inviolable, We noblemen, barons, gentlemen, burgesses, ministers and commons under subscribing, considering divers times before and especially at this time, the danger of the true reformed religion, of the king's honour, and of the public peace of the Kingdome by the manifold innovations and evils . . . mentioned in our late supplications, complaints, and protestations, do hereby profess, and before God, his angels, and the world solemnly declare,

That, with our whole hearts we agree and resolve, all the days of our life, constantly to adhere unto, and:

to defend the foresaid true religion, and (forbearing the practice of all novations, already introduced in the matters of the worship of God, or approbation of the corruptions of the public government of the kirk, or civil places and power of kirk-men, till they be tried and allowed in free assemblies, and in parliaments)

to labour by all means lawful to recover the purity and liberty of the Gospel, as it was established and professed before the foresaid novations and because, after due examination, we plainly perceive, and undoubtedly believe, that the innovations and evils . . . have no warrant of the Word of God, are contrary . . . to the intention and meaning of the blessed reformers of religion in this land, to the above written acts of parliament, and do sensibly tend to the re-establishing of the popish religion and tyranny, and to the subversion and ruin of the true reformed religion, and of our liberties, laws and estates . . . [We] therefore from the knowledge and consciences of our duty to God, to our king and country, without any worldly respect or inducement, so far as humane infirmity will suffer, wishing a further measure of the grace of God for this effect . . . promise, and swear by the great name of the Lord our God,

To continue in the profession and obedience of the foresaid religion [and] that we shall defend the same, and resist all these contrary errors and corruptions, according to our vocation, and to the uttermost of that power that God hath put in our hands, all the days of our life.

And in like manner with the same heart, we declare before God and men that we have no intention nor desire to attempt any thing that may turn to the dishonour of God, or to the diminution of the king's greatness and authority:

But on the contrary, we promise and swear, that we shall, to the uttermost of our power, with our means and lives, stand to the defence of our dread sovereign, the king's majesty, his person, and authority, in the defence and preservation of the foresaid true religion, liberties and laws of the kingdom . . .

We . . . faithfully promise, for our selves, our followers, and all other under us, both in public, in our particular families, and personal carriage, to endeavour to keep ourselves within the bounds of Christian liberty, and to be good examples to others of all godliness, soberness, and righteousness, and of every duty we owe to God and man, and that this our union and conjunction may be observed without violation, we call the living God, the searcher of our hearts . . . who knows this to be our sincere desire, and unfeigned resolution, as we shall answer to Jesus Christ, in the great day, and under the pain of Gods everlasting wrath, and of infamy, and loss of all honour and respect in this world . . .

Most humbly beseeching the Lord to strengthen us by his holy Spirit for this end, and to blesse our desires and proceedings with a happy successe, that religion and righteousnesse may flourish in the land, to the glory of God, the honour of our king, and peace and comfort of us all. In witnesse whereof we have subscribed with our hands.

SOURCE: Dickinson, WC 1954 *A Source Book of Scottish History*. London, iii, 95–104.

The Solemn League and Covenant, 1643

Building upon the aims of the National Covenant, and following the outbreak of the Wars of the Three Kingdoms, the Solemn League and Covenant reflected the strength of the Scottish Covenanters, who were in a position to give aid to the English Parliamentarians. This Covenant prescribed the maintenance of the presbyterian Church of Scotland and further reformation in England and Ireland. Its impact was limited in England, where congregational independence quickly overtook presbyterianism as the preferred destination of reformation, but in Scotland, among the Covenanters, its obligations were treated as sacred and binding, although they were unworkable. The paragraph structure of this document has been altered to aid comprehension.

We noblemen, barons, knights, gentlemen, citizens, burgesses, ministers of the Gospel, and commons of all sorts in the kingdoms of Scotland, England and Ireland, by the providence of God living under one king, and being of one reformed religion,

Having before our eyes the glory of God, and the advancement of the kingdom of our Lord and Saviour Jesus Christ, the honour and happiness of the king's majesty and his posterity, and the true public liberty, safety, and peace of the kingdoms,

And calling to mind the treacherous and bloody plots, conspiracies, attempts and practices of the enemies of God against the true religion and professors thereof in all places, especially in these three kingdoms, ever since the reformation of religion, and how much their rage, power and presumption are of late, and at this time increased.

We have now at last . . . for the preservation of our selves and our religion from utter ruin and destruction, according to the commendable practice of these kingdoms in former times, and the example of God's people in other nations, after mature deliberation, resolved and determined to enter into a mutual and Solemn League and Covenant, wherein we all subscribe [sign], and each one of us for himself, with our hands lifted up to the most high God, do swear:

1. That we . . . [will] endeavour in our several places and callings, [to bring about] the preservation of the Reformed Religion in the Church of Scotland . . . against our common Enemies; The Reformation of Religion in the Kingdoms of England and Ireland, in Doctrine, Worship, Discipline and Government, according to the Word of God, and the example of the best Reformed Churches; And shall endeavour to bring the Churches of God in the three Kingdoms, to the nearest conjunction and uniformity in Religion . . .

2. That we shall in like manner, without respect of persons, endeavour the Extirpation of Popery, Prelacy . . . Superstition, Heresy, Schism, Profaneness, and whatsoever shall be found to be contrary to sound Doctrine, and the power of Godliness; Lest we partake in other men's sins, and thereby be in danger to receive of their plagues . . .

3. We shall . . . endeavour . . . to preserve the Rights and Privileges of the Parliaments, and the Liberties of the Kingdoms, and to preserve and defend the King's Majesty's Person and Authority, in the preservation and defence of the true Religion, and Liberties of the Kingdoms; that the world may bear witness with our consciences of our Loyalty, and that we have no thoughts or intentions to diminish his Majesty's just power and greatness.

4. We shall also . . . endeavour the discovery of all such as have been, or shall be Incendiaries, Malignants, or evil instruments, by hindering the Reformation of Religion, dividing the King from his people, or one of the Kingdoms from another, or making any faction, or parties . . . contrary to this League and Covenant, That they may be brought to public trial, and receive condign [severe] punishment . . .

5. And whereas the happiness of a blessed Peace between these Kingdoms, denied in former times to our Progenitors, is by the good Providence of God granted unto us, and hath been lately concluded, and settled by both Parliaments, we shall each one of us, according to our place and interest, endeavour that they may remain conjoined in a firm Peace and Union to all Posterity . . .

6. We shall also according to our places and callings in this Common cause of Religion, Liberty, and Peace of the Kingdoms, assist and defend all those that enter into this League and Covenant . . .

And shall not suffer our selves directly or indirectly by whatsoever combination, persuasion or terror, to be divided and withdrawn from this blessed Union and conjunction, whether to make defection to the contrary part, or to give ourselves to a detestable indifference or neutrality in this cause . . .

And because these Kingdoms are guilty of many sins, and provocations against God, and his Son Jesus Christ, as is too manifest by our present distresses and dangers, the fruits thereof:

We profess and declare before God, and the world, our unfeigned desire to be humbled for our own sins, and for the sins of these Kingdoms,

That the Lord may turn away his wrath, and heavy indignation, and establish these Churches and Kingdoms in truth and Peace . . . and [that he may] bless our desires and proceedings with such success, as may be deliverance and safety to his people, and encouragement to other Christian Churches groaning under, or in danger of the yoke of Antichristian Tyranny, or to join in the same, or like Association & Covenant,

To the Glory of God, the enlargement of the Kingdom of Jesus Christ, and the peace & tranquillity of Christian Kingdoms, and Commonwealths.

SOURCE: Dickinson, WC 1954 *A Source Book of Scottish History*. London, iii, 122–5.

Letters and Journals of Robert Baillie

These extracts from the letters and journals of Robert Baillie (1602–62) give insights into the Covenanting mind, as in 1639 he savoured victory for the presbyterian cause and the prospect of more complete reformation; and in 1644–45 his cause experienced reversals due to the military prowess of the royalist marquis of Montrose. The fact that Montrose's army consisted of Highlanders and Irishmen, and that it was jointly led by Alasdair MacColla, a Northern Irish descendant of Clan MacDonald, was a source of particular angst for Baillie, as he wrestled with the question of how the Covenanters and the Campbell earl of Argyll could be defeated on successive occasions by a seemingly ungodly rabble.

A) LETTER FROM ROBERT BAILLIE TO WILLIAM SPANG, 28 SEPTEMBER 1639

The accidents of our land this seven months bygone has been very many and very strange. I doubt if the providence of God sheltering a poor church from imminent ruin with a power, wisdom, goodness, clearly divine has ever in any land shined so brightly as in ours these days. The hand of our God has now well near led us all down from the stage of extreme danger [so] that we may all go about in our old security, every one [to] his own neglected affairs, with a mutual amity and a most universal joy. Our prince is brought off so well as may be, and much more honourably than any could have dreamed, from the pursuing the revenge of enraged church men, who would neither endure to amend their crimes nor suffer the censure of their obstinacy. Our state is secured from the wrath of our misinformed prince, from the arms of our neighbour kingdoms and a strong faction among our self. Our church has got a full purgation and has cast forth freely all the corruptions that did infect either doctrine or discipline. We are put in possession of general assemblies and parliaments according to our mind, the sovereign medicines against the sudden return of such mortal diseases amongst us. The . . . faction in our land, which with full sails was hauling us all away to Rome for our religion . . . [which] was not careful much to cover their intention to have our church presently popish and our state slavish . . . is now broken, lying in the pit of shame and poverty in a strange land . . . pitied by none, helped by very few . . .

B) ROBERT BAILLIE'S JOURNAL, 25 OCTOBER 1644
Montrose and his forces defeated the Covenanters at Tippermuir (1 September) and Aberdeen (13 September).

[The marquis of] Argyll was at their heels. They got up to the mountains [but] many of their followers left them. Yet Montrose, with two or three thousand of most desperate and cruel villains, came back on the hills so far as Atholl . . .

This is the greatest hurt our poor land got these fourscore years, and the greatest disgrace befell us these thousand. If we get not the life of these worms chirted [squeezed] out before they creep out of our land the reproach will stick on us for ever. It hath much diminished our reputation [in London] already, being joined with the length of the siege of Newcastle. Many things here have deceived our hopes, the enemy within [Newcastle] desperately resolute, with frequent sallies kept our people night and day in duty. Our mines, the most part, after all our labour, were countermined or drowned, our soldiers for want of pay and clothes were worn to rags, sundry of our best regiments and officers were of necessity gone to Scotland. Besides, winter and ill weather now comes on.

C) LETTER SENT BY ROBERT BAILLIE TO GLASGOW, 10 AUGUST 1645
Montrose's remarkable series of victories continued at Inverlochy (2 February 1645), Auldearn (9 May) and Alford (2 July).

When the singular favours of God do lift up our hearts in praises here, and in confidence of a happy issue of this troublesome work, our spirits are deeply wounded within us and broken by what we hear from time to time from dear Scotland. We are amazed that it should be the pleasure of our God to make us fall thus the fifth time before a company of the worst men in the earth, and besides all the calamity which the sword of these barbarous men doth bring, that our angry God should send upon us a more furious pestilence than I ever heard of in our land. For these things we weep, our eyes run down with water. We cannot but think there is love at the bottom of all this bitterness. The cause here and there is one, if there be any odds, surely the enemy in Scotland, for all kinds of wickedness has it. That the Lord thought fit to call them down here [England] and set them up there [Scotland] is one of the deeps of divine wisdom, which we will adore. The constant practise here [England], on the least appearance of any public danger, is to flee [resort] both to public and private fasting on the least appearance of any publick danger . . . If the godly there [Scotland] have the like care, and if the magistrate [state] be alike industrious, to crave the assistance of gracious people's fasting and praying . . . [perhaps] God would make clear, what the cause may be that so long he deserts us. Whatever the matter may be, were I this night to die; my heart does not smite me for any wrong I know our Nation has done in arms against the Malignant party . . . for dayly more and more it appears to the world, that the design of the misled Court was, and is, by all means out of hell, to fasten the yoke of tyranny on the necks both of our bodies and souls, for our times, and the days of our posterity . . . Whatever troubles God has cast upon us for our present triall, we expect ere long a comfortable conclusion . . . [Those who] are the instruments of Scotland's woe, if yet they will not waken . . . will perish, not only without any wise man's compassion, but with a mark of infamy on their persons and families for ever . . . We hope the Lord will not forget to be merciful for ever.

SOURCE: a) Reid, D (ed) 1982 *The Party Coloured Mind. Selected Prose relating to the conflict between Church and State in Seventeenth Century Scotland.* Edinburgh, 53–4; b) and c) Baillie, R 1841–2 in Laing D, (ed) *Letters and Journals.* Bannatyne Club, ii, 234, 306–8.

Restoration to Revolution: 1660–1690

DOCUMENT 85

Extract from the Act Rescissory, 28 March 1661

The Act Rescissory was the most far-reaching piece of legislation approved by the first parliament of the Restoration era. The act annulled all legislation passed in parliament since 1633 including all legal guarantees for presbyterian church government. The act also offered an indemnity to those who had acted on the authority of these parliaments but ominously indicated that there could be exceptions.

Thairfor the Kings Majestie and estates of Parliament doe heirby Rescind and annull the pretendit Parliaments kept in the years 1640, 1641, 1644, 1645, 1646, 1647 and 1648 and all acts and deids past and done in them and declare the same to be henceforth voyd and null; and his Majestie, being unwilling to take any advantage of the failings of his Subjects dureing those unhappie tymes, is resolved not to retaine any remembrance thairof but that the same shall be held in everlasting oblivion and that, all differences and animosities being forgotten, his good subjects may in a happie union under his Royall Government enjoy that happines and peace which his Majestie intends and really wisheth unto them as unto himselff.

SOURCE: 1814–75 *Acts of the Parliaments of Scotland.* Edinburgh, vii, 86–8.

Act Concerning Religion and Church Government, 28 March 1661

This act placed the final decision on the preferred form of church government in the hands of the king.

. . . as to the Government of the Church his Maiestie will make it his care to satle and secure the same in such a frame as shall be most agreeable to the word of God most suteable to monarchical Government, and most complying with the publict peace and quyet of the Kingdome.

SOURCE: 1814–75 *Acts of the Parliaments of Scotland.* Edinburgh, vii, 86–8.

Act Restoring Episcopal Government, 1662

Despite the attempts of the presbyterians, on 14 August 1661, a proclamation indicated that the king wished to restore episcopacy, effectively re-establishing royal control of the church. This decision was codified in the following act of parliament.

Forasmuch as the ordering and disposall of the externall government and policie of the church doth propperlie belong unto his majestie as ane inherent right of the croun, by vertew of his royall prerogative and supremacie in causes ecclesiasticall; and in discharge of this trust his majestie and his estates of parliament takeing to their serious consideration that . . . by the late rebellion within this kingdome in the yeer 1637 the ancient and sacred order of bishops wes cast off, their persons and rights wer injured and overturned and a seeming paritie among the clergie factiously and violently brought in, to the great disturbance of the publict peace . . . and therwithall considering . . . what prejudice the libertie of the subject hath suffered by the invasions made upon the bishops and episcopall government, which they find to be the church government most aggreeable to the Word of God, most convenient and effectuall for the preservation of treuth, order and unity and most suteable to monarchie and the peace and quyet of the state: Thairfor his majestie, with advice and consent of his estates of parliament . . . doth heirby redintegrat the state of bishops to their antient places and undoubted priveledges . . . [including] power of ordination, inflicting of censures and all other acts of church discipline, which they are to performe with advice and assistance of such of the clergie as they shall find to be of knoun loyaltie.

SOURCE: 1814–75 *Acts of the Parliaments of Scotland.* Edinburgh, vii, 372–4.

Test Oath, August 1681

The Test Act established that office-bearers in both church and state were obliged to take an oath acknowledging the royal supremacy, repudiating the Covenants and swearing not to attempt any alteration in either church or civil government. The Test was a means of establishing loyalty and exposing religious nonconformity which was rigorously punished.

And I farder affirm and swear by this my solemn oath that I judge it unlauful for subjects upon pretence of reformation or any other pretence whatsoever, to enter into Covenants or Leagues, or to convocat, conveen or assemble in any Councills, Conventions or Assemblies, to treat, consult or determine in any matter of State, civil or ecclesiastick without his Majesties special command or express licence had thereto, Or to take up arms against the king or those commissionated by him: And that I shall never so rise in arms or enter into such Covenant or Assemblies: And that ther lyes no obligation on me from the National Covenant or the Solemn League and Covenant (so commonlie called) or any other manner of way whatsoever, to endeavour any change or alteration in the Government, either in Church or State, as it is now established by the Laws of this kingdom.

SOURCE: 1814–75 *Acts of the Parliaments of Scotland*. Edinburgh, vii, 244–5.

Extract from William of Orange's Declaration for Scotland, 10 October 1688

In his Declaration for Scotland, William stressed the reasons behind his decision to intervene in Britain – ostensibly the preservation of liberty and the Protestant religion. He mentions his wife's place in the succession but is careful to avoid any overt reference to the overthrow of King James.

It is both certain and evident to all men that the public peace and happiness of any State or Kingdom cannot be preserved wherever the Laws, Liberties, and Customs, established by the lawful authority in it, are openly transgressed and annulled: more especially where the alteration of Religion is endeavoured, and that a Religion which is contrary to Law is endeavoured to be introduced. Upon which those who are most immediately concerned in it are indispensably bound to preserve and maintain the established Laws, Liberties, and Customs; and above all the Religion and Worship of God that is established among them: and to take such an effectual care that the inhabitants of the said State or Kingdom may neither be deprived of their Religion, nor of their Civil Rights. Which is so much the more necessary because the greatness and security both of Kings, Royal Families, and of such as are in authority, as well as the happiness of their subjects and people depend, in a most especial manner, upon the exact observation and maintenance of these their Laws, Liberties, and Customs. Upon these grounds it is that We cannot any longer forbear to declare that to our great regret We see that those Counsellors who have now the chief credit with the King have no other design but to overturn the Religion, Laws, and Liberties of those realms, and to subject them in all things relating to their Consciences, Liberties, and Properties to arbitrary government; and that, not only by secret and indirect ways, but in such an open and undisguised manner that their designs are now become visible to all that consider them . . . And since our dearest and most entirely beloved Consort, the Princess, and likewise We ourselves have so great an interest in this matter and such a right as all the world knows to the succession of these kingdoms which those men have attempted to violate, for preventing of all redress of miseries, by the lawful successors of the Crown, educated by the good providence of God in the true profession of the Protestant Religion, We cannot excuse ourselves from espousing the true interest of these nations in matters of such high consequence, and from contributing all that lies in Us for the defence of the Laws and Liberties thereof, the maintaining of the Protestant religion in them, and the securing the people in the enjoyment of their just rights. But that our intentions may be so manifest that no person may doubt or pretend to doubt thereof, to excuse themselves from concurring with us in this just design for the universal good of the nation, We do declare that the freeing that Kingdom from all hazard of Popery and arbitrary power for the future, and the delivering it from what at the present doth expose it to both, the settling of it by Parliament upon such a solid basis as to its religious and civil concerns, as may most effectually redress all the above mentioned grievances, are the true reasons of our present undertaking as to that nation.

SOURCE: McCrie, CG 1888 *Scotland's Part and Place in the Revolution of 1688.* Edinburgh, 214–22.

The Humble Adress of the Noblemen, Gentilmen and Royal Borows, within the Shyre of East Lowthian, To His Highness the Prince of Orange, December 1688

This address, promoted by John Hay, second earl of Tweeddale, was sent by the shire of East Lothian to the Prince of Orange at the end of December 1688. It received broad support with only five recorded as having refused to sign. The document not only highlights concern for liberty and religion, it also suggests a closer union between the kingdoms of Scotland and England – a subject that few historians have seriously considered in the context of the Revolution.

Wee the Noblemen Barons, Freeholders, and Royal Burghs of the shyre of East Lowthian Being highly sensible of the mercy and Goodness of Almighty God; who hes put it in your Highness heart to designe the rescueing of those Kingdoms particularly us of Scotland from the danger of Popery and Slavery And with so much labour and toyle and expense of Treasure to prepare ane Army and fleet for so great ane undertaking, And at length to expose your Person and Army to so great hazard by Sea and Land Which work he hath crown'd with so great Success in so short a time by your favourable reception in our Neighbour Kingdome of England and the remoovall of all impediments out of your way as is matter of wounder And wherin wee Acknowledge Gods great goodness and under him do owne and Acknowledge our deliverance and preservation to have come from your Highness, And therefore in all humility desire you will be pleas'd to take us under your protection and perfect so great a work so happily begune and fairly advanc'd by procuring unto us a free Parliament and that it may be so, restoring the severall Burghs of this Kingdome to their Antient Priveledges of Choising there owne Magistrats whereby there elections may be free and uncoacted and that your Highness will take it into your consideration by what wayes and means these Kingdoms of Scotland and England may be united in a more strict and inseperable Union then they have ben as yet that wee be not heir after left open by the advantage may be taken of our distinct and different Laws and Customs and exercise of Government whereby methods are taken by the Enemies of our peace and Tranquility to raise standing Armys in either Kingdome by which the other may be thretned or enforc'd to submit to Alterations in their Religion or diminution of there Liberty or fforaigne fforces brought in to either for the subversion of the Religion and Liberty of both which were a work worthy of your Highness and would highly advance the Security of the Protestant Religion within

this Island and through the whole Christian world and posterity to all Generations will bliss your Memory for it as wee at present who are, May it please your
Highnesse, Your Highnes's most humble and Faithfull Servants.

SOURCE: National Library of Scotland, Yester Papers, 7026/94A.

Electoral Summons Addressed to the Royal Burgh of Dysart, 5 February 1689

The general election of 1689 was subject to considerable innovation. Considering James VII's recent attempts to pack the burgh councils with his supporters and as a result gain control of the burgh electorate, it was decided that for the first time all Protestant burgesses should receive a vote. In addition the limits imposed by the Test Oath were also ignored. Unprecedented numbers participated in the burgh elections, the majority of which were won by Revolutioner candidates.

WHEREAS the Lords and Gentlemen of the Kingdom of *Scotland*, met at *White-Hall*, at Our desire, to Advise Us what is to be done, for Securing the Protestant Religion, and Restoring the Laws and Liberties of that Kingdom, according to Our Declarations, have desired Us, for the attaining of these Ends, to call a Meeting of the Estates, to be holden at *Edenburgh*, in *March* next.

WE being Desirous to do every Thing that may Tend to the Publick Good and Happiness of that Kingdom, have Resolved to call the said Meeting against the fourteenth Day of the said Month of *March* next; and do therefore in pursuance, and according to the Tenor of the said Advice, Require you upon the Receipt of this Our Letter, to make Publick Intimation of the same on the first Mercat Day at the Cross of the Royal Burrough of Dysert in the usual manner, and to appoint a Day, to be at least fyve Days after the said Intimation for the whole Burgesses to meet and Chuse their Commissioners for the said Meeting of the Estates at *Edinburgh* the said fourteenth Day of *March*, a Copy of this Our Letter and of your Intimation, containing the Day of Election to be left affixt on the said Cross. The Burgesses and Commissioners being Protestants, without any other Exception or Limitation. And that you Report your Diligence herein to the Convention. *Given at* St James's the fifth Day of Feb. *in the Year of Our Lord* 1689.

SOURCE: NAS, Supplementary Parliamentary Papers, PA 7/25/58/10/2.

Colin Lindsay, Third Earl of Balcarres' Account of the Opening of the Convention Parliament, March 1689

Balcarres sat in the convention of estates and left a reasonably detailed account of events. The following extract, although coloured by his Jacobite sympathies, is an accurate description of contemporary politics. He comments on the significance of the burgh elections, the irregularity of proceedings and the apparent confusion of the Jacobite party.

Some days before the convention met, the Duke of Hamilton and some Lords and Gentlemen brought to Edinburgh several companies of foot, which they quartered in the town, beside a great number of rabble that they kept concealed in vaults and cellars, till some day after the convention had met. The loyal party were not a little alarmed with that illegal beginning, but much more with the illegal methods they had taken in electing members for the convention; they had very well foreseen, that if the legal way had been observed in elections, (which was that both electors and elected should take the test), none of their party had been chosen, therefore it was ordered by the Prince of Orange that all Protestants without distinction should have a vote in the elections; by this, and many of the Episcopal party their having scruples to meet upon the Prince's orders, they secured many of the boroughs which was a great addition to them. The first thing proposed, in this meeting of estates, after the Prince of Orange's letter had been read, was the choice of a President. Both parties saw well the consequence of getting one chosen of their own principles, and both looked upon this as a decisive stroke. The loyal party had great difficulty to pitch upon any of their own number [who] was not obnoxious to the Presbyterians, which obliged them to propose the Marquis of Atholl, – not that they were satisfied with him, but his early appearance for the Prince of Orange made the other party have the less to object against him. The Duke of Hamilton, [however,] having a considerable interest, and the Marquis of Atholl giving his own and friends' for him, got himself chosen President. This unexpected accident made above twenty forsake us, finding we had lost a vote so material, and that the other party would have both forces and authority upon their side. The next thing proposed was a Committee of Elections, which they likewise gained, and had all of their party named, which gave them such assurance, that all things thereafter were instantly put to the vote, which they were sure to carry, but in so tumultuous and irregular a way, that even the Duke of Hamilton himself, who knew the laws of our country and the force of reason and decency better than any of his party, could not help being ashamed at their scandalous behaviour, and did his endeavour often to hinder it; nor can it be denied, if his cause had been good, that he behaved himself with great prudence and moderation, insomuch that many of his own party began to repent of their choice. Some few days were passed in deciding the differences in elections, which would have required a much longer time if most of your friends had not yielded their claims, perceiving nothing of justice was so much as pretended to be done. Of the debateable elections, none was more remarkable than that of Mr Charles Hume; after the death of his elder brother, the title of Earl of Hume fell to him, but from the great debts upon his estate, he did not assume it, having an estate left him, which was to go to a younger brother if he came to be Earl: so, not pretending to be a peer, he was chosen for the shire he lived in; but the majority of the convention, finding he would not be of their party, rejected him. When the sentence was given, he told the President, that, since they had taken one way of sitting from him in the convention, he would try another which they could not take from him, – so went and took his place as Earl, with loss of the best part of his estate.

SOURCE: Lord Lindsay (ed) *Memoirs Touching the Revolution in Scotland 1688–1690*. Bannatyne Club, 24–5.

Act of the Estates of Scotland Establishing the Government hereof. Draft of an Act Put Before the Convention of Estates, c.March 1689

This is an extract from a piece of draft legislation that dates from the period immediately before the Scottish throne was settled on William and Mary. While a large part of the content was reproduced in the Claim of Right (see Document 94 below), the concluding section on union is unique. This was not something demanded by William of Orange but an idea strongly endorsed by the Scottish nobility and gentry who assembled in London in late 1688. This draft never became law.

Wee The Lords and Commissioners of Shyres and Burroughs assembled upon the call of the Prince of Orange who came with ane army to restore and preserve our religion Laues and Liberties Against arbitrary government Idolatrie and superstition Which call hath been generallie accepted of by the nation ffor which and for his just and gracious declarations Wee doe render our most hearty thanks never to be forgotten ... After most serious consideration and deep sense of our present condition wee doe find and declare That this nation is and ever hath been a free comonwealth under no despotick or arbitrary government but by a monarchy governable only by Law comprehending long and free customes all which wer introduced by the express or tacite consent of the nation ... And now being convinced by just and evident motives and reasons of the deplorable condition of the nation which wee have been under and which may easily recurr if there be not ane union als well of the bodys politick of the nations in this Island as in the royall head governing both and withall considering That wee doe live in the bowells of the same Island have the same language and the same common interest for religion and liberty and the same friends and foes and having the fullest affection to and confidence in the said prince of Orange now King of England and the princes Mary now Queen of England his consort and withall considering That no free people over whom a title of right of government is acquyred or rendered to soveraigns doeth not *ipso facto* become a part of and is incorporat with the comon wealth wherof that soveraign is supream head and governour partakeing of the common priviledges of the commonwealth Therfor wee doe hereby Enact consent and agree That the body politick of this nation be and is unite with the body politick of England and that wee be under the same soveraign authority and in the same commonwealth with them to be henceforth intituled and denominat the Kingdom of great Brittain ffrance and

Ireland or the Kingdom of England and Scotland unite and of ffrance and Ireland as shall be most acceptable to the King and parliament of England provydeing allways and upon special conditions That this nation shall enjoy their established judicatures their lawes and customes as to privat rights with the priviledge of *de non evocando* [the right of nationals of a state to enjoy the legal protection of that state] in any tyme comeing, And that the church of this nation shall perpetuallie enjoy its government by church sessions presbitries synods and by ane unsubordinat convocation thereof, And that rules for discipline shall be established by commissioners from the severall synods that non may have cause to complain or be afrayed of rigour or arbitrary government in church or state. Lykeas wee doe consent and agree That all publick impositions in kind by custome excise etc: be the same as it is now or shall be in England Provyding allwayes that the proportion of members in both houses of parliament of the unite kingdom to serve for Scotland shall be the twentieth part to witt ten peers in the house of peers fifteen Knights of Shyres and twelve burgesses of burroughs in the house of comons as shall be ordered by us dureing this meeting and that the proportion of the assessments and of all aides subsidyes and taxes upon Lands and Burroughs shall in no tyme exceed the twentieth part of what shall be imposed upon the united Kingdom ffinally that there may be no more ranckor but a universall amitie in the nation Wee humbly beseach The King to give a generall Indemnitie and act of oblivion with exception only of murthers and such other crymes as use to be excepted in all indemnities being confident his Majestie will intrust none in the government who may be unacceptable to the nation.

SOURCE: NAS, Leven and Melville Muniments, GD 26/7/20.

Extract from The Declaration of the Estates of the Kingdom of Scotland containing the Claim of Right and the Offer of the Crown to the King and Queen of England, 11 April 1689

The Claim of Right clearly documented the various transgressions of James VII and asserted the rights and liberties of the Scottish people. After considerable debate it was found that James VII had 'forfaulted', i.e. forfeited, his right to the throne. This was a far more radical term than 'abdicated', the expression used by the English parliament to justify the Revolution. There was also a strong contractual flavour to the Claim of Right, which was presented to William of Orange along with the Articles of Grievance, the acceptance of which was a condition of his being offered the throne.

Wheras King James the Seventh Being a profest papist did assume the Regall power, and acted as King without ever takeing the oath required by law, wherby the King, at his access to the government is obliged to swear, To maintain the protestant religion, and to rule the people according to the laudable laws; And Did By the advyce, of wicked and evill Counsellors, invade the fundamentall Constitution of this King-dome And altered it from a legall limited monarchy, to ane Arbitrary Despotick power; and in a publick proclamation, asserted ane absolute power, to cass annul and dissable all the lawes, particularly arraigning the lawes Establishing the protestant religion and did Exerce that power to the subversion of the protestant Religion, and to the violation of the lawes and liberties of the Kingdome . . . Therfor the Estates of the kingdom of Scotland Find and Declaire That King James the Seventh being a profest papist, Did assume the Regall power and acted as king, without ever takeing the oath required by law, and hath by the advyce of Evill and wicked Counsellors, Invaded the fundamentall Constitution of the kingdome, and altered it from a legall limited monarchy To ane arbitrary despotick power, and hath Exercised the same, to the subversione of the Protestant religion, and the violation of the laws and liberties of the Kingdome, inverting all the Ends of Government, wherby he hath forfaulted the right to the Croune, and the throne is become vacant.

SOURCE: 1814–75 *Acts of the Parliaments of Scotland*. Edinburgh, ix, 37–9.

Acts Concerning Prelacy, Presbyterianism, and Patronage, 1689–90

William II was no different from most monarchs in preferring the episcopalian system of church government, where bishops could be useful in facilitating crown control of the church. However, the bishops and much of the episcopalian clergy were strongly coloured by Jacobitism, and William had had contact with presbyterian exiles in the Netherlands before the Revolution of 1688. He therefore decided to settle the established Church of Scotland as a presbyterian church. It is open to debate, however, whether this was the arrangement that was most agreeable to the inclinations of the people.

The king and queens majesties doe declaire that they, with advyce and consent of the estates of this parliament, will settle by law that church government in this kingdome which is most aggreeable to the inclinations of the people.

Their majesties . . . do establish, ratifie and confirme the presbyterian church government and discipline, that is to say the government of the church by kirke sessions, presbyteries, provinciall synods and generall assemblies . . .

Their majesties . . . declare that in case of the vacancie of any particular church and for supplyeing the same with a minister, the heretors of the said parish (being protestants) and the elders are to name and propose the persone to the whole congregation to be either approven or disapproven by them . . .

SOURCE: 1814–75 *Acts of the Parliaments of Scotland.* Edinburgh, ix, 104, 133–4, 196.

The Crisis of the Regal Union: 1690–1707

DOCUMENT 96

Scotland's Wish for a Prosperous Voyage to Her African and Indian Fleet

In 1693 the parliament passed a general act to encourage foreign trade and in 1695 the company of Scotland Trading to Africa and the Indies was established. What was later and better known as the Darien Company attracted considerable public enthusiasm in Scotland, which was matched by a massive investment of around £400,000 from a total of some 1,400 subscribers. The attempt to establish a Scottish settlement – Caledonia – at Darien in Panama aroused powerful passions in Scotland, particularly as King William was perceived to have been forced to withdraw his support for the Scottish venture by English mercantile interests. This document illustrates the public mood in June 1699 as the first ships set sail for Darien.

In Ages past, when Men desir'd no more
But the improvement of their *Native* Store;
My *Spotless Fame*, Wide through the World was spread
Virtue and *Valour* grac'd my hoary Head.
No State around, cou'd e're pretend to be
More Ancient, Warlick, Royal, and Free:
Ev'n Mighty *Rome*, whose All-conquering Pride
Was never with her Triumphs satisfy'd,
In me to Crown her Conquests oft essay'd
Yet all in vain: as the proud Waves that roar,
Foam, and Recoil from the resisting Shoar.
      But since, of late Man's ever-teeming Brain
Has found a Way to tread the *Wat'ry* Main,
And search for Wealthy Climates, where, of old,
Men never dream'd of finding Land or Gold.
Great cause I've found to lye obscure and see,
My Neighbouring States admit'd Prosperity.
Oft have I sigh'd, oft did I deeply groan
My MONARCH's *Absence*, and my *Widow'd* Throne.
Oft mourn'd to see my *Ebbing* Wealth should flow
Through Channels I desir'd it *least* to go.
      But Heav'n at last has Smil'd, and seems to be

Propitious to my fam'd *Antiquity*.
My *Gracious* PRINCE, tho' *Absent*, yet doth share
His God-like *Bounty*, with an *equal* Care.
    Prosperity and Bless attend the Man,
And all his Race, that first the Work began:
Some *Divine* Motive, surely, *touch'd* his Soul
At first, and did *direct it* in the whole,
To bring me this Contentment: May he still
Enjoy, as he deserves, my best Good-will.
    Nor let me e're to *These* ungrateful prove,
Who best deserve their Country's dearest Love.
Those *Noble Souls*, I mean, whom Heaven inclin'd
To *act* what in my favour *it design'd*:
May they a Thousand-fold receive again,
The In-comes of their Loyal Toil and Pain
    And you *Brave Youths*, whose Nobler Souls Possess,
Your great Ancestors *Matchless* Hardiness;
Who for your Country's *Wellfare* can defy
The utmost spight of threatning Destiny.
May *Smoothed* Sea's, and *Prosp'rous* Gales attend
Your Sails, on whom my Swelling *Hopes* depend.
    What *Panting Joys!* What *soft Desires* shall seize
Each generous *Scot*! when that enticing Breeze
Shall Welcome you to roam the Spacious Seas.
    My Rev'rend FORTH, Proud of his Lordly Load,
Thinks now he may be term'd a *Demi-god*:
And melting all in Love, along He Slides,
Kissing his Lovely CALEDONIA's Sides.
    Safe may you *Go*, and safe may you *Import*
Rich *Indian* Gold, and Wealth of every sort.
    The Blinded *Pagans* too, shall Bless the Day
On which your happy Sails did bend that way,
T' *enlighten* them with a *Celestial* Ray.
    So shall loud *Fame* your lofty Praise resound,
    And both the *Poles*, our Trade and Travels *Bound*.

SOURCE: 1699 *Scotland's Wish for a Prosperous Voyage to Her African and Indian Fleet*. Edinburgh.

An Exact List of all the Men, Women, and Boys that Died on Board the Indian and African Company's Fleet, during their Voyage from Scotland to America, and since their Landing in Caledonia; Together with a particular account of their qualities, the several Days of their Deaths, and the respective Distempers or Accidents of which they Died, 1699

By September 1699, news was filtering back to Scotland that the Darien adventure was failing. A second expedition failed to rescue the situation and the colony was finally abandoned in April 1700 when those who had survived the sea voyage surrendered to the Spanish, into whose territorial interests the Scots had intruded.

Nota. By Volunteers are meant such Young Gentlemen as went in no particular station, but only in hopes of preferment as opportunity should offer.

July 23	Alexander Pierty, a Planter	Fever
August 8	Daniel Martin, a Sailer	Flux
23	Robert Donaldson, a Planter	Flux
30	John Forrester, a Planter	Flux
September 11	John Forrester, a Planter	Flux
16	James Dunnie, a Planter	Flux
19	Robert Hardy, a Volunteer	Fever
21	John Stewart, Volunteer	Fever
	Robert Baillie, a Planter	Fever
23	John Smith, Sailer	Fever
25	Alexander Elder, Sailer	Fever
27	Jeromy Spence, Sailer	Fever
28	Andrew Baird, Sailer	Flux
29	Walter Johnstoun, Chirurgeon's Mate	Fever
October 1	John Duffus, Sailer	Fever
5	Thomas Dalrymple, Planter	Fever
7	James Paterson, Volunteer	Flux
10	Charles Hamilton, Mid-shipman	Flux
11	Jacob Yorkland, Volunteer	Flux
15	James Davidson, Planter	Flux
16	Henry Charters, Volunteer	Flux
19	Lieutenant John Hay's Wife	Flux

20	Adam Hill, a Planter	Flux
	Walter Eliot, a Midshipman	Fever
22	Adam Cunningham, a Midshipman	Fever
	Adam Bennet, a Midshipman	Fever
23	Mr Thomas James, Minister	Fever
	Peter Mackintosh, Sailer	Flux
24	John Daniel, Planter	Flux
25	David Henderson, a Sailer	Flux
	James Graham, Volunteer	Flux
26	William Miller, Volunteer	Fever
27	John Chiefly, Volunteer	Flux
28	Mr John Malbon, Merchant	Fever
	Alexander Tailor, Sailer	Fever
	Robert Gaudie, Planter	Flux
	John Aird, a Planter	Decay
	Lieutenant Hugh Hay	Fever
	Peter Paterson, a Sailer	Flux
	James Montgomery	Flux
31	John Luckison, Volunteer	Flux
November 1	David Hay, Volunteer	Flux
2	Thomas Fenner, Clerk to Mr Paterson	Fever
3	Lieutenant James Inglis	

After Landing

November 5	Hugh Barclay, Sailer	Fever
	Henry Grapes, Trumpeter	Fever
6	Archibald Wright, Volunteer	Flux
7	James Clark, Volunteer	Flux
9	James Weems, Volunteer	Flux
11	John Fletcher, a Planter	Flux
14	Mr Paterson's Wife	Fever
15	Archibald Mosman, Volunteer	Flux
16	John Cannie, Sailer	Flux
	John Sim, Sailer	Flux
20	Mr Adam Scot, Minister	Flux
22	Roger Munckland, Volunteer	Flux
	Andrew Hamilton, a midshipman	Fever
24	William Baird, Sailer	Flux
27	James Young, Sailer	Fever
29	James Montgomery, a Planter	Flux
	John Burrol, a Sailer	Fever
December 3	James Borthwick, a Sailer	Fever
6	David Miller, Planter	Flux

	Ensign William Hallyburton	Flux
7	William Erskin, Planter	Flux
8	Robert Bishop, Chirurgeon's Mate	Flux
10	Recompence Standburgh, one of the Mates on Board the St Andrew	Fever
11	Robert Pendreick	Drown'd
	William Tenter	Drown'd
	William Maclellan, a Boy	Drown'd
	David White, a Planter	Fever
17	William Barron, a Planter	Flux
24	Alexander White, a Planter	Flux
	Andrew Brown, a boy on board the French Ship	Drown'd
	Peter Telfer, a Planter	Flux
25	Captain Thomas Fullarton, commander of The Dolphin	Died suddenly after warm walking

No doubt, every one will justly Regret the loss of his own nearest Friend, but it's a great and General Mercy that, of so many as went Crowded in Five Ships, upon so long and tedious a Voyage as they had, so few are dead; Especially considering, that on their way they had the misfortune of taking in bad Water, upon an Uninhabited Island, in the beginning of the Rainy Season, which occasioned general Sickness among them; tho' soon after their Landing in Caledonia (thanks be to GOD) they Recovered their Health so much (even beyond expectation) that, when the Express came away, there were but Five of all our Men who were not at Work in Building of Forts and Houses. And as even a greater Number of so many as went, might have died by this time, had they all remain'd at Home, so it may be some Satisfaction to the nearest Friends of the deceased that their Names shall stand upon Record as being amongst the first Brave Adventurers that went upon the most Noble, most Honourable, and most Promising Undertaking that Scotland ever took in hand.

SOURCE: 1699 *An exact list of all the men, women and boys that died on board the Indian and African Company's fleet, during their voyage from Scotland to America, and since their landing in Caledonia.* Edinburgh.

Letters to the Duke of Hamilton on the Famine of the 1690s

The 1690s was one of the most difficult periods in Scottish history. The country suffered a series of blows to overseas trade owing to the dislocations caused by the Nine Years War and the actions of French privateers; the eventual loss of the Scots colony at Darien; and the economic and social as well as the political consequences of a series of poor harvests which resulted from a prolonged spell of colder and erratic weather during what is termed The Little Ice Age. Historians differ about the length, extent and severity of the period of dislocation, which in some years was a full-blown famine. What is certain is that contemporaries became fully aware that something serious was happening by the summer of 1696, although in some places there are signs of distress two years earlier.

A) EXTRACT FROM A LETTER, DANIEL HAMILTON TO THE DUKE OF HAMILTON, EDINBURGH, 7 AUGUST 1696

. . . There was never such difficulty of getting money since I be in the world nor greater hardships for people to live in it this 300 years there being a general famine through the whole country for want of victual in so much that peas and barley have been sold here from 18 to 20 pounds [Scots] per boll and not a grain to be had of any kind but what is brought from the north of England and Ireland yea from Norway. We have an appearance of a good crop but it will be very late by reason of cold weather and gray frosts of which we had plenty in the first three weeks of July almost every night, as for the fruit I caused two neutral men value it and I gave it over to the gardener at the price they put upon it which is only 20 pounds Scots for gooseberries currants and all except what is in the north garden which I reserved to send to Hamilton . . .

B) EXTRACT FROM A LETTER, DAVID CRAWFORD TO THE DUKE OF HAMILTON, EDINBURGH, 8 JUNE 1699

The condition of the shire of Clydesdale is so bad that the poor are dying every day by the dyke sides and on the highway for mere want, especially in several parishes who have not taken such a regular course for providing their poor as Hamilton has done. Wherefore her grace as Sheriff caused warn all the Commissioners of Supply within the shire to meet at Hamilton last week to see what course to take thereanent.

And they have drawn up a petition to the Privy Council with several very good proposals for preventing so many to starve for want; occasioned by the negligence of parishes who will not follow the method that Hamilton does which her grace sent me in [yesterday] . . . to present to the Council in the name of her grace and the shire . . .

c) EXTRACT FROM A LETTER, EARL OF RUGLEN TO THE DUKE OF HAMILTON, EDINBURGH, 23 AND 25 MARCH 1699

. . . affairs here are in great disorder and we have frequent tumults on the account of our great scarcity albeit it be represented for other ways. Above this day an extraordinary Council was called on the account of a great tumult at St Andrews they having broke up all the houses when they suspected any kind of victual would be found and seized it and in Dundee there has been the like so you may judge what a lamentable condition the country is in the prices of corns being excessive and the people crying out upon the impositions.

SOURCE: a) NAS, Hamilton MSS, GD 406/1/4128; b) NAS, Hamilton MSS, GD 406/1/4402; c) NAS, Hamilton MSS, GD 406/1/6368.

Extract from Kirk Session Records, Kilmartin, Argyll, 23 December 1697

This document sheds further light on the famine years of the 1690s, and on the attempts by the main relief agency – the Church – to cope with the crisis.

The session taking to their serious consideration the great number the distressed and indigent condition of the poor of the land and laying to heart the sad case want and straits of their own native poor within this parish and the common regrets of the people, that the generality of them are out of capacity to supply their own through the great distress the land is in, by reason of the general and universal scarcity that is through the whole kingdom and that there is a great resort of stranger poor that throngs into the country that is much neglected thereby in regard the commonality cannot well supply both their own and foreign poor therefore they have enacted and appointed that hereafter special care be taken of their own poor and a method taken for supplying duly the most indigent and necessitous of them.

SOURCE: NAS, Church of Scotland Records, CH 2/793/1, Kilmartin (Argyll) Kirk Session Minutes, 1691–1706.

A Representation to the Royal Burghs of the State of this Town and People of Borrowstouness, 1705

Historians of this period debate whether Scotland's economy was 'sinking', in which case the prospect of Union may have been perceived as a deliverance, or whether Scotland's situation was stronger than it appeared, with prospects for European trade, in which instance the case for incorporation becomes less robust. This source, which can illuminate the condition of Scotland on the eve of the Union, is one of a number of petitions sent to the Convention of Royal Burghs seeking tax relief. But we have to be aware of the contemporary purpose of this source. We know less about conditions in the newer burghs of barony, which were often established by landowners to rival the older, chartered, royal burghs, with their monopolies of certain trades and exclusive trading rights. The royal burghs complained that the new burghs were thriving, but we might expect them to say this.

Whereas we are threatened by your Agent to be pursued for 7 years stent [tax] for your relief, which doth amount to a considerable sum wee have judged it proper briefly to lay before you a true account of the present state of the place –

Since the year 1698 whence commenced our present payment, this town has sustained several very great losses, partly by the loss of our ships that went to Caledonia and never returned and where many of our seamen belonging to the said ships died, partly by several of our ships being cast away at sea and all the cargo lost and some of them with not one person saved partly by others of them being taken by privateers to the great impoverishing of the place so that whereas 7 years ago we had near to 30 sail of ships we have now but 10 left of which 10 upon enquiry we apprehend it will be found that not above 16/16 parts [shares] which makes but one ship belongs to owners living in this place –

By reason of the great losses the number of our poor widows & orphans is greatly increased so that of about 557 families we reckon to be in the town there are 205 widows very few of whom are able to bear any part of the burden of the stent yea many of them are supplied out of poor boxes and the necessitous and indigent case of them and their fatherless children calls for more than we are in a capacity to give and among the remaining 352 families we are able to instruct that many of them are single persons in a very poor condition of whom some have weekly pensions.

Our trade is much decayed and become very low and though this be the common and universal complaint of the nation yet it doth more nearly wreak and affect us so that with greater reason to our grief we can use it than most places in the nation: we stand by the sea, our ships reduced to a few the import and export of what belongs to the place very inconsiderable and whereas in time of peace we could have made several voyages in a year, now in war we make but one or two at most, whereby many of our seamen who have families are not and others scarce able to subsist whereupon many of them are obliged to repair to Newcastle and take on with the Coaliers who using to return to their families against winter do then spend any little thing that have gained in the summer.

We having hinted in the preceding paragraph that the import and export of what belongs to the place is very inconsiderable for clearing of this particular it would be considered that the ships belonging to Bo'ness are employed in carrying home and abroad the goods belonging chiefly to the Royal Burghs such as Ayr, Glasgow, Stirling, Linlithgow, Dumfries etc as can be made appear by the custom house books that will be entered . . . [illegible] 7, 8 or 900 pack of goods and not one pack belonging to the inhabitants of Bo'ness from all which it is plain that . . . [illegible] Royal Burghs have the real trade and we but their servants from whose representatives as we desire so we would expect a kind treatment.

SOURCE: Edinburgh City Archives, Moses Collection, Convention of Royal Burghs, SL 30/222, Burgh reports and petitions, 1705.

A Letter on Anglo-Scottish Tensions: from Roderick Mackenzie of Prestonhall to William Bennet of Grubbet, Edinburgh, 9 December 1703

The disasters of the 1690s, including the failure of Darien, continued to have reverberations into the early years of the eighteenth century. Anger in Scotland about William's role in the Darien affair and the widespread belief that his withdrawal of support for the venture, and order that the masters of Scottish vessels should not be permitted to obtain water and provisions from English colonies in the region, had produced a wave of popular patriotism, perhaps even what can reasonably be described as a Scottish national political movement. The following extract provides an illuminating insight into Scottish attitudes to their southern neighbours in 1703.

We have no foreign mails since my last. As to that great defeat of the Germans by the French, it can not be but thought a very mortifying blow to the Confederacy in general, as being prejudicial to the common liberties of Europe when there is not strength enough to maintain an equal balance between the two chief potentates: but as to the particular interest of Scotland, whose circumstances have a certain peculiarity in them different from the general interest of all its neighbouring nations, several judicious well-wishers to it are of opinion that anything that tends to the humbling of that haughty insolence so natural to our imperious and purse-proud neighbours must of course prove for our ease and quiet: so that indeed some of those politicians do not tick to say they had rather wished the foresaid loss and indignity had fallen more immediately to England's share than to that of the Empire, while England treats us as it does, and has done for many years, to the immortal scandal and reproach of our poor deserted nation in general, but more especially to that of such of its most superlatively scandalous and unnatural brood whom for the viciousness of their morals, the debauchery of their principles and the too too openly avowed prostitution of their mercenary and slavish tempers, England has singled out now for a course of years together as the most thorough-paced instruments and tools that they could think for completing that yoke of bondage under which we have laboured too too long, by reason of a certain unaccountable base creeping mean spirit of despondency that has insensibly and by degrees stolen upon the gross of our unthinking people.

SOURCE: NAS, Ogilvy of Inverquharity MSS, GD 205/34.

Two letters on the Prospect of Union

The details of the proposed Union seemed to some Scots at least to be very much in Scotland's interest. These letters were written by William Bennet of Grubbet, a member of the small but politically significant Squadrone Volante party in the Scottish parliament. Grubbet therefore represents only one strand of opinion in Scotland about the best course for the country. Even so, Grubbet, a staunch presbyterian, had also been a Scots émigré in the Low Countries when James VII was monarch of Scotland and, along with several leading figures in Scotland who had also suffered under the Stuarts and had a deep fear of 'popery', was inclined to favour the Hanoverian succession and looked to union with Protestant England as a means of securing his religion.

A) WILLIAM BENNET OF GRUBBET TO WILLIAM NISBET, MARLFIELD, 10 MARCH 1706

I shall not speak of news, only we have seen the list of the Commissioners for a union treaty, and since you are all silent above, 'tis felt we should follow your example here, so I shall say nothing, as to the sentiments of people here, on that choice, the time will come, when we shall know, what is kept so mysterious and secret at present, and I pray God that all may end well, to the happiness of this sinking nation, which unless it get a sudden crisis, must perish under the disease of its manifold grievances, having languished so long that 'tis now at its latter grasp . . .

B) WILLIAM BENNET OF GRUBBET TO WILLIAM NISBET, MARLFIELD, 13 APRIL 1706

We had all hoped, to have seen you here sooner, as the end of May, but I still fancied, that being on the stage of business, you would not leave it until you saw what course matters were like to take in this great business, now under agitation and management, for my own share I think a fair bargain, with our neighbour nation, the best handle, to give us peace, and save us from anarchy, and confusion. We have long gone astray, and been bewildered in a maze of perplexities and misery, had nothing left us, but to complain, and no view how to be better at the long run, as to the general concern of the nation, what ever designs and advantages private men might have projected for themselves, at certain events, but if we are now to have compensation, for what we have suffered from our neighbours, in the matter of

Darien and the like, and the advantages of their trade, and plantations, as also hard and piquant things removed . . . we then see the end of our journey, and what this time may not conclude, another day may effectuate towards a full union, when such obliging preliminaries pave the way thereto, as nobody can doubt, but this will be advantageous to us, labouring under so many hardships and miseries, so it will be most important, for the happiness of our neighbours, since if we go not along with them, it may be in our hands to do them far more mischief, than we can do ourselves good . . .

SOURCE: NAS, Ogilvy of Inverquharity MSS, GD 205/38.

The Western *Gáidhealtachd*

DOCUMENT 103

The Lordship of the Isles, 1545

The Lordship of the Isles had been annexed to the Scottish crown in 1493, although in terms of military power and manpower the region from Islay in the south to Lewis in the north remained strong, and was persistently troublesome to the Stewart monarchs. The early 1540s were a time of great upheaval in Scotland as a whole and in the Highlands, following the death of James V in 1542 and the 'Rough Wooing'. Donald Dubh, a pretender to the Lordship of the Isles, revived the Council of the Isles and united most of the chiefs of Clan Donald to intrigue with Henry VIII against the Scottish crown. Ultimately, however, their unity could not hold, and their rebellion disintegrated. The Book of Clanranald, produced in the seventeenth century, is a work of poetry, history and genealogy, laid down by the MacMhuirich bards in the service of Clan MacDonald.

A) THE BOOK OF CLANRANALD

During the time that Donald Dubh had been in custody there was a great struggle among the Gael for power, so that Mac Ceaain of Ardnamurchan almost destroyed the race of John Mor, son of John of Isla, and of Kintyre. John Cathanach . . . John Mor . . . and Donald Balloch, son[s] of John Cathanach, were treacherously taken prisoners by Mac Ceaain . . . he conveyed them to Edinburgh . . . and they were executed . . .

   In a similar manner a misfortune came over the Clann Donald of the north side, for after the death of John of Isla, Earl of Ross and the killing of Angus, Alexander son of Gillespie, son of Alexander of Isla, took possession of the Earldom of Ross and of the northern Oirir [mainland possessions] entirely . . . However, some of the men of the northern side came . . . the Mackenzies . . . and fought a battle against him, which they call Blar na Pairce . . . Alexander came to the coast after that to seek for a force in the Isles . . . and . . . was killed by Mac Ceaain and by Alexander, son of John Cathanach . . . Donald Gallda, son of Alexander, son of Gillespie, came of age; and he came from the Lowlands by the direction of the Earl of Moray, until he came to the Isles; and he brought Macleod of Lewis with him, and a good number of the nobles of the Isles. They went out on the Point of Ardnamurchan, and there they met Alexander, son of John Cathanach, and he and Donald, son of Alexander, made a compact and agreement with each other; and they together attacked Mac Ceaain at a place called Creagan Airgid, and he and his three sons and many of his people were slain there.

Donald Gallda was nominated Mac Donald of this side of the Point of Ardnamurchan, and the men of the Isles submitted to him; but he did not live after that but
seven or eight weeks . . .

With regard to Donald Dubh, son of Angus, son of John of Isla . . . the lineal
lawful heir of the Isles and of Ross, on his release from confinement he came to the
Isles, and the men of the Isles gathered about him; and he and the Earl of Lennox,
made an agreement to raise a large army for the purpose of his getting into
possession of his own property; and a ship came to them from England to the
Sound of Mull, with money to help them in the war. The money was given to Mac
Lean of Duart to divide among the leaders of the army; they did not get as much as
they desired, and therefore the army broke up.

B) ARTICLES PROPOSED TO THE COUNCIL BY THE COMMISSIONERS OF THE LORD OF THE ISLES, 23 AUGUST 1545

'My Lordis, thir ar the artikillis concernyng or besynes diffen be us as commissio-
naris to my lord erll of Ros and lord of Iles of Scotland', viz.:

1. The Earl desires the King [Henry VIII] to send to Lennox with an army now
instantly and promises that then the most part of Scotland will come to the King's
obedience. 2. To be supported, now that he is become the King's subject, against
all Scottish enemies, and provided for if the King agree with the Scots. 3.
Especially not to agree with Argyll until the Earl recovers the possessions which
Argyll falsely took from him while he was in prison. 4. To have surety for the
pension of 2,000 cr. promised him by the Council in the King's name. 5. Of the
8,000 men whom he promises the King, he desires wages for 3,000, who being
gentlemen must be sustained and helped, and will hold the rest ready at his own
expense.

C) THE LORD OF THE ISLES, 4 SEPTEMBER 1545

Promise by Rose Macallister, elect of the Isles, and Master Patrick Maclane,
brother germane to the lord Maclane, bailye of Ycomkill and justice clerk of the
South Isles, commissioners sent by 'lord Donald of the Ilis and erll of Ros' to
present to Henry VIII a 'writing of an oath' and to make covenants for him, that
(the King having granted the earl a pension of 2,000 cr. by letters patent, and
undertaken the protection of him and his adherents) the said Earl and his
adherents will serve the King in Scotland, annoy the Governor there and his
part-takers, and make no agreement with Huntlie or Argyill to the King's
prejudice. And whereas the King now sends Lennox, as his lieutenant, with
Ormond and a number of men, to invade Scotland, and penetrate as far as
Sterling if it be feasible, the Earl of Ross will join that enterprise with 8,000 men
so long as Lennox remains in Argyll's country, and with 6,000 men when he is in
any other part of Scotland (employing the other 2,000 in annoying Argyll). For

this the King will allow, besides his men in wages out of Ireland, wages for 3,000 of their men for two months at the same rate as his own.

SOURCE: a) Macbain, A and Kennedy, J (eds) 1894 'The Book of Clanranald', *Reliquiae Celticae*. Inverness, i; b) and c) Brewer, JS (ed) 1864–1932 *Letters and Papers, foreign and domestic, of the reign of Henry VIII*. London.

DOCUMENT 104

Government Perceptions of the Highlands, 1597–99

These acts of parliament and the comments of James VI in Basilikon Doron *give some indication of the attitude of the crown towards the Highlands and Islands and identify lack of commerce, industriousness and godliness as particular problems of the region.*

A) ACT OF PARLIAMENT, 1597

. . . considering that the inhabitantis of the Helandis and Iles of this Realme quhilkis are for the maist part of his Hienes annext propertie hes not onlie frustrat his Majestie of the yeirlie payment of his proper rentis and deu service properly addebtit be thame to his Maiestie furthe of the saidis landis bot that they have lykwayis throche thair barbarus inhumanitie maid and presentlie maikis the saidis Hielandis and Iles quhilkis are maist commodious in thameselves alsueill be the fertillitie of the ground as be riche fischeingis be sey altogidder unprofitable baith to thameselffis and to all uthers his Hienes liegis within this Realme thay nathair intertening onie civil or honest societie amangis thame selfis naythir yit admittit utheris his Hienes liegis to trafficque within thair boundis with safetie of thair lives and gudes . . .

B) ACT OF PARLIAMENT, 1597

for the better intertening and continuing of civilitie and policie within the Hielandis and Iles hes statute and ordanit that thair be erectit and buildit within the boundis thairof Thre Brugheis and Burrow Townes in the maise convenient and commodious pairtis meit for the samyn; To wit ane in *Kintyre* ane uthir in *Lochaber* and the third in *the Lewis* . . .

C) ACT OF PARLIAMENT, 1598

. . . the landis and Iles of the Lewis and Ronalewis and Trouternes [on Skye] . . . to mak the samyn commodious and profitabill to his hienes his realme and leigis quhilk hes bene the mair difficill hitherto to be accomplischit be reasoun of the evill dispositioun and barbaritie of the peopill inhabitantis of the saidis landis and Iles . . . quha hes euer opponit thame selfis directlie to suffer or permit ony policie or civilitie to have ony entrie or place amangis thame . . . understanding that the saidis landis and Iles ar be speciall providence and blissing of God inrychit with ane incredibill fertilitie of cornis and store of fischingis and vtheris necessaris surpassing far the plantie of ony pairte of the inland And yit nonetheless the same ar possest be inhabitantis quha ar voyd of ony knawledge of God of his Religioun and naturallie abhoiring all kynd of civilitie quha hes gevin thame selfis ovir to all kynd of barbarietie and inhumanitie . . . And now the gentilmen abone namit being maist willing at the uttermast of thair power to advance and set fordwart the Glorie of God and honour of thair natiue cuntrey and his maiesties seruice And heirwith to augment the yeirlie rent and revenew of the croun . . . bot alsua in the planting of kirkis and uther polices within the landis and Iles forsaidis.

d) JAMES VI, *Basilikon Doron*

As for the Hie-lands, I shortly comprehend them al in two sortes of people: the one, that dwelleth in our maine land, that are barbarous, and yet mixed with some shewe of ciuilite: the other, that dwelleth in the Iles, and are alluterly barbares, without any sort or shew of civilite. For the first sort, put straitly to execution the Lawes made alreadie by mee against their Over-lords, and the chiefs of their Clannes, and it will be no difficultie to dantone [daunt] them. As for the other sort, thinke no other of them all, then as Wolves and Wild Boares: And therefore follow foorth the course that I have begunne, in planting Colonies among them of answerable In-lands subiects, that within shorte time may roote them out and plant ciuilitie in their roomes.

SOURCE: a)-c) 1814–75 *Acts of the Parliaments of Scotland.* Edinburgh, iv; d) James VI 1599 *Basilikon Doron.* Edinburgh, 42–3.

The Statutes of Iona

The Statutes of Iona represent a change in policy of the government of James VI towards the Highlands and Islands, moving away from attempts to coerce the Highlands or instigate plantations of Lowland subjects in the region, towards seeking accommodation with the chiefs. While there was an element of coercion in the new policy – the chiefs had essentially been kidnapped and imprisoned in the Lowlands prior to their agreement to negotiate with the crown – there is also a sense that the crown did not demand as much as it might have done from the chiefs. Note, for example, the conspicuous absence of any demand that the chiefs pay the rents they owed on crown property.

The Court of the South and North Illis of Scotland haldin at Icolmekill

[1] They haif all aggreit in ane voice, lyk as it is presentlie concludit and inactit, that the ministeris alswele plantit as to be plantit within the parrochynis [parishes] of the saidis Illandis salbe reverentlie obeyit, thair stipendis dewtifullie payit thame . . .

[2] . . . certane oistlairis [innkeepers] to be set doun in the maist convenient placeis within every Ile, . . . furnitour sufficient of meit and drink to be sauld for reasonable expensis.

[3] . . . for releif of thair said intollerable burdyn, that na man be sufferit to remaine or haif residence within ony of thair boundis of the saidis Iles without ane speciall revenew and rent to leive upoun, or at the leist ane sufficient calling and craft quhairby to be sustenit . . .

[4] . . . that quhatsumevir persone or personis . . . found soirning [extorting free quarters], craveing meit, drink or ony uther geir . . . salbe repute and haldin as thevis and intollerable oppressouris, callit and persewit thairfore before the judge competent as for thift and oppressioun . . .

[5] . . . that no persone nor personis indwellairis within the boundis of the saidis haill Iles bring in to sell for money ather wyne or acquavitie, undir the pane of tinsale [loss] of the samyn . . .

[6] . . . everie gentilman or yeaman . . . haveing childreine maill or famell, and being in goodis worth thriescore ky [cows], sall put at the leist thair eldest sone, or haveing

no childrene maill thair eldest dochter, to the scuillis on the Lawland, and interteny and bring thame up thair quhill thay may be found able sufficientlie to speik, reid, and wryte Inglische . . .

[7] . . . in respect of the monstrous deidlie feidis [feuds] . . . intertenyit within the saidis Ylis . . . na persone nor personis . . . beir hagbutis [a kind of gun] nor pistolletis furth of thair awne housis and dwelling places . . .

[8] . . . na vagabound, baird, nor profest pleisant pretending libertie to baird and flattir, be ressavit within the boundis of the saidis Yllis . . .

[9] . . . the principall of every clan man be ansuerable for the remanent of the samyn, his kin, freindis, and dependairis . . .

SOURCE: 1877–98 *Register of the Privy Council of Scotland*. Edinburgh, ix, 26–30.

Letter from Iain Muideartach, Twelfth Chief of Clanranald to Pope Urban VIII, 1626

The Protestant Reformation had limited penetration in remote areas of the western Highlands and Islands, where Catholicism persisted. This letter records the promise of the chief of the powerful Clanranald, a branch of Clan MacDonald, to advance the interests of the Counter-Reformation in Scotland.

I . . . with the rest of the nobles and other classes, pledge and promise . . . every help for the greater spread and preservation of the faith among us as we shall prove beyond doubt by deeds, by a perilous war, by the shedding of blood and, should it be necessary, by our own death for the defence of the faith . . . we, the aforementioned clan . . . shall with the help of our kinsfolk and friends subdue the greater part of Scotland . . . though we could not keep it long against the power of the King unless aided by your Holiness or by the power of Catholic kings. Wherefore we humbly beseech Your Holiness that if matters should ever reach this state (as we think they undoubtedly will) your patronage and assistance will not be wanting to us . . . The greatest hope of success is in the fact that this part of Scotland, always accustomed to arms, has become warlike, strong in battle . . . Our country and islands are in themselves difficult for an enemy to approach . . . All the Gaelic-speaking Scots and the greater part of the Irish chieftains joined to us by ties of friendship . . . will begin war each in his own district to the glory of God . . . However . . . whether the above mentioned help is given or denied, I, the nobles and the above mentioned people, are prepared one and all to endure by the grace of God . . . every temporal loss and discomfort for the faith we have received . . . professing and offering obedience to Your Holiness, to the apostolic Roman see . . . for ever . . .

Given in the great island called Uist the 5th February, 1626

SOURCE: Campbell, JL 1953 'The Letter sent by Iain Muideartach, twelfth chief of Clanranald, to Pope Urban VIII, in 1626', *Innes Review*, xv, 110–16.

DOCUMENT 107

Letter from the Marquis of Hamilton to Charles I, 15 June 1638

As conflict loomed between Charles I and his Scottish presbyterian subjects, this document foreshadows the events of the Wars of the Three Kingdoms by highlighting the probable loyalty of many Highlanders to the king, and their antipathy to the acquisitive and presbyterian Clan Campbell. This document also illustrates the presence of Gaelic interests and, more narrowly, MacDonald interests, in both Scotland and Ireland. The earl of Antrim hoped to regain former MacDonald lands in the south-west Highlands and Islands by allying with the king against the Covenanters and the Campbells.

. . . the Iyles men . . . the mynd therof . . . is reasonabill good . . . can not say for anie greatt effection they cayrie to your Majestie bot becaus of ther splen to Lorne [Archibald Campbell, later earl of Argyll] and will dou if they durst just contrarie to whatt his men doueth . . .

I cannot negleckt the representing to your Majestie thatt the Earle of Antrim may be of yuse in this busines, for [he] is belouved by divers of his name, and heath sume pretentiounes to lande in Kintyre, Iyles, and Heaylands, and will no dout repare to Iyrland and bring shuch foors with him as will put thoes countries in that disorder.

SOURCE: Gardiner, SR (ed) 1880 *The Hamilton Papers.* Camden Society, 9–13.

Allegiance to William and Mary, 1690–91

Aware that their title to the throne was parliamentary rather than strictly hereditary, and conscious of the Jacobite threat in the Highlands in particular, William and Mary took steps to secure allegiance. They insisted upon receiving oaths of allegiance in successive waves, culminating in the final demand that all oaths be tendered by 1 January 1692.

A) ACT FOR SECURITY OF THEIR MAJESTIES GOVERNMENT, EDINBURGH, 22 JULY 1690

I . . . doe in the sincerity of my heart assert, acknowledge, and declare, that their Majesties King William and Queen Mary, are the only lawful undoubted Soveraignes, King and Queen of Scotland, alse well *de jure* as *de facto*, and in the exercise of the government. And therefore, I doe sincerely and faithfully promise and engage, that I will, with heart and hand, life and goods, maintaine and defend their Majesties title and Government against the late King James, his adherents and all other enemies who, either by open or secret attempts, shall disturb or disquiet their Majesties in the exercise thereof.

B) CORRESPONDENCE FROM THE PRIVY COUNCIL TO THE QUEEN, 29 JULY 1691

The Highland rebels have been of late very peaceable, acting no hostility . . . Severall of them accepted of an oath tendered to them . . . never to ryse in armes against their Majesties or the Government; uthers were living in such quyett, that except an invasione had happened, they seemed resolved to have continued so . . .

C) PROCLAMATION OF INDEMNITY, 27 AUGUST 1691

William and Mary, by the grace of God, King and Queen of Great Brittaine, ffrance and Ireland . . . Whereas we did allow John, Earle of Breadalbane, to meet with the Highlanders . . . we understand their willingness to render themselves in subjectione to our authority . . . humbly asking . . . our assistance for accommodating some differences and ffeuds . . . we being satisfied that nothing can conduce more to the peace of the highlands . . . then the taking away of these differences and feuds which prevail with them, to neglect the opportunities to improve and cultivat their countrie, and to accustome themselves to depredationes and idleness . . . we are resolved graciously, to pardone, indemnifie, and restore all . . . who shall take the oath of alleadgance . . . before the first day of January next . . . And we . . . doe assure and declare all such persones . . . by suearing and signing, as said is the said oath of alleadgance to us, that they shall be altogither free, safe, and secure from all maner of punishment, paines, and penalties that can be inflicted upon them for open rebellione, or any other of the crymes above specified.

SOURCE: a) 1814–75 *Acts of the Parliaments of Scotland*. Edinburgh, ix, 223; b) and c) Gordon, J 1845 *Papers Illustrative of the Political Conditions of the Highlands of Scotland, 1689–96*. Maitland Club.

Correspondence Relating to the Massacre of Glencoe

These documents outline the fate of a clan that failed to take the oath of allegiance by the deadline of 1 January 1692. John Dalrymple, master of Stair, who enjoyed considerable political advancement under the Williamite regime, had, even before the passing of this deadline, shown his intent towards the MacDonalds of Glencoe in letters to the Campbell earl of Breadalbane, and to Lieutenant-Colonel James Hamilton, deputy governor of the garrison of Fort William. The Massacre took place on 13 February 1692, and in the political outcry and inquiry that followed, the king was unsurprisingly acquitted of any culpability.

A) FROM JOHN DALRYMPLE, MASTER OF STAIR TO JOHN CAMPBELL, EARL OF BREADALBANE, 2 DECEMBER 1691

I think the clan Donell must be rooted out . . .

B) FROM JOHN DALRYMPLE, MASTER OF STAIR TO LIEUTENANT-COLONEL HAMILTON, 3 DECEMBER 1691

The M'Donalds . . . the only popish clan in the kingdom, and it will be popular to take severe course with them. Let me hear from you with the first whether you think this is the proper season to maul them in the cold long nights . . .

C) ADDITIONAL INSTRUCTIONS FROM KING WILLIAM II TO SIR THOMAS LIVINGSTONE, 16 JANUARY 1692

But, for a just example of vengeance, I intreat that the thieving tribe in Glenco may be rooted out in earnest.

SOURCE: Gordon, J 1845 *Papers Illustrative of the Political Conditions of the Highlands of Scotland, 1689–96.* Maitland Club.

The Church and Religion

DOCUMENT 110

Sir David Lindsay of the Mount, *Ane Satyre of the Thrie Estaitis*

David Lindsay's play Ane Satyre of the Thrie Estaitis *was performed in an embryonic version in 1540, and more fully in Cupar in 1552, and then in Edinburgh in 1554, before the regent, Mary of Guise. It was primarily concerned with the ideal of a king as a central figure in the commonwealth, but this extract also reveals that Lindsay was influenced by Protestant criticisms of the corrupt lives of some of the Catholic clergy, who are here proud to boast of their womanising, drinking, gambling and enriching themselves.*

Spirituality:
... of my office, gif ye wald have the reill,
I let yow wit, I have it usit weill:
For I tak in my count twyse in the yeir,
Wanting nocht of my teind ane boll of beir.
I gat gude payment of my Temporall lands ...

gif: if; reill: truth
wit: know

boll of beir:
  large measure
  of barley

Abbot:
Tuiching my office, I say to yow plainlie,
My Monks and I, we leif richt easelie:
Thare is na monks, from Carrick to Carraill,
That fairs better, and drinks mair helsum aill

. . .

My paramours is baith als fat and fair,
As ony wench, intill the toun of Air.
I send my sons to Pareis, to the scuillis,
I traist in God that thay sall be na fuillis.
And all my douchters, I have weill provydit,
Now, judge ye, gif my office be weill gydit.

Scrybe:
Maister Person [parson], schaw us gif ye can preich.

Person:
Thocht I preich not, I can play at the caiche:
I wait thair is nocht ane amang yow all,
Mair ferilie can play at the fut-ball;
And for the carts, the tabils, and the dyse,
Above all persouns, I may beir the pryse.

caiche: tennis

SOURCE: Laing, D (ed) 1871 *The Poetical Works of Sir David Lindsay*. Edinburgh, ii, 262–4.

First Bond of the Lords of the Congregation, 1557

Along with preachers such as John Knox, the Lords of the Congregation were a principal driving force behind the Reformation. Bonds were common among members of the nobility who pledged loyalty to allies in the face of threats and enemies. In this First Bond of the Lords of the Congregation, five powerful members of the landed class declared their intent to bring about reformation. This Bond has been seen as an origin of the covenanting tradition that developed in the seventeenth century.

We, persaving how Sathan In his membris the Antechristes of oure tyme, crewellie dois Raige seiking to downetring [overthrow] and to destroye the Evangell of Christ, and his Congregatioune: awght according to our bownden dewtye, to stryve in our maisteres Cawss, even unto the deth . . . We do promis before the Maiestie of God, and his Congregatioune: that we (be his grace) sall with all diligence continewallie applie oure hoill power, substaunce, and oure very lyves to mentene, sett forwarde, and establische the MAIST BLISSED WORDE OF GOD . . . to haif faithfull ministeres purelie and trewlie to minister Christes Evangell and Sacramentes to his Peopill: We sall mentene thame, nurys thame, and defende thame, the haill Congregatioune of CHRIST, and everye member therof, at oure haill poweres, and waring of oure lyves aganis Sathan and all wicked power that dois intend tyrannye or troubill aganis the forsaid Congregatioune. Onto the quhilk holie worde and Congregatioune we do Joyne us: and also dois forsaik and Renunce the Congregatioune of Sathan with all the superstitioune, abhominatioune, and Idolatrie thereof . . .

SOURCE: Innes, C (ed) 1872 *Facsimiles of National Manuscripts of Scotland.* Southampton, iii, no. xl.

First Book of Discipline, 1561

The Reformation Parliament of 1560 discussed religion without the sanction of the crown and was packed with Protestant sympathisers and supporters and dependants of the five noblemen who had signed the First Bond. While the Confession of Faith outlined the religious beliefs of the new reformed Church of Scotland, the Book of Discipline *was commissioned by the parliament to define the policies and structure of the church, and was written by a team of six reformers, including John Knox.*

It apperteneth to the Pepill, and to everie severall [separate] Congregatioun, to Elect thair Minister . . .

Everie severall Churche have a Scholmaister appointed . . . Yf it be Upaland [rural], whaire the people convene to doctrine bot once in the weeke, then must eathir the Reidar or the Minister thair appointed, take cayre over the children and youth of the parische, to instruct them in thair first rudementis, and especiallie in the Catechisme . . .

Men of best knowledge in Goddis word, of cleanest life, men faithfull, and of most honest conversatioun that can be found in the Churche, must be nominated to be in electioun [as elders] . . . The Elderis being elected, must be admonischeit of thair office, which is to assist the Minister in all publict effares of the Churche; to wit, in judgeing and decernyng causes; in giving of admonitioun to the licentious liver; in having of respect to the manneris and conversatioun of all men within thair charge . . . [and] to tak heyde to the life, manneris, diligence, and studye of thair Ministeris. Yf he be worthie of admonitioun, thei must admonische him; . . . of depositioun, thay with consent of the Churche and Superintendent may depose him, so that his cryme so deserve.

Everie Maister of houshald must be commandit eathir to instruct, or ellis caus [to] be instructed, his children, servandis, and famlie, in the principallis of the Christiane religioun; without the knowledge whairof aught none to be admitted to the Tabill of the Lord Jesus . . .

SOURCE: Laing D (ed) 1895 *The Works of John Knox*. Edinburgh, ii.

Selections from Elgin Kirk Session Minutes, 1593–99

This document details the impact of the Reformed Church discipline upon the community of Elgin.

11 May 1593 – It is appointit that the Communioun be ministrat upon Sondaye the 27th day of this instant and for the better preparatioun thairunto they haif appointit ane fast and abstinence to be upoun Sondaye the 20th day of May and preiching upoun Wedinsdaye and Fryday thairefter . . . and fast and preiching to be preceislie keipit the saidis dayis through owt the haill broghe and landwart [urban and rural parts of the parish]

20 June – The Catechisme is appointit fra Sondaye nixt cuming to be teacht at efter noonis in the kirk ilk Sondaye . . .
   Margaret Greiff confessis she sufferit her bairne to be smoirit [suffocated] through negligence upoun the nycht. She is ordanit to stand three Sondayis in sackclothe bairfut and bairleggit in the kirk befoir the congregatioun . . . all the quhyill of the preaching and prayeris and in the haill meintyme of the making of hir repentance appoynts ane mytre of papir upoun hir head or breist, with ane inscriptioun thairupoun conteining the cause of hir being thair . . .

6 March 1594 – The examinatiounes of the toun to begin on Mondaye nixt, the maisteris of the fameleis befoir noone and the servandis efternoone, and the communion to be ministrat to the landward on Sondaye cum aucht dayis [i.e. a week] and to the toun the Sondaye thaireftir and for the better preparatioun thairunto a fast to be upoun Wedinsdaye and Frydaye the ouk [week] befoir . . .

24 April – It is appointit that the commoun ordour be usit anent the barroun of Sanquhir for committing fornicatioun with Janet Cuik . . .

11 August 1596 – Issobell and Margaret Tailyeour . . . to do thair repentance on Sonday nixt for thair publict flytting [railing at each other] and frequent skailding on the calsay [high street] under the payne of fyve pundis . . .

18 August – Sic yettis and durris [Such gates and doors] as ar found stekit [locked] upoun the officiaris quhen thei pas through the toune on the sabboth daye with the

visitours for inbringing the peopill to the sermon salbe callit dissobediens and puneist thairfoir . . .

19 January 1597 – Comperit Walter Hay, goldsmith, accusit for playing at the boulis and golff upoun Sondaye in the tym of the sermon, and hes actit himselff fra this furthe under the paynes of £5 nocht to commit the lyik outher afoir or eftirnone the tym of the preaching . . .

22 April – Issobell Barry hir head to be scheavin and stand in the joggis [an iron collar chained to the kirk gate] two houris and gif scho be found relapsit in fornicatioun to be baneist furth of this toun.

25 May – The names of the new eldaris and deacones to be proclamit from the pulpit that all personis that hes ony thing to say aganis them cum on Wedinsdaye . . .

5 August – Tua honest men to go through the toun upoun the sabbothe daye with the officiaris for visiting of the absents remanaris from the kirk as they had wount to do fra the last bell be rung to the sermone quhill the sermone be endit and that the saids visitors try all uther enormiteis and faultis as far as they can persave.

28 August – Elspet Mill complenit to the sessioneris upoun Stephin Jhonestoun quhome scho allegis molestit hir in the place quhair scho satt the tym of the sermone this day and gaif hir injurious wordis quhilk the elderschipe hes tryit and fand the same to be trew . . . for the whilk he is appointit on Sonday nixt to confess his offens and crave pardon thairfoir . . .

12 October – The deacounes ar augmentit with Thomas Richartsone quha haiffing the cair of the puir of this burgh, quhais names ar contenit in ane roll, assistit with a baillie and tua eldaris sall sit doun and convein ilk Wedinsday eftir sermone in the kirk and call the said puir afoir thame and try thame quhow they have keipit the sermones, morning and evening prayeris and behaved themselves utherwayis . . .

12 September 1599 – Isbell Foularton to pay 40d for selling of drink the tym of the sermoun . . .

21 December – All prophane pastyme inhibited to be usitt be any persones ather within the burgh or college and speciallie futballing through the toun, snaw balling, singing of carrellis or uther prophane sangis, guysing, pyping, violing, and dansing . . . under paynis of publict repentans, at the leist during this tyme quhilk is superstitiouslie keipitt fra the 25th day of December to the last of Januar . . .

SOURCE: NAS, MS CH2/145/1–2.

The Ordour Appoyinted by his Majestie for the Apparrell off Churchemen in Scotland, 1633

While James VI had the power to direct what the clergy of Scotland should wear during ceremonies, he diplomatically chose not to exercise it. He was keenly aware of presbyterian sensitivities, and tended to pick his battles carefully, focusing on bringing the structure and ceremonies of the church to a more episcopalian footing. His son Charles I, however, was less tactful in his dealings with Scottish presbyterians, and he did issue an order laying down a form of uniform for the clergy. The wearing of surplices would be seen as a step towards Catholicism, and would be highly unpopular.

It is our pleasure that all the lords Archbischops and Bischops within that our Kyngdome off Scotland sall in all publick places weare gownes with standing capes and cassocks . . . [and] lords Archbischops and Bischops sall in all churches where they come in tyme of divine service or sermoun be in whytes, that is in a rochett and sleeves as they weare at the tyme off our coronatioun, and especiallie whensoever they administer the holy communioun or preach . . . And for all inferiour clergymen we will that they preach in thair black gounes; bot when they reade dyvine service, christen, burye or administer the sacrament off the lords supper, they sall weare there surplices, and if they be doctours there tippets over thame . . .

SOURCE: 1814–75 *Acts of the Parliaments of Scotland.* Edinburgh, v, 20–1.

Spiritual Exercises of Katharine Collace, Mistress Ross (d. 1697)

This personal narrative gives valuable insights into the religious conversion and experience of a woman in the seventeenth century. Katharine Collace endured an unhappy marriage and the birth of twelve children, none of whom outlived her, and the document outlines the comfort and anxiety that her faith brought to her life.

The Lord trysted me with suitable education relating to things spiritual and temporal, and preservations from manifold hazards. But what I especially remark is, his great and wonderful work in dealing effectually with my soul about the fourteenth year of my age, and this is the more remarkable because being religiously educated . . . winning to a form of godliness and lookt upon as religious by others – yet I got not leave to rest there, but by a word of a sermon was made suspicious of my state . . . and so came to be exercised with the necessity of a change, which I sought after, and was much encouraged therein by the Lord, who made my work, though sharp, yet very pleasant that I loathed all divertissements . . . so that for some considerable time together I was so filled with joy unspeakable that the ordinances [preaching and sacraments] became like a little heaven to me; and I loathed all the vanities of this life as hell . . . But being ignorant of the life of faith . . . I turned less diligent in secret prayer, which was an inlet to backsliding . . . All this time I much question[ed] if I had closed with Christ . . .

After this, I was sore tried with subtle tentations to sin, but the Lord graciously preserved me. I also met with some trials of affliction. One was (besides the death of two fine children in that place, and two before in Ross . . . I had a young one overlaid [smothered] by his nurse . . . And then a hell arose in my conscience for blood-guiltiness, and sin against light. I roared through the disquietness of my heart, and Satan was also let loose upon me . . . Only that word kept me up insensibly, Christ's soul was troubled . . .

Another remarkable passage was this: having a sweet child threatened with death, I was somewhat troubled about her eternal salvation . . . she being of more age than the rest that died before, being three years and a half old, and so guilty of actual sins, at least in words, being very capable to discern between good and evil, [yet] the Lord did wonderfully condescend to me, and made her to speak to admiration . . . She began to commend heaven, saying, The Lord is there, and the Father of the Lord Jesus Christ is there, and all the holy angels are there, and all the bonny things are there. She says moreover, this is the Lord's day, and we may not sing nor speak our

own words, but we may sing spiritual songs and we may sing hallelujahs this day . . .
I lookt on this as an evidence of [God's] condescension.

SOURCE: Mullan, DG (ed) 2003 *Women's Life Writing in Early Modern Scotland:
Writing the Evangelical Self c.1670–c.1730*. Aldershot, 43, 47–8, 54–5.

The Sanquhar Declaration, 1680

The government of Charles II and the remnants of the Covenanters fought inter-mittent military and ideological battles in the Restoration period which culminated in the Battle of Bothwell Brig in June 1679, after which, the Covenanting movement splintered further. The Cameronians published this declaration in their heartland of south-western Scotland, renouncing their allegiance to the regime of Charles II. They were followers of the field preacher Richard Cameron, who was shortly afterwards killed in a skirmish with government troops.

Although we be for government and governors such as the word of God and our covenant allows, yet we for ourselves and all that will adhere to us, as the representative of the true presbyterian kirk and covenanted nation of Scotland, considering the great hazard of lying under such a sin any longer, do by thir presents disown Charles Stuart, that has been reigning (or rather tyrannizing as we may say) on the throne of Britain these years bygone, as having any right, title to, or interest in the said crown of Scotland for government, as forfeited several years since by his perjury and breach of covenant both to God and his Kirk . . . [We] do declare a war with such a tyrant and usurper and the men of his practices, as enemies to our Lord Jesus Christ, and his cause and covenants . . . As also we disown . . . the Duke of York, that professed papist . . .

SOURCE: Wodrow, R 1721–22 *History of the Sufferings of the Church of Scotland.* Edinburgh, appendix xlvii.

Scotland and Europe

DOCUMENT 117

The Riksråd Debates, 1638–40

These documents illustrate the central importance of Sweden to Scottish politics at a time of serious upheaval within the British Isles. Two Scottish envoys, General Alexander Leslie and Colonel John Cochrane, sought to explain the Scottish opposition to Charles I to the Swedish state council, the Riksråd, while appealing for military aid. Once in Scotland Leslie remained in contact with the Swedish Chancellor, Axel Oxenstierna, and the first surviving letter dated June 1638 stated that the two causes of conflict in Scotland were religion and national liberty. This letter was read out in the Riksråd meeting on 28 June and the issues of the national and religious freedoms in Scotland came to be repeatedly discussed in the Riksråd.

A) RIKSRÅD, 28 JUNE 1638

The State Marshal [Jacob de la Cardie] mentioned that Field Marshal Leslie's request was, that after he spoke so highly implying otherwise he has reversed his decision and must return quickly to Scotland again. For this he must receive his licence with haste to set about his discharge before the King in England surrounds Scotland with his ships and launches an attack.

It was decided that they shall write to the State Chancellor [Axel Oxenstierna] and advise him that the disposition and turbulent state in Scotland has occurred for the sake of religion and freedom, and ask his opinion on Herr Leslie's supplication.

B) RIKSRÅD, 9 AUGUST 1638. SEVERAL DISCUSSIONS FOLLOWED, WITH THE MOST INTENSIVE DEBATES ON 9 AND 10 AUGUST, REGARDING THE RELEASE OF LESLIE FROM SWEDISH SERVICE

There followed a discourse on Field Marshal Leslie's insistent request: 1. To receive decommissioning from Her Majesties service to [serve] another to help his fatherland Scotland which is now threatened by the king in Britain in respect to his intrusion into their religious affairs. Or, if he can not gain perpetual release, that he may be absented for as long as it takes to ensure the preservation of his fatherland. 2. That he may be in receipt of some ammunition and weapons.

Regarding the decommissioning, it has merits and would be hard to deny him as he has 1. Long and faithfully served the Swedish Crown. 2. He has always been, and still is well liked. 3. He says now that his fatherland is in a turbulent state, which does seem likely to continue as it has already gone so far that the king has been presented with conditions with which he is not satisfied but will debate; therefore it is only the love of patria that drives him [Leslie], without hope of compensation from Scotland, that he cannot give it up. 4. He has placed all his goods, earned with blood and sweat, in Scotland and bought property there. 5. His son has a wife in Scotland who is the daughter of an earl. 6. If his decommissioning was denied he would become unwilling and slow to provide any further service to the Swedish Crown. 7. Now we do not have such great need of his service as the government [in Germany] is run by Herr Johan Baner. If Leslie were used in Westphalia the situation would become difficult for us and his service would become impossible and impractical.

On the other hand it would be a huge consideration to decommission him at this time. [1.] For if we offend the king in England we would become suspected of fomenting tumults [rebellion]. 2. If the king in England got the upper hand over the Scots, as he is not a good Swede [i.e. pro-Swedish], he would probably become an official enemy to us.

It was resolved thereupon that Leslie should be told that although his service to us [Sweden] was dear and we did not want to lose it, similarly as he insists upon it, awoken by his fatherland's troubled state, we could not deny or hinder him from serving his fatherland for the reasons noted above. However it was deemed more suitable that he should receive a total decommissioning than a temporary one so that we would not be suspected to be encouraging our subjects to arm against their king due to the service Leslie does the Swedish Crown. But once he is free from service we can say that he has departed and is no longer our subject; he is now free and in Scotland a landed man and therefore no-one can reasonably find fault with us; and we cannot reasonably reject his request. Thus as long as Leslie is in service we cannot make preparation in Westphalia, and similarly he cannot go there in person without damage to his reputation.

As for the rest, regarding the muskets, rifles and pieces, it is no less considerable a request than the first. However it is a question of whether we can lend them to him under pretext of compensation and thus supply him with weapons.

It could be reasonable that he, Leslie, got a bonus from the Crown this time as he is completely resigning from the Crown's service and that he is similarly told that what he gains serves the Crown after the Scottish trade is claimed.

C) RIKSRÅD, 10 AUGUST 1638, AFTERNOON

Field Marshal Herr Leslie came in and the Scottish situation was discussed with him as well as his decommissioning.

It was all round agreed that when his fatherland had settled into a peaceful state he would again serve no other state rather than the Swedish Crown.

The government's resolution for him was this: As he has such high respect for his fatherland's service, they do not want to deny him his decommissioning. It would be a great consideration to allow him to receive any of the ammunition etc publicly from the Crown; if we could bear testimony to him privately we would rather do that. Thus for his faithful service he will be given 2,000 muskets as long as he makes an agreement with some merchant here for them, who would get them from the Crown first. If there are cannon makers amongst his compatriots he can be assisted with copper; however we would like to receive some of them [cannon].

Leslie commented that Northampton, a town in England, had been upset in its religious rites by the king, which would cause not a little upset.

It is of some consideration to allow Leslie to receive ammunition from here, as nothing is getting through the Sound, however as Herr Leslie wants to try his luck with it he can receive a letter from the Krigsråd providing him with 2,00[0?] muskets with accompanying bandoleers, forks and 'potter' from here to Jacob Makler [James Maclean]. As for the rest it will be provided for him from Örebro [and shipped] to Gothenburg, to the merchant who lives there [John Maclean].

D) RIKSRÅD, 22 AUGUST 1638

Field Marshal Leslie came before the government and took his leave, and the government bore witness to him of their affection for him, which they wanted to demonstrate on the next [possible] occasion and they wished him much luck. He thanked them for their appreciation, promising his service to the Swedish Crown, always ready when it was required.

SOURCE: Kullberg, NA *et al* (eds) 1878–1959 *Svenska Riksrådets Protokoll, 1621–1658*. Stockholm, vii, 252–326. (In translation from the original Swedish.)

The Second Riksråd Debate

On conclusion of the First Bishops' War in 1639, it was apparent to both Royalist and Covenanter alike that the truce would not last. Colonel John Cochrane, a veteran of both the Danish and Swedish armies, was chosen to represent the Covenanter committees on an official embassy to seek foreign aid. Various Scottish Covenanting nobles signed his travel pass to Scandinavia in April 1640, including Argyll and Montrose, who continued to play significant roles in Scandinavian relations and later became enemies. Chancellor Axel Oxenstierna informed the Riksråd on 8 July 1640 of Colonel Cochrane's arrival.

A) RIKSRÅD, 8 JULY 1640, MORNING

His Excellency the State Chancellor recounted that a Scottish colonel, John Cochrane, had arrived here from Scotland on a mission from the 'Directors of the Scottish League', and the same Cochrane's letters of credit were read out from the aforementioned Directors to Her Majesty, and two letters to the State Chancellor, one from the Directors, the other from Field Marshal Leslie, which commended Cochrane to the Chancellor and to the Queen.

B) RIKSRÅD, 9 JULY, AFTERNOON

John Cochrane, Colonel, entered and had an audience in the name of the Directors of the Scottish People. After a greeting and good wishes for a good and happy rule [to Queen Christina], he excused the Directors greatly that they had not earlier notified Her Majesty of the condition of their fatherland, saying that they had always believed that the misunderstanding which had arisen between their king and them, would be – as had already begun – resolved. But now they could not take comfort from that, but rather see daily that disagreement grows. They are therefore forced into sending out envoys to neighbouring foreign potentates and republics to inform them of their fatherland's condition, namely that there are two areas in which they are badly pressed; Religion and religious services are being replaced by some new and Papist decrees; unusual offices are being forced upon them against their church hierarchy, and everything is being directed in such a way that it is feared that nothing other than the Spanish inquisition is imminent. The polity is being changed, their jurisdiction and liberty curtailed, the kingdom is being reduced into the form of a province, and other unusable and unacceptable changes have been introduced into it. Under these conditions the Estates have convened, deliberated what to do and could see no other way forward than either to averting their eyes to allow their religion and religious services to be destroyed and the polity, with a kingdom's jurisdiction and liberty, be anguished; or to be timely and considered about the ways to meet such danger with appropriate resistance. While pity itself and everyone's innate duty to his fatherland does not allow it, one in such cases can conspire. Although it has been thought out that it will be difficult to rectify, the Scottish nation's Directors have ventured on their good and just cause and taken to defence, thereby allowing it to be seen that they are ready to overturn all that is dear for God and fatherland. Therefore, they had not wanted to inform the neighbouring potentates and republics, particularly her Majesty in Sweden, not only because the Scottish nation has now, for a good time, enjoyed from Her Majesty and from her Majesty's ancestors all benevolence and friendship, and that her Majesty tends to support others who are weighted down and in need with her defence with all Royal affection. In the same comfort he [Cochrane] said he was sent to Her Majesty to ask her for advice and help in this their sorry state, by which the Scottish nation is obliged to Her Majesty, and hereafter remains bound in Her Majesty's eternal service, gratitude and promise.

After this the government and the Council convened and after a discussion the State Chancellor responded that on behalf of Her Majesty, our most gracious Queen, and in her name the Royal government and present Council, have heard and understood what he, John Cochrane, on behalf of his principals, the Directors in Scotland, had presented. That his principals congratulate Her Majesty on her happy rule and success against her enemies, with best wishes, that what has begun well and now for a long time on behalf of Christianity may in the same manner happily continue, for which the Royal government is thankful and promises the aforementioned Scottish nation all good-will and whatever both nations longstanding and good friendship can require. We understand that the noble gentlemen, the Directors in Scotland, had sent the gentleman to our fatherland, that what we until now from others, sometimes passionately, have heard about your state, can now by you verbally and clearly understand. And as the Scottish nation has now for a long time, circa 60 years, had a strong relationship and experience of us, and a good portion of the Scottish nation has shown our previous kings and Crown worthy services; for this reason their success and wellbeing has not been any less desired by us than the Scottish nation itself. Thus we unhappily hear and understand what the gentleman now verbally tells us about the misunderstanding and disunity that has arisen between His Majesty in England, your king, and the Scottish nation. Her Majesty our gracious Queen and the Royal government wishes nothing better than that they could come up with some means and advice to fix such disputes. If the gentleman gives Her Majesty a reason he could be certain that Her Majesty's good will shall not fail. What the gentleman conveys about Her Majesty wanting to support and help his nation would require more consideration, and until that has been undertaken, the gentleman should be told in the meantime that in whatever manner we can help the Scottish nation and honour we will not be slow to act.

Johan Cochrane thanked Her Majesty and the government for such good and friendly comfort and said that the help he requests on behalf of his principals did not involve money or people. Both of these he hoped that his nation would have in great store, and reminded what the war required, with which her Majesty is now long familiar, but hoped Her Majesty, through royal benevolence, could spare us some ships and accompanying ammunition. The Directors promise that the same ships and artillery will be returned without fraud. This was what he was commanded to find out from Her Majesty and Your Excellency [Axel Oxenstierna].

The State Chancellor: We will not keep you any longer at this time but as the issue in itself is important and worthy of consideration and [Cochrane] was perhaps keen to be quickly dealt with, therefore we would like to discuss it amongst ourselves and then give you our answer.

Cochrane left.

The State Chancellor: It is an important question posed to us. I do not think it is impractical in itself if it regarded 40– or 80,000 riksdaler which we could spend on them, if we did not have to consider the present condition of our state and fear the outcome the situation in Scotland will produce. Therefore it is safer not to directly declare our partiality. Nothing is more dangerous or to be more feared than that the Scottish nation, which is now united, should be oppressed and thus everything would be upset, which is what I said to Leslie when he was here. If the king in England does not allow himself to be ruled by the advice of the clergy, but will use moderation, compromise, win the English to him and exaggerate the difficulties in Scotland, he would soon turn the situation to his favour.

Field Marshal: If we do not wisely direct this advice we will obtain new difficulties.

State Chancellor: I will see to it, while you are away, to speak individually to Cochrane to get a better understanding of the issue and to show him that events are too new for us to get involved and certainly not to enter into any hostile act. If he would like to have ships and artillery that can be considered further. In the meantime, it is best and safest to cease discussion until we see how the course of events run.

C) RIKSRÅD, 18 JULY 1640, MORNING

The State Chancellor recounted to the Senate his private discussion that day with the Scottish colonel, John Cochrane, regarding the Scottish situation. I, said the Chancellor, declared to Cochrane Her Majesty our most gracious Queen's affection for the Scottish nation and that she wanted to support them in their requests where the condition of the Scottish state was understood. We have had news that things now have again come to a happy conclusion. He thanked us for the Queen's affection and said that his principals and the entire Scottish nation are determined to maintain the same favour with ready service; they bear confidence in us through the long services that a good number of their nation have shown the Swedish Crown. He said that Scotland has never been so well provided with officers as now and that was through the relationship with Sweden for which he, on behalf of his principals' and nation's name, thanked Her Majesty most humbly. Regarding the news we had received of a reconciliation he assured me that it could not be such as the king in England had made up his mind to go against the Scots; indeed the most distinguished of the English lords are in agreement to reduce the kingdom of Scotland into the form of a province and remove other privileges. I repeated Her Majesty's goodwill to support them, but that it is difficult because of this state's inconveniences and the great trouble of the war [in Germany]. However, it is of no small consideration for us to put ourselves between the king in England and the Scottish nation which now, after this misunderstanding has been concluded, has promised to recognise the king in England and his descendants as their rightful lord and sovereign. Should we now support you, the whole burden of war and unrest could fall on us. To make oneself judge in this case, where all potentates are keeping a distance, is of no less consideration. We are engaged in war against the House of Austria, are not in such good standing with the King of Poland, and Denmark [Christian IV] would like for us to end up in some labyrinth. If we were to take this on for your sake they might well announce their answer and intention [against Sweden]. If it were such that we did not have to fear for our neighbours on both sides, but that we could use our power in this German war we would not lack people to send to complete our two main armies, one going directly to Austria and Meren[?], without getting approached to support others who might need our help. But we must always keep ourselves in such a posture that we, along with the enemy, keep an eye on discontented neighbours. If we therefore, to our great damage, should enter into your cause and make few advances on your behalf, I truly believe that you would not request our help so strongly. He [Cochrane] said he could see this from all sides and therefore he had received orders from his principals to obtain artillery with all haste as the Scots are completely bereft of any so that they hardly had fieldpieces, much less the ability to defend themselves in castles and on the seas.

The State Chancellor discussed if one could support these requests. There are two things to consider: 1. Whether we should do it or not, 2. If we resolve to go ahead it must be carefully thought out so that it will not come to anybody's notice.

Herr Claes Fleming: 1. I do not think we should rule it out; 2. The best method would be to use Scottish merchants at Gothenburg who love their fatherland and who would trustworthily and loyally fulfil their duties. It would also be a means for us to sell our pieces and get good prices for them.

The State Chancellor continued on about his conversation with Cochrane who said that the Scots' resolution was to remain constant in their longstanding alliance with France and that where England [Charles I] could cause trouble for it he would do his utmost to upset it. If England [Charles I] overpowered the Scots we [the Swedes] would also not be unmolested. The State Chancellor replied [in Latin] it is not future worries that we are considering but present ones. We must see what is of use for you and for us to both our advantage 2 [sic]. The war will not end soon. If the war continues various potentates will become involved for their own interest. A fire might be lit in the middle of the sea which may set all surrounding lands alight.

Britain is a harbour out of which all military expeditions at sea can leave. All those who are powerful at sea lie around England, which is by nature safe and secure. Spain is 2 days' journey from there, France, the Netherlands, the Hansa towns all lie round about her. If your king cannot be reconciled to you then the kings of Spain and Denmark will also be drawn into the affair, and on the other side the opposing party who is allied to France, so that from this a great fire erupts. You only had to see the smoke that was around Holland now – how highly it went into the eyes of all the neighbouring potentates and republics. Had Spain put its foot down then one would have seen that almost all the nations would have become involved for their own interests.

This is what the Chancellor said he had discussed with Cochrane and then departed.

D) RIKSRÅD, 27 JULY 1640, AFTERNOON

The State Chancellor said that the other thing pressing on us is the Scottish situation and Colonel Cochrane's mission from the Directors in Scotland, who had requested help in the name of his principals. We deliberated it before we went our separate ways.

In the meantime I have conferred with him and shown that 1. It would be dangerous for us to be involved in the war, 2. If we did become engaged both England and Spain would come after us, 3. This might be an anticipation of the situation, as it is not known which way it will go – to war or not. And thus I asked him not to seek to damage us and lead us into circumstances where we would rather not be.

Cochrane asked me to rethink 1. That their loss (to England) would not be a little damaging to us, 2. War was certainly imminent, 3. They did not seek to damage Sweden, no troops or money, just some ships and artillery and even that not yet now but when the situation had deteriorated further.

The State Chancellor asked the other good gentlemen of the Council what their advice was.

Herr Axel Baner thought it was a consideration to let ships go before it could be seen which way the Dutch situation would go [in the intervening weeks there had been Riksråd discussions about an alliance with the Netherlands].

The State Chancellor: They have not asked for anything yet, only if it comes to pass that they get tangled up with England. We do not know how it will go, if it comes to a rupture then it may be that all neighbours will get involved as a consequence, including us. The most important things to consider are 1. That it is uncertain whether they will end up in war, 2. The Scottish people are the underdog. 3. If the king should win Sweden would pay dearly.

Herr Johan Skytte believed that one consideration in supporting the Scots was to remember that they have rebelled against their sovereign.

State Chancellor: It is a point of contention to speak about the motivations of subjects. If you go along with it, civil unrest will happen, if you deny that subjects in such cases may not speak out, then you support and encourage a tyrant in a republic and all things get confused. Now, in brief, we must remember how the king in England has played in this situation. 1. He has made the most noble gentlemen obliged to him, or he has entirely disassociated from them, 2. He has taken on all rights of [Scottish] kingship and taken them to England, left nothing in Scotland but the Privy Council and even that has only been left in name. What deliberations there are of war, peace, alliances – all that is agreed in England. Noble families were, by right of birth, in the Privy Council; those he has ejected from the Council and installed new members, including other bishops with a view to conformity in the Anglican and Scottish church. He also made an Archbishop a chancellor, and the Treasurer of the kingdom is a knight of the garter and in his place in Scotland he has placed a bishop. He has given the clergy the authority to hold inquisition and examine whomever they like, high or low, and deliver him of life, property and honour. While all this was going on nobody dared to resist until the matter of religion was taken up. Then the common man began to grumble and the nobility, with the gentry, raised their heads. And after they saw that the longer it continued the more dangerous it became, they convened and formed a League [The National Covenant]. In such a case when one sees one's fatherland oppressed, all rights of kingship trampled, their sovereignty dismissed and the whole kingdom reduced into the form of a province, could you then be persuaded into silence? This is an enterprise that will cost many their throats. Had not our forefathers taken such a firm resolution under Engelbrekt and old King Gustav, we would today be lying under Denmark in the same condition as Norway. He, Cochrane, requests all this *sub specie emptionis* [with an eye to making appropriate purchase].

It was resolved to assist the Scottish nation by means of the merchants noted and through Gothenburg harbour.

E) RIKSRÅD, 18 AUGUST 1640, MORNING

The State Chancellor informed the Senate 1. How Colonel John Cochrane had requested an answer to his requests on behalf of the Administrators from Scotland and 2. How His Excellency had responded to Cochrane, namely, 1. That the turn of events in England must be considered to see where they go, 2. Made a declaration of the government's willingness to support the Scots in the manner possible, 3. It caused difficulties *commeandi* [coming and going], that one could not so easily support them *portubus omnibus obsessis* [with all the ports blockaded].

Cochrane recounted that 1. Now all appearances toward reconciliation were gone and war was at hand, as the Directors have firmly entered into the matter, 2. He thanked him [Oxenstierna] for the good news, 3. He requested to be furnished with some ships, artillery and copper, out of which artillery could be made in Scotland.

These requests were deliberated and the considerations were 1. How England had always, particularly in this war, been against us [Sweden], had not wanted to allow the recruitment of Scottish troops in England when Herr Johan Oxenstierna as a legate sought permission from him [Charles I] to do this, even less to allow the recruitment of entire regiments. 2. The Scots, on the contrary, have been long used in the service of the Swedish Crown and even at present worthy cavaliers are to be found in the army here at home [in Sweden], 3. Doing this would oblige the Scottish nation to us to undertake further services. 4. He is not requesting the ships immediately either.

It had then been resolved that he would receive [the support requested] on behalf of the Scottish nation and under the names of the merchants [blank spaces] . . .

F) RIKSRÅD, 28 AUGUST 1640, MORNING

Amongst other items dealt with letters were read and signed to the Directors of the Scottish kingdom with Colonel Cochrane.

It was resolved to give the aforementioned Colonel Cochrane a golden chain of 200 kronor value and 300 Rixdaler in coin to pay for his stay at the hostel.

SOURCE: Kullberg, NA *et al* (eds) 1878–1959 *Svenska Riksrådets Protokoll, 1621–1658*. Stockholm, viii, 97–217. (Translation from the original Swedish by S Murdoch.)

Urban Society and Economy

DOCUMENT 119

Taylor the Water Poet, 1618

John Taylor 'the Water Poet' (1578–1653) was a keen entrepreneur, whose lively personality was his greatest asset. His practice was to publicise his journeys in advance and collect money from sponsors who would receive a published account of his travels upon his return. His journey to Scotland The Pennyles Pilgrimage *(1618) was the most successful of his adventures.*

I came to take rest, at the wished, long expected, ancient, famous city of Edenborough, which I entred like Pierce, penniless, altogether moneyless, but I thanke God, not friendelesse; for being there, for the time of my stay, I might borrow (if any man would lend), spend if I could get, begge if I had impudence, and steal if I durst adventure the price of a hanging, but my purpose was to house my horse, and to suffer him and my apparel to lye in durance, or lavender in stead of litter, till such time as I could meete with some valiant friend, that would desperately disburse . . . At last I resolv'd, that the next gentleman that I met withal, should be acquaintance whether hee would or no: and presently fixing mine eyes upon a gentleman-like object, I looked on him, as if I would survay something through him, and make him my perspective: and hee, much musing at my gazing, and I much gazing at his musing, at last he crost the way and made toward me, and then I made downe the street from him, leaving to encounter with my man, who came after me leading my horse, whom he thus accosted, My friend (quoth he), doth yonder gentleman (meaning me) know me, that he lookes so wistly on me? Truly Sir, said my man, I thinke not, but my master is a stranger come from London, and would gladly meete some acquaintance to direct him where he may have lodging and horse meate. Presently the gentleman (being of a generous disposition) over-tooke me with unexpected and undeserved courtesie, brought me to a lodging, and caused my horse to bee put into his own stable, whilest we discoursing over a pinte of Spanish, I related as much English to him, as made him lend me tenne shillings (his name was Master John Maxwell), which money I am sure was the first that I handled after I came from out the walls of London: but having rested two houres and refreshed myselfe, the gentleman and I walked to see the city and castle, which as my poore and unable and unworthy pen, I will truly describe.

The castle on a loftie rocke is so strongly grounded, bounded, and founded, that by force of man it can never be confounded; the foundation and walls are impenetrable, the rampiers impregnable, the bulwarkes invincible, no way but one to it is or can be possible to be made passable. In a word, I have seene many straights and fortresses in Germany, the Netherlands, Spaine, and England, but they must all give place to this unconquered castle, both for strength and situation . . .

So leaving the castle, as it is both defensive against any opposition, and magnificke for lodging and receite, I descended lower to the city, wherein I observed the fairest and goodliest streete that ever mine eyes beheld, for I did never see or heare of a street of that length (which is halfe an English mile from the castle to the faire port which they call the Nether-bow), and from that port, the street which they call the Kenny-hate [Canongate] is one quarter of a mile more, downe to the kings palace, called Holy-rood-house, the buildings on each side of the way being all of squared stone, five, six, and seven stories high, and many by-lanes and closes on each side of the way, wherein are gentlemens houses, much fairer then the buildings in the high-street, for in the high-street marchants and tradesmen do dwell, but the gentlemens mansions and goodliest houses are obscurely founded in the aforesaid lanes: the walles are eight or tenne foote thicke, exceeding strong, not built for a day, a weeke, or a moneth, or a yeere; but from antiquitie to posteritie, for many ages; there I found entertainment beyond my expectation or merit, and there is fish, bread and fruit, in such variety, that I think I may offencelesse call it superfluity, or saciety. The worst was, that wine and ale was so scarce, and the people were such misers of it, that every night before I went to bed, if any man had asked me a civill question, all the wit in my head could not have made him a sober answer.

I was at his Majesties palace, a stately and princely seate, wherein I saw a sumptuous chappell, most richly adorned with all appurtenances belonging to so sacred a place, or so royall an owner. In the inner court, I saw the kings armes cunningly carved in stone, and fixed over a doore aloft on the wall, the red lyon being the crest, over which was written this inscription in Latine, 'Nobis haec invicta miserunt 106 proavi.' I enquired what the English of it was? It was told me as followeth, which I thought worthy to be recorded: '106 fore-fathers have left this to us unconquered.' This is a worthy and memorable motto, and I thinke few kingdoms or none in the world can truly write the like, that notwithstanding so many inroads, incursions, attempts, assaults, civill warres, and forraigne hostilities, bloody battles, and mighty foughten fields, that maugre the strength and policie of enemies, that royall crowne and sceptre hath from one hundred and seven descents, kept still unconquered, and by the power of the King of Kings (through the grace of the Prince and peace), is now left peacefully to our peacefull king, whom long in blessed peace, the God of peace defend and governe.

SOURCE: Hume Brown, P 1891 *Early Travellers in Scotland*. Edinburgh, 108–11.

Sir William Brereton, 1636

Sir William Brereton was a wealthy and cosmopolitan landowner from Cheshire in England, who travelled extensively in the Netherlands and Ireland, as well as in Scotland, and owned property in New England. He was a Puritan by inclination, which may explain his interest in the minister at Ayr. He opposed Charles I's religious policies in the Long Parliament from 1640, and afterwards served as an officer in the Parliamentary army.

A) GLASGOW

We came to the city of Glasgoaw, which is thirty-six miles from Edenburgh, eighteen from Failkirke. This is an archbishop's seat, an ancient university, one only college consisting of about one hundred and twenty students, wherein are four schools, one principal, four regents. There are about six or seven thousand communicants, and about twenty thousand persons in the town, which is famous for the church, which is fairest and stateliest in Scotland, for the Toll-boothe and Bridge. This church I viewed this day, and found it a brave and ancient piece . . .

Here I visited the Archbishop of Glasgoaw's palace, which seems a stately structure, and promises much when you look upon the outside. It is said to be the inheritance of the Duke of Lennox, but the archbishops successively made use of it. Here I went to see the hall and palace, and going into the hall, which is a poor and mean place, the archbishop's daughter, a handsome and well-bred proper gentlewoman, entertained me with much civil respect, and would not suffer me to depart until I had drunk Scotch ale, which was the best I had tasted in Scotland, and drunk only a draught of this ale in this kingdom.

B) AYR

Coming late to Aire, we lodged in one Patrick Mackellen's house, where is a cleanly neat hostess, victuals handsomely cooked, and good lodging . . . No stable belonging to this inn; we were constrained to seek for a stable in the town, where we paid 8d a night for hay and grass for an horse, and 1s a peck for base oats. This also is a dainty, pleasant-seated town; much plain rich corn land about it; and better haven, there being a river, whereon it is placed, which flows much higher than the bridge, which is a great and fair neat bridge, yet nevertheless it is but a bare naked haven, no pier, nor defence against the storms and weather. Better store of shipping than at

Erwin [Irvine]. Most inhabiting in the town are merchants trading into and bred in France.

Enquiring of my hostess touching the minister of the town, she complained much against him, because he doth so violently press the ceremonies, especially she instanced in kneeling at communion; whereupon, upon Easter day last, so soon as he went to the communion-table, the people all left the church and departed.

SOURCE: Hume Brown, P 1891 *Early Travellers in Scotland*. Edinburgh, 150–3, 156.

Richard Franck, 1656

Richard Franck (c.1624–c.1708) was an Englishman who is believed to have served in the Parliamentary army during the wars against Charles I. His Northern Memoirs narrated his journey from Glasgow to Caithness and his return to England via Aberdeen and Edinburgh. It has been seen as an idiosyncratic work, largely because his preoccupation with angling intrudes (although more commonly in discussions of rural areas) at every possibility in the narrative.

A) GLASGOW

Now, let us descend to describe the splendour and gaity of this city of Glasgow, which surpasseth most, if not all the corporations in Scotland. Here it is you may observe, four large fair streets, modell'd, as it were, into a spacious quadrant; in the centre whereof their market-place is fix'd; near unto which stands a stately tollbooth, a very sumptuous, regulated, uniform fabrick, large and lofty, most industriously and artificially carved from the very foundation to the superstructure, to the great admiration of strangers and travellers. But this state-house, or tollbooth, is their western prodigy, infinitely excelling the model and usual built of town-halls; and is, without exception, the paragon of beauty in the west; whose compeer is no where to be found in the north, should you rally the rarities of all the corporations in Scotland . . .

In the next place, we are to consider the merchants and traders in this eminent Glasgow, whose store-houses and ware-houses are stuft with merchandize, as their shops swell big with foreign commodities, and returns from France, and other remote parts, where they have agents and factors to correspond, and inrich their maritime ports, whose charter exceeds all the charters in Scotland . . .

B) STIRLING

So let us pass on with our travelling design . . . to the ports of Sterling; where stands a beautiful and imbellished Castle, elevated on the precipice of an impregnable rock, that commands the vallies (as well as the town) and all those habitable parts about it: those are the turrets that present before us, let us enter her ports, both strong and spacious; whose incircling arms surround a city (but not a great one) that's built all with stone; so is here castle; and situated close by the river Firth [Forth], as above explain'd, upon lofty, craggy, and mountainous rocks, almost inaccessible. More southward yet the city spreads itself into many sweet situations, that invigorate the inhabitants, and accommodate the Low-land merchant rather than the mariner with profitable returns from the hills, by the Highlander. The Firth runs here that washeth and melts the foundations of the city, but relieves the country with her plenty of salmon; where the burgomasters (as in many other parts of Scotland) are compell'd to reinforce an ancient statute, that commands all masters and others, not to force or compel any servant, or an apprentice, to feed upon salmon more than thrice in a week.

c) DUNBLANE

Dirty Dumblain; let us pass by it, and not cumber our discourse with so inconsiderable a corporation . . .

I think it but time lost, to survey the reliques of a ruinous heap of stones, that lean o're the verge of a river, facing the mountains. The houses, it's true, are built with stone, but then to consider them low and little, it plainly demonstrates there's nothing eminent but narrow streets, and dirty houses; a convincing argument there's no scavengers amongst them. And for their housewifery, let that alone; for if you touch it, you sully your fingers. There is a market-place, such an one as it is; but as for merchants, there's no such thing in nature. But a palace there is, and a cathedral too, otherwise Dumblain had nothing to boast of.

d) EDINBURGH

Welcome to these elevated ports, the princely court of famous Edinburgh. This city stands upon a mighty scopulous mountain, whose foundations are cemented with mortar and stone; where the bulk of her lofty buildings represent it a rock at a reasonable distance, fronting the approaching sun; whose elevations are seven or eight stories high, mounted aloft in the ambient air. But the length, as I take it, exceeds not one mile, and the breadth on't measures little more than half a mile; nor is there more than one fair street, to my best remembrance. But then it's large and long, and very spacious, whose ports are splendid, so are her well-built houses and palaces, corresponding very much to compleat it their metropolis.

SOURCE: Hume Brown, P 1891 *Early Travellers in Scotland*. Edinburgh, 191–5, 215.

Register Containing the State and Condition of Every Burgh Within the Kingdom of Scotland, in the Year 1692

Royal burghs, in theory, held a monopoly on foreign trade, but these rules were often flouted due to the rise of new trading centres such as Greenock. The Convention of Royal Burghs, keen to demonstrate the effects of this problem on their prosperity, and that of the nation, commissioned this survey of the state of the Scottish burghs. The reliability of these accounts may be questioned, then, because the burghs had a vested interest in portraying a decline in their trade. The fact that Scotland was at war in this period, as the three kingdoms joined other European powers in an alliance against France, should also be taken into account for its effects on trade.

A) BURGH OF EDINBURGH

The Annwall Revenewes off the Good Towne of Edinburgh

	Marks		Marks
Meall marcat	1,600	Mark upon the pack to Edinburgh	450
Netherbow, Cowgait, and New ports	1,250	Mark upon the tun and pack to Leith	3,600
West port	1,800	Shoar dewes at Leith	7,700
Societie and Potteraw ports	1,200	Weighouses of Edinburgh and Leith	5,100
House of Moore	2,000	Timber bush	1,200
Tallow trone	110	Imposition on forraigne cloath	2,500
Flesh and cloath boards	1,700	Annuity and seat rents	20,300
Fish marcat	870	Elleaven common milns	15,600
Corn and leather marcats	450	Old imposition on wines	37,850
Sheep flecks	400	New imposition	14,750
Poultray and bread marcats	1,600		
Veal boards	500		
Shoad carts	1,050		
Fruitte metts	300		
		TOTAL	109,230

	Lib.	S.	D.		Lib.	S.	D.
Societie	2,333	6	8	South kirk inclosurs there	30	0	0
Grass of Grayfrier yeard	166	13	4	Gallow green	72	0	0
Fore Moore	60	0	0	Colledge and kirk rents	5,264	0	0
Back Moore	33	6	8	Few duties of Canongait, Leith			
				and Portsburgh	700	0	0
Boningtoun milns	933	6	8	Houses and chope rents	1,767	2	4
Borrow Loch	800	0	0	Silver deutie	81	0	0
Fleshers of Edinburgh	200	0	0	South Links of Leith and house ther	203	6	8
				TOTAL	85,464	11	9

Victwall rent, 307 bolls 1 firlott 2 pecks bear.

Accompt of the Ships of Leith the 17th May 1692

Skippers of Ships	Burden Tons	Value	Skippers of Barks	Burden Tons	Value
Captain James Kendall	90	8000	John Barr	40	1000
Captain James Simson	120	5000	John Mill	15	300
Alexander Tait	150	8000	John Haigs	40	2000
Robert Gray	100	6000	John Achinmutie	36	1500
Thomas Whyt	90		David Riehaye	25	900
Thomas Riddell	100	3500	Charles Ranie, ane wark	2	
Thomas Weir	90	3000	Thomas Hendersone	25	900
Androw Simsone	70	3000	John Gair	16	500
Alexander Stivenson	130	5000	John Kay	12	300
James Sutherland	90	6000	John Sime	30	1000
John Tait	60	4000	Gilbert Dick	20	600
James Law	90	6000	Walter Graige	15	500
John Browne	140	8000	Matthew Barton	24	900
Williame Browne	24	900	Malcolm Macalla	30	1200
Alexander Gerve	16	700	Walter Lesly	14	500

Accompt of Shiping belonging to the Merchants of Edinburgh for twelve moneths by past

Kendalls ship twice to Holland, with lead ure and sheep skins.

Simpsons, trade twice to Holland with coalls and wooll.

Alexander Tait, twice to Holland with coalls, at present ane transact ship in France with Canon and Buchan.

Robert Gray, twice to Holland with coalls, sheep skins, and wooll.

Thomas Riddell, once to Hamburgh with returns of mumbear, some quantity of brandie, and once to France with returns of wyne.

Thomas Weir, twice to London with coalls and some packs of linen cloath, quhereof the most pairt belonged to Glasgow.

Andrew Simson to London, with coalls and some packs of linen cloath, whereof the most pairt belonged to strangers, with some packs of drest leather belonging to merchants heir.

George Wood, twice to Holland with coalls and sheep skins.

Alexander Stevinsone, twice to Amsterdam with coalls.

James Sutherland, once to Hamburgh with returns of mumbear and some brandie, and now at Spain.

John Tait, imployed by the publict at Innerlochie.

James Law, once at London with shouldiers, being balanced with coalls.

John Brown, once to Bilbo and not yeit reteired.

Item, thrie Swades or Damask ships, in all thrie hunder tunns, with wynes from France.

Item, three ships belonging to the merchants all lost comeing from France with wynes.

Item, as to the consumption of malt, the same is computed to be about 500 bolls per week.

Item, to the trade with the barks the same is all inland trade with corns and coalls, except two barks who are at present in the Sound with herrings on the merchants accompt.

B) BURGH OF GLASGOW

The toune of Glasgow for its constant yearly expence:-

Debitor

	Lib.	S.	D.
To the stipends of 5 of ther ordinary ministers, each being at 1080 lib. yearly, is	5,400	0	0
To the stipend of the barronie minister	950	0	0
To the master and two doctors of the grammar school ther salary	593	6	8
To the keeper of the toun cloacks yearly	133	6	8
To few duty paid to the colledge of Glasgow yearly	166	13	4
To the tack duty of the teynds of the baronie	200	0	0
To the salary of the precentars of the 4 churches	320	0	0
To the salary of the keeper of the high church	133	6	8
To the few duty paid out of the aikers of the new greenes	66	13	4
To the touns quarter master his salary	180	0	0
To the townes postmaster	120	0	0
To the doctor, cutter of the ston gravel	66	13	4
To James Porterfield, schoolmaster, of pension	52	0	0
To upholding of the great church and other churches	666	13	4
To coall and candle furnished to the toun guaird	800	0	0
To the master of works compt about the publick works of the toune	4,400	0	0
To the touns chirurgeon for the poor	133	6	8
To the toun drummers ther pension and cloaths	100	0	0
To the severall ringers of the touns bells	50	13	4
To the servants and keepers of the tollbooth	66	13	4
To the magistrats, theasurer, master of works, &c., ther yearly fiall	165	0	0
To the clerk's servants yearly	180	0	0
To the officers ther cloaths and pensions	740	0	0
To the touns agent at Edinburgh his sallarie	100	0	0
To the yearly news letters and gazettes	60	0	0
To the touns eique and eique of Provand	180	0	0
TOTAL	15,994	6	8

The toun of Glasgow creditor by ther wholl common good:-

	Lib.	S.	D.
By the duty of ther milns valued one year with another yearly	5,333	6	8
By the duty of ther ladles	2,333	6	8
By the duty of ther pecks	566	13	4
By the deuty of ther tron	500	0	0
By the deuty of ther bridge	733	6	8
By the fourth pairt of the Gorball teynds	200	0	0
By ther walk milne			
By the drawen teynds about the toun	800	0	0
By the rent of the barronie of Provand	3,333	6	8
By ther 4th pairt of ther Gorball lands	666	13	4
By sewerall small ground anwalls	400	0	0
By their miln lands	133	6	8
By the rent of Petershill	66	13	4
By their common lands	72	0	0
By their two greens yearly	1,000	0	0

By the flesh marcat	200	0	0
By the royall companies house free	180	0	0
By the correction house and yeard	50	0	0
By burges fiynes yearly one year with another	333	6	8
TOTAL	16,902	0	0

There are lyckwayes some houses and salaries at Port Glasgow, but by reason of the great decay of trade ther is nothing gott for them, yea not soe much as it cost the toun in upholding them.

Accompt of Ships belonging to the towne of Glasgow for the present at home:-

	Burden (tunns)	Value
The James; Alexander Stewart, commander	100	5000 merks
Elizabeth; John Millar, master	150	6000 lib.
Friendship; Archibald Yuill, master	80	4000 merks
Lark; Robert Galbraith, master	80	6000 lib.
Grissell; John Taillyer, master	30	2000 merks
Amity; Lott Gordon, master	80	6000 lib.
James; now bought be George Lockhart	160	6000 lib.
Fortoun; Hugh Campbell, lait master	50	2000 lib

Accompt of Ships belonging to the toun of Glasgow for present abroad and are uncertain of ther home comeing because of the warr, and the owners declair they are content to take ther stocks imployed in the voyadges:-

	Burden (tunns)	Value
The Concord, George Lyon, master	150	
James of Glasgow, James Wilson, master	80	
The James	36	
The William and Marie, belonging to George Lockhart and partners	36	
The Margaret, belonging to James Walkinshaw and partners, burden	50	
The Robert to Hugh Montgomerie	70	
The small yaught to James Gibsone	30	

C) BURGH OF INVERNESS

Accompt of the common good belonging to the burgh of Invernes, few dewties, and other caswalties belonging therto, for the year 1691

	Lib.	S.	D.
The peck and firlott pettie custome and tole mony of the bridge, rouped [auctioned] for	1,010	0	0
The weighouse and salt measour rouped for the said year	40	0	0
Flesh stocks and shambles rouped for	46	0	0
The anchorage and shoar dewes rouped said year for	190	0	0
The few dewties yearly, and what is paid to the towne by the weivers	359	10	8
TOTAL	1,645	10	8

Accompt of the yearly debursements of the toun of Invernes to their ministers and other servants, out of the common good of the burgh, having no other way to pay the same

	Lib.	S.	D.
Imprimis, to the ministers yearly	133	6	8
To the master of the grammar school	133	6	8
Item, for ther eiquie	61	12	0
Item, for the missive dewes	77	8	0
Item, the four officers salaries	40	0	0
Item, for the red coats to them yearly	26	13	4
Item, the drumers sallarie	40	0	0
The provost and four baillies salaries	33	6	8
The thesaurers salary	40	0	0
The clerks sallarie	66	13	4
Item, the annual rent of 11,841 lib. 72 s. Scots of debt resting be the toune yearly is	710	0	0
Item, for keeping the touns knock yearly	80	0	0
Item, the executioners sallarie yearly	16	0	0
Item, for coall and candle to the sewerall gairds from Michaelmes 90 to Michaelmes 91, per the thesaurers accompt thereof	460	0	0
Item, for repairing the peer and harbour from Michaelmes 90 to Michaelmes 91, per the thesaurers accompt thereof	90	0	0
To Mr William Robertson of Inshes, for the rent of the house and close quher the peits for the severall gairds are keeped	10	0	0
Item, to William Cuthbert, merchant, for the rent of ane seller for a meill mercat yearly	12	0	0
TOTAL	3,030	15	8

The magistrats declair that the balance betuixt the charge and discharge is raised by cess on the inhabitants of the burgh.

SOURCE: 1881 *Miscellany of the Scottish Burgh Records Society*. Edinburgh, 55–8, 71–5, 94–5.

Rural Society and Economy

DOCUMENT 123

Tackholding Tenants

These entries in landlords' rentals illustrate both the early granting of tacks (leases) for life and the family circumstances of the grantees.

Glossary: ferme – rent; brukit, brukand – enjoyed, enjoying; atis – oats; gresum, gersum - entry money; heratour – besides; othir – either; quhilk – which; chese – choose.

A) COUPAR ANGUS ABBEY

Be it kend to al men be thir present lettres, us David . . . Abbot of . . . Couper and our convent . . . to have grantit, set and for *ferme* lattyn, To Androw Gibsoun a quarter of our landis of our Grange of Kincreich . . . as he *brukit* of befor, for al the dayis of his lyve: he payand tharfor yerly to us 8 merkis of usuale mone . . . a dusane capons . . . and twa bollis of *atis* . . . with aucht and wont servys. And he sal pay at his entrie 8 merkis in name of *gresum*. *Heratour*, we have grantit to hym in the sam tak, to ane to succed hym, *othir* his wife or ane of his sonnys *quhilk* he wil *chese*, for al the dayis of thar lyve . . . 21 April 1477.

B) ALLOWAY (AYRSHIRE)

(Whitsunday court, 1533): The provest and bailies [of Ayr] . . . sett with consent of auld Wille Patersone and his wyff, all and haill the said Willeis maling in Mekle Cortone . . . to Robert Pawtersone thar sone for all the dayis of his lyff; the said Wille his fader and his wyff brukand samekle as thai dow labour . . . for al the dayis of thar liffis . . . the said Robert payand therfor to the gude town sax merkis of gersum . . . viz: ane third in hand to the officiaris, ane third at Mychaelmas nixt hereftir . . . and the lattir third . . . at Witsonday nixt thareftir . . .

SOURCE: a) Rogers, C (ed) 1879–80 *Rental Book of the Cistercian abbey of Cupar Angus*. London, i, 207; b) *Alloway Barony Court Book*: former NAS ref. B6/28/1, fos 1, 5. Now in Carnegie Library, Ayr.

Kindly Tenancy

This rental of the fourth earl of Morton's lands of Preston (Stewartry of Kirkcudb-right) names the occupants and at the same time notes through whom the kindly tenancy is passed on and to whom it now belongs. It also shows that the kindness might be sold. The entries have been summarised.

Glossary: oxgait, oxgang – one eighth of a ploughgate, c.13 acres; bere – barley; maill – rent, in this context, money rent.

A) THE TERMS OF KINDLY TENANCY IN THE 1570S

John Hannah, *kindly tenant* to two *oxgait* there; who occupies one himself and has made over to Thomas Dickson his son-in-law his kindness to the other. Thomas Newell, occupier of three oxgaits there; of which he is kindly tenant to two, and bought the kindness of the third from Joke Gibbonson, paying yearly 1 boll 3 firlots *bere* and 10 shillings *maill*, with service. Thomas Maxwell, occupier of half an oxgait and a quarter. Who is entered [tenant] through his wife's kindness, Marion Gibbonson; and John Maxwell their son who is kindly therto.

B) THE TERMS OF KINDLY TENANCY IN THE 1590S

Kindly tenants, although enjoying a customary right to inherit and pass on their holdings, nevertheless had still to honour the terms of their tacks. This is made clear in the admission of a kindly tenant by William sixth earl of Morton on 29 July 1594. Note that the kindness, being a heritable right, is not said to expire automatically like the rental; rather, Hannay agrees to renounce it. The text has been summarised.

    I William earl of Morton . . . receive and admit William Hannay, *brother germane* [full brother] to Michael Hannay sometime in Preston, under the sett and kindly tenancy of . . . all and whole the said Michael's two oxgaits of Preston . . . during all the days of the said William [Hannay's] lifetime. Providing always in case the said William fails in thankful payment of his said service and duty . . . [he] shall lose this his rental [i.e. tack for life], to expire in itself, and [he] shall renounce his right and kindness of the said land.

SOURCE: a) NAS Morton Muniments, GD 150/2079/1, undated [1570s]; b) NAS Morton Muniments, GD 150/1514.

DOCUMENT 125

Family Provision: Bequests from the Will of Sir Andrew Kerr of Hirsel (d. 1573)

This extract highlights the kind of provision made for the support of family members, in youth and old age. The texts have been summarised.

He leaves £40 each to three servants, 'to help them to steadingis and thay to be gud servandis to the hous'. Leaves his son to his wife 'with 500 merkis to kepe him at the scolis [university] quhill he be twentie yeiris of age'. Leaves his own younger brother Robert certain rents to repay him for a bed canopy and curtains and his own heir, Walter, to provide Robert with 'ane ploughgate of land for the uphald of his bairnis'.

SOURCE: NAS, Commissariot of Edinburgh, Register of Testaments, CC8/8/2, fo. 359r.

Standard of Living: a Tenant Farmer, 1560

The inventory of Patrick Robertson in Finmouth (Fife), tenant of Sir William Kirkcaldy of Grange. His goods, crops, stock and household furnishings, seem a little at odds with travellers' descriptions of the miserable living conditions of the country people. He appears to have been a reasonably prosperous farmer. The text has been summarised.

Testament dative of Patrick Robertson in Finmouth, died August 1560.
Inventory:

Sown on the lands of Finmouth and Leslie – 8 chalders oats, estimated to 20 chalders, at 26s 8d per boll = £3426 13s 4d; 16 bolls bere, estimated to 60 bolls, at 44s per boll = £132; 6 firlots rye, estimated to 6 bolls, at 33s 4d per boll = £10; 4 bolls peas, estimated to 6 bolls, at 40s per boll = £12.

In his girnell [granary] – 2 chalders of meal at 33s 4d per boll = £53 6s 8d. 8 bolls malt at 44s per boll = £17 12s.

1 gray horse = £16; 1 'white-gray' horse = £8 13s 4d; 1 dun horse = £10; 1 black horse = £10; 1 'broken' mare = £8.

19 drawing oxen at £5 6s 8d each = £101 6s 8d; 6 other oxen at £4 each = £24; 6 newly-calved cows and calves at £5 each = £30; 4 forrow cows [not in calf] at £4 13s 4d each = £18 13s 4d; 4 three-year old stots [bullocks] at £3 6s 8d each = £13 6d 8d; three two-year old stots and three quoys [heifers] of the same age at 50s each = £12; 34 ewes at 16s each = £27 4s; 30 old yield [barren] sheep at 16s each = £24; 40 lambs at 6s 8d each = £13 6s 8d.

Household plenishings (not counting the reserved 'heirship goods').
4 standing beds; 5 feather beds; 5 bolsters; 24 coddis [pillows]; 30 pairs sheets; 16 pairs blankets; 5 wardouris [bed-covers]; 2 pairs linen curtains [for beds]; 2 comptaris [side tables]; 12 board cloths [table-covers]; 24 serviettis [table napkins]; 6 washing cloths (for use at table?); a Flanders kist; a meal kist; an iron chimney [fire-basket]; a basin; a dozen pewter plates; a dozen pewter trenchers; 3 quart stoups [measuring vessels]; 3 tin pint stoups; 3 silver spoons; an iron pot, of 3 gallons; 2 brass pots, of 3 gallons; 1 pot, of 2 gallons; 2 brass pans, of 1 gallon; 6 chandlers [candlesticks]; 4 lengths of ash wood sawn for building-couples; 3 chairs; 2 forms; 2 spits; 2 sacks; 3 canvases; 2 sewing sheets [for sowing seed]; 2 harrows; 6 sleds; all worth £40.
Total inventory = £998 12s 8d.

SOURCE: NAS, Commissariot of Edinburgh, Register of Testaments, CC8/8/1, fo. 49v.

The Coming of Feu-ferme: the Dark Side

Parliament, privy council and the pre-Reformation church council were aware of the opportunity feuing afforded land-speculators, some of whom took the land over the heads of tenants, then resigned it to them for compensation which represented a profit on the transaction. Note that as Bellenden had paid the commendator of Scone £1,000 for his charter, he made himself a profit of 100 merks (£66 13s 4d) on the transaction. The text of the following contract has been summarised.

Contract between Sir John Bellenden of Auchnoule, justice clerk, and William Soutar, John Dickson, John Soutar of the Hill and Alexander Mackie, equal portioners and inhabitanis of the toun of Wester Banchory, in the barony and regality of Scone.

Forasmuch as it was complained and lamented by the said persons that Sir John had taken the said toun of Wester Banchory in feu to his son Lewis in fee and to himself in liferent over their heads, they being now presently possessors of a quarter thereof, like as they and their predecessors have been of old possessors and kindly tenants to the abbey of Scone, and having no other steadings to live upon, earnestly desiring Sir John, feuar, to resign and overgive all title that he and his son have obtained from the commendator and convent of Scone . . . that they might be heritably infeft in feu-ferme therein . . . Offering also to the said Sir John to pay such sums of money as he had deburfed thereon. Which desire the said Sir John gladly accorded unto in manner as after follows:

Sir John shall resign the lands in favour of the said inhabitants and their heirs, to each of them a quarter, and shall cause the commendator receive his resignation.

Each grantee to receive a separate charter for payment as set out in Sir John's feu charter. They shall also pay Sir John 1,600 merks (£1,066 13s 4d) in three instalments. At Edinburgh 15 May 1562; the tenants, who are unable to write, subscribe with the help of the notary.

SOURCE: NAS, Register of Deeds, first series, RD 1/5, fo. 164r.

A Household Headed by a Widow: Marion Cochrane in Lessudden (Roxburghshire)

The texts of these family documents have been summarised. The Stodart daughters were joint-heiresses, their only brother having died, but the younger is compensated by the elder daughter's future father-in-law for allowing her older sister to succeed. Marion Cochrane died in November 1559. The descendants of Christian and Robert held the land until it was sold to Scott of Raeburn, a local laird in 1672, by two other joint-heiresses. Lessudden is now St Boswells.

A) 5 JANUARY 1555

Contract between Ninian Bryden in Rutherford and Robert his son on the one part, and Marion Cochrane, widow of the late John Stodart in Lessudden and Christian Stodart her daughter on the other, by which Robert Bryden shall, God willing, complete the band of matrimony with Christian and come to Marion in household and enter to the steading which Marion occupies in Lessuden, Marion to be the principal disponer of the stock and goods of the steading during her lifetime. After her death Robert and Christian and their heirs to succeed to it. In return, Ninian shall give Marion towards the marriage of her younger daughter Katherine £40.

B) 22 FEBRUARY 1556/7

Feu charter by James [Stewart] commendator of Melrose and the convent to Marion Cochrane in liferent and to Christian Stodart her daughter and Robert Bryden the latter's husband heritably, of one and three quarters husbandlands in the toun of Lessudden, lordship of Melrose (Roxburghshire), reserving the fishings in the River Tweed, belonging to the lands, to the abbey. Which lands were feued to Mr Henry Sinclair, dean of Glasgow Cathedral, and were resigned by him in favour of the present grantees.

Paying therefore yearly, £3 4s 9d and 3s 6d commutation for 7 poultry, with carriage service and to have their corn ground at Newtoun mill. Double feu-duty at the entry of heirs. The charter to be cancelled if they fall into arrears for three terms and 40 days.

c) 1556/7

Document setting out that the lands shall be held by Marion Cochrane for life, then by Christian and her husband Robert Bryden, whom failing the heirs of Katherine Stodart, Christian's younger sister, whom failing to the nearest heirs of Christian and Katherine on their father's side, he having been the kindly tenant through whose family the land had come.

SOURCE: a) NAS, Scott of Raeburn Muniments, GD104/3; b) NAS, Scott of Raeburn Muniments, GD 104/5; c) NAS, Scott of Raeburn Muniments, GD104/9.

Improving the Landscape

The feuing programme in the barony of Glasgow came comparatively late, from about 1580 onwards. The statement by the author of this passage, that the feuars of Glasgow paid only their 'ancient rent' by way of feu-duty, is corroborated by the fact that the amount of 'augmentation', that is the element of increase in the feu-duty which proved that the feu was not 'in diminution' of the old rent, was so small in Glasgow feu charters as to be nominal.

Govan parish lyeth upon the south side of the river of Clyde a great way, betwixt the parishes of Rutherglen and Ranfrew; and is just opposite to the citie of Glasgow. All the parish is kirk land, anciently belonging to, and lately holden of the Archbishops of Glasgow; and is a part of the lordship, regalitie and barronie of Glasgow, whereof the Dukes of Lennox have for many ages been heretable baillies. The parish lies in a pleasant, low and fertile soill, along the river; and is mostly possessed by small fewars . . . there was a commission granted to Walter commendator of Blantyre, to few the haill lands of the lordship and regalitie of Glasgow, without demunition of the old Rentall; to the effect that the Tenents, being thereby become heretable possessors of their severall possessions, might be incouradged by virtue and politie to improve that countrie. Conform whereto all this regalitie was fewed to the severall possessors, about the year 1590, for payment of their ancient rent by way of few duties; which is the occasion that this parish is divided amongst so many small heritors.

SOURCE: Hamilton W (ed) 1831 *Description of the Sheriffdoms of Lanark and Renfrew*. Glasgow, 27–8.

Late-seventeenth-century Tenancy Patterns

These entries from the poll tax records for Aberdeenshire illustrate the population pattern on multiple-tenant and single-tenant farms. Note the names of servants without a fee, who 'served for their meat'.

THE MUIR

Alaster and James Miches, tennents, their general poll themselves, wives,	£4 4 0
Item, John Michie, their servant, his fee £6 per annum, the fortieth	
pairt whereof and the general poll is	£0 9 0
Item, Elspeth Gordon, his servant (no fee), her generall poll	£0 6 0
Item, Alaster Sandesone, tennent ther, his generall poll for himself	
and his wife is	£0 12 0
Item, William Michie, *alias* Bayne, and his wife, their poll is	£0 12 0
[Total]	£3 15 0

COBLETOUNE

Donald Farquharson, tennent ther, his generall poll for himself	
and his wife	£0 12 0
Item, Elspet McGrigor, his servant (no fee), her generall poll is	£0 6 0
Item, John Riach, tennent, and his wife, their poll is	£0 12 0
[Total]	£1 10 0

MILLTOUNE OF WHITEHOUSE

Imprimis, John Stewart, tennent and gentleman ther, his poll £3	
and the generall poll 6s, both is	£3 6 0
Item, his wife and his children, John, William, Charles, Margaret	
and Sarah Stewarts *in familia*, their poll is	£1 16 0
Item, James McAllan, Patrick McIntire, John Grant, William	
Andersone and Duncan Grant, his servants, each of their fees	
per annum, £14, the fortieth pairt wherof and generall poll	£3 5 0
Item, Isobell Stewart, her fee 10 merks per annum, the fortieth	
pairt whereof and the generall poll is	£0 9 0
Item, James Gordon, his servant, his fee £6 per annum,	
the fortieth pairt whereof and generall poll is	£0 9 0
[Total]	£9 5 4

SOURCE: Stuart, J (ed) 1844 *List of Pollable Persons in the Shire of Aberdeen, 1696*. Aberdeen, i, 156–7.

DOCUMENT 131

The Problem of Vagrancy

These documents outline both the letter of the law on vagrancy, and the way it was applied in the localities. Many property owners were unwilling to resort to a formal 'assessment' of the parish but preferred to work out local ways of dealing with the problem, even in times of exceptional dearth and hardship.

A) ACT OF PARLIAMENT, 1574

Item, that nane be sufferit to beg bot cruikit [crippled] folk and waik [infirm] folk.

Item, that nane be tholit [suffered] to beg in ane p[a]rochyn [parish] that ar borne in ane uther. That the heidismen of ilk parochin mak takynnis [tokens] and gif to the beggaris of that parochyn . . .

It is tho[ch]t expedient and ordanit alsweill for the utter surpressing of the saidis strang and ydill beggaris, sa outrageous enemies to the commoun weill, as for the cheritabill releving of the aigit and impotent puyr people that . . . all personis being above the aige of 14 and within the aige of 70 yeris, that heireftir ar declairit . . . vagabondis, strang and ydill beggaris . . . eftir the first day of June nixtocum, to be wandering and misordering thame selffis . . . salbe apprehendit . . . brocht befoir the sheriffis, stewartis, bailies or lordis of regaliteis to landwart or . . . provest and bailies within burgh, and . . . committit in ward [prison] . . . quhill thay be put to the knawlege of ane assyis . . . within sex dayis . . . And gif thay happin to be convicted, to be adjugeit to be scurgeit and burnt through the girsill of the ryt eare . . . except sum honest and responsall persoun will of his cheritie . . . tak and keip in his service the offender for ane haill yeir . . . and bring the said offender to the said court at the yeiris end, or . . . gude prufe of his death . . . [For the third offence of vagrancy the death penalty].

B) DECISION OF THE BARONY COURT OF URIE, 1698

24 May 1698 . . . the haill heritors within the parish of Fetteresso [Kincardineshire] having unanimouslie, with concourse of minister, elders and kirk sessione . . . agreed . . . that ilk ane of thame shall maintaine the poor within thair particular lands by themselves and thair tenents, and to give badges to such as are travelling within ther own grounds . . . Ane peck and ane half peck of meall to be given to Rachel Lightoune in Glithno, blind woman, and ane servant to attend her . . . half ane peck of meal weekly to be given to Alexander Burnet in Powbair, his children,

and ordains badges to be given to the persons following [5 names] . . . which quantity of victual to be given out to beddells [licensed beggars] . . . extends weekly to two pecks, half peck meal . . . and ordains the said beddalls to begin at William Gibsone at Mill of Cowie and receave from him the saidis two pecks, half peck meall, commensing upon the twentie third of May instant, which compleits his payment to them for fyftine weekis next therafter . . .

SOURCE: a) 1814–75 *Acts of the Parliaments of Scotland*. Edinburgh, iii; b) Barton, DG (ed) 1892 *The Barony Court Book of Urie in Kincardineshire, 1604–1747*. Edinburgh, 102–10.

Seventeenth-century Landlord and Tenants

These extracts from the Barony Court Book of Urie highlight tenant-debt, the commutation of dues in kind, and the tenants' duties towards improvement of the landscape.

Glossary: elne (ell) – measure of length, the Scots ell was about 0.8 of an English ell; sarking lyneing – shirt linen; poynding – confiscation; brew talloun – tax paid in tallow for privilege of brewing; restand – remaining to be paid; birkes – birches; rountrie – rowan; geintrie (geantree) – wild cherry; grasman – landless tenant with only pasture rights.

1625 November 30 The said day Stephane Forbes in Cowie is decernit to pay twentie markis money for his maill of the yeiris of God 1624 and 1625 . . . with 2 dozen elnes of sarking lyneing or the said yeiris, or 6s 8d for ilk elne thairoff, within the terme of law, under pain of poynding . . . to pay to the laird five markis money for ilk stane of brew talloun for . . . 1623 and 1624 . . .

The said day Archebald Murrey is decernit to pay to the laird 40s money for the maill of ane piece fischerland, with 30s for thrie capounes restand be him that he became debtour for John Mowatt for 1624 yeiris . . .

1682 July 29 The said [day] in presence of the said David Barclay [laird of Urie] and his balyie and als the heall tennentis . . . the laird and baliyie ordained [them] to set and plant trees yeirlie in their respective yeardes, to wit, ashes, plaines, birkes, fir or rountrie, geintrie . . . everie husbandmane yeirlie sex trees, everie cottar three and everie grasman two . . . and to come and receive [the trees] from the laird or his gairdner yeirlie at Michalmas and March . . . wherof the heall tennentis acceptes . . .

SOURCE: Barton, DG (ed) 1892 *The Barony Court Book of Urie in Kincardine-shire, 1604–1747.* Edinburgh, 60, 96–7.

Renaissance Architecture

The House of Tyrie, Buchan, 1723

No trace remains of the House of Tyrie near Fraserburgh in Buchan, and indeed it has been questioned whether its construction was ever completed. This document of 1723, however, gives a description of it as it stood in the eighteenth century, along with accounts of other notable buildings in the vicinity.

The Gentlemans houses in this Parish are Tyrie about ½ mile East from the church, being an avenue the whole way. It is a large Edifice of 40 foot square, and a large round on every corner with a pavilion roof. The upper story of 3 being one roume of 40 foot square having 4 large chimneys and 8 windows and so many in each of the lower stories with a coat of armes well cutt for the lintels as the branshes of the family.

This house not being finished in the rounds throw the death of J. Fraser of Tyrie the founder *in anno* 1690 is like to turne ruinous throw disorder of his sons affairs now abroad. It hes large orchards and arming of barren planting and at foot of the parks below the house eastward is a pretty cannal or water draught of 12 foot broad, near a mille in lenth, running eastward and falling in below Philorth and Cairnbulg into the sea.

The other remarkable house in this Parish is that of Boynlie, built *in anno* 1660 by Boynlie the late Tutor of Pitsligo in the year 1660, But much augmented and beautified by Captain Forbes of Boynlie his son, by the addition of 2 Jambs and a fore parlour or vestibule twixt them, and a balcony above, making the house double, and is situat in the center of a Rock in the middle of a Glen, which affords terraces on either side. On[e] in the middle of the entrie and a pair of stairs ascending by 12 steps to the hous from a handsome avenue and square from the utter gate. The east side or back of the house is a story higher by the cellars being cutt out of the Rock, and below are 3 handsome terraces, and ane opposite bank, where as many are designed. Ther runs a handsome brook northwards thorow a large low orchard which has its rise from 2 springs half a mile or more above the house. The one whereof within a large inclosure of a den called Wellmurnan remarkable for sending out such a great quantity of fyne water from a fountain head fronting eastward, that it chiefly supplies a corn milne lately built near the hous and foot of the said inclosure. This is the head of the water which passes northward to the church and hous of Tyrie falling into the forsaid Canale. From this hous invironed with fyne gardens well planted and walled with Rounds on every corner half rounds on the side, of fore and back entries, on the East and West, with a summer hous and ducat [dovecote] on the

South and North and standing in the low parlour, hes a small visee [hole] to[wards] each airth [compass point], there are some remarkable eccho's which will repeat severall words distinctly.

SOURCE: Mitchell, A (ed) 1906 *Geographical Collections Relating to Scotland.* Edinburgh, i, 53–4.

Chancellor Seton's Inscription in the Wall at Pinkie House

Alexander Seton (1556–1622), earl of Dunfermline and lord chancellor of Scotland was a typical aristocrat of Renaissance Scotland. He made his home at Pinkie, near Musselburgh in East Lothian, which he remodelled between 1607 and 1613. His statement that his home was not to be a place connected to war is particularly poignant given that the Battle of Pinkie of 1547, in which the Scots were disastrously defeated by the English, took place within sight of it.

D.O.M. For his own pleasure, and that of his noble descendants and all men of cultivation and urbanity, Alexander Seton, who above all loves every kind of culture and urbanity, has planted, raised and decorated a country house, gardens, and suburban buildings. There is nothing here to do with warfare; not even a ditch or rampart to repel enemies, but in order to welcome guests with kindness and treat them with benevolence, a fountain of pure water, a grove, pools and other things that may add to the pleasures of the place. He has brought everything together that might afford decent pleasures of heart and mind. But he declares that whoever shall destroy this by theft, sword or fire, or behaves in a hostile manner, is a man devoid of generosity and urbanity, indeed of all culture, and is an enemy to the human race.

SOURCE: Bath, C 2003 *Renaissance Decorative Painting in Scotland*. Edinburgh, 99–100.

Poem by Alexander Montgomery to Sir Robert Drummond of Carnock

The poet and courtier Alexander Montgomery (d. 1598) wrote these lines to celebrate the achievements of Sir Robert Drummond of Carnock who was royal master of works from 1579 to 1583 and who undertook surveys of the royal palaces of Falkland, Linlithgow, Edinburgh Castle, Stirling Castle and Holyroodhouse, and recommended how they might be improved.

All buildings brave bid DRUMMOND nou adeu;
Quhais lyf furthsheu he lude thame by the lave.   Whose life demonstrated he
Quhair sall we craiv sik policie to haiv?   loved them more than the rest.
Quha with him straiv to polish, build or plante? Where now shall we
These giftis, I grant, God lent him by the laiv.   seek such improvement?

SOURCE: Montgomerie, A 1887 *Poems*, Cranstoun, J (ed). Edinburgh, 221.

The Earl of Strathmore's Account of Renovations to his Property

Patrick Lyon, third earl of Strathmore and Kinghorne (1642/3–95) set about improving his estates and homes, Castle Lyon (later named Castle Huntly) and Glamis Castle, in the years down to 1689. Here his own records explain his decision to design the renovations himself, without the help of architects.

The house itselfe was extreamly cold and the hall was a vault out of which since by the stricking [making an opening] thereof I have gained the rowmes immediately now above it. No access there was to the upper part of the house without goeing thorrow the hall, even upon the most undecent occasions of Drudgerie unavoidable to be seen by all who should happen to be in that rowme nor was there any other to reteer to, till the rowme which is off it was changed as it now is, for att that time it was not above fourteen feet broad. However for the first ten years of my life I lived there and had enough to doe for the first seven years of these ten to gett together as much as did compleitly furnish that house, and were as much strangers to Old Glammiss as if it had not been. And for the first three years of my life which I only reckon since the year 1660 I could not endure allmost to come near to, or see it, when the verie Mains [home farm] was possessed by a wedsetter [someone who holds land as security for a loan], so, when my wife after the end of the first seven years considered that nothing contributes so much to the distruction and utter ruine of furniture than the transporting of it, I was induced by her to make my constant abode att Castle Lyon for some time longer till she gott together some things necessary to be had before we could think of comeing to Glammiss which she provided with so much care as that for our first comeing to Glammiss where I proposed to live for some time as reteeredly as I did att first when I took up house at Castle Lyon having scarce a spare rowme furnished to lodge a stranger in. And tho it was my resolutione to follow my father's way of living constantly at Castle Lyon in summer and att Glammiss in winter yet the reforming of my house at Castle Lyon which I was fully bent to doe in the way and manner as it now is, was a work of such difficulty to be done and took up so much more time than att first I apprehended it should that my family stayed here full three years before it was possible for me to reduce that place again into any order. Perhaps in the summer time My wife and I and the children might goe doune sometimes, they for their diversione but I to give necessarie directions for the advancing of the work which I declare had I known of what difficultie it was befor I undertook it I had never enterprised the same . . .

Now as is before writtin I remaind constantlie from the sixtie yeare of God that I first took up house att Castle Lyon till the yeare 1670, in so much, that during the whole space My wyfe never saw Glammiss but once. Not that I resolved to continue still to neglect this the ancient seat of my family, whereabout the greatest parte of my estate lyes, but that being quitt spoiled in both houses and nothing remaining but the bare walls and having with great difficulty, trouble, and charge gott together as much as made Castle Lyon habitable, and not being resolved to spoyle it by the frequent transporting thereof, there we remained till some more was provided then served our turn att that place. And in the yeare 1670 we came here as new beginners where we past that winter and lodged our selves all in that storry of the old house which is on the top of the great staircaice, for that storry was the only one glazed att that time. The nixt summer being impatient to see the ruins of the place, for the east wing of the house was no better then if it had had no roofe at all, so I entered to work and gott on a roof upon it after I had highted the walls of the great round and erected two new little geivels [gables] on the syd wall making out more lights in the second and third storry which are easie to be knoun at this day by the newness of the work, putting out the grats out of the window of the third storry lykways with severall altrations of the contrivance within doors too tedious here to sett doune. And whereas the third storry was cymsylled [a sloping ceiling] above which sort of sylling is commonly a nest for ratts I gested [joisted] it over and gain'd rowms above within the roofe, highted the staire of that syd of the house on turn, so that these roums now above add not a little to the conveniencie of our present dwelling lodgeing the younger children and such of the wemen servants as are of the best account who have private access by a back stair to these roumes my wyfe makes use of her selfe. To the syd of the house I have clapp'd to a new building which answears to the three storrys and is covered with lead which platforme goes off the fourth storry, and is of great convenience and use to us who live for the time in this syd of the house . . .

It is hardly possible by any descriptione which I can now make to give any impressione to my posteritie what the place was lyke when I began first my reformations for there remains nothing of it but the great old house allenerly. The old chattered and decayed trees which surrounded the house, yet there were not many, and the most of these that were, were to the southward, a common mistake of our ancestors whereas reasonably any thickets or planting that are about any man's house ought rather to be upon the north, northeast, and northwest, neither was the planting which was here of any bounds. The whole planted ground not exceeding four aikers att most, verie disproportionable to the greatness of the place with a verie low wall of dry stone scarce sufficient to hold out any beast. There was but one entrie to the house which was to the southeast with an utter gate att no greater distance then much about the place where the bridge is over the ditch hard by the round upon the corner of the gardin from which to the inner gate of the Court there was a Rasso [projection], and a low wall such as I told you off before in each syd till you com to the gate of the closs or Court, where there was a bridge with a pend over a mightie, broad and deep ditch which surrounded the house upon the inner brink whereof there was a high wall, a gate forenent [in front of] the bridge and over the gate a little lodge for the porter. There was upon the east syd of the gate houses two roums in lenth which joyned to the great east round of the house so that you may guess by this how strangely near and untowardly this wall and this gate stood with the house itselfe, upon the west syde of the gate within the wall beforementioned there was [a] row of byres and stables and att the tourne, the walls and ruins of a spatious old hall and off it the thing which they called the chamber of Dess, but upon this I never saw a roofe, upon the inner wall of this there was a too fall [lean-to] and the geival thereof open fitt to receive a coatch which I supposed never had a door, of this the Inglish garrison made a smiddy, upon the end of the old hall which made the turne there were other buildings where the women house was and lodgings for serving men, nixt to this there was the chief stable with travesses for horses fitt for to hold seven or eight but the lofting of these was quitt rotten, then did the building turn and joyned to the inmost corner of the weast geivall of the great house of the house where there was a brewhouse and a baick-house which had been of my father's building. All this before mentioned was within the bounds of that which you now see is the fore-court where the two greens are on each syde of the pav'd walk a strange confused unmodel'd piece of business and was to me a great eye sore, these houses also upon the east syd of the gate of the entrie were also in the time of the Inglish garisone consumed with fire, for in the loft they keeped hay where the fire was first keneled, which is commonly the end of all hay Lofts, and a foolish thing it is to house hay unless a man will be so provident as to build a house particularly for it separate from all others . . .

But to returne to Glammis. Tho it be ane old house and consequentlie was the more difficult to reduce the place to eny uniformity, yet I did covet extremely to order my building so as the frontispiece might have a resemblance on both syds, and my great hall which is a rowme that I ever loved having no following was also a great inducement to me for reering up that quarter upon the west syde which now is, so having first founded it I built my walls according to my draught and form'd my entrie which I behoved to draw a little about from the west else it had run directly thorrow the great victual house att the barns which my father built and I was verrie loath to destroy it; verie few will discover the throw in my entrie which I made as unsensible as possiblie I could. Others more observing have challenged me for it but were satisfied when I told them the cause, others perhaps more reserved take notice of it and doe not tell me and conclude it to be an error of ignorance but they are mistaken. I confess I am to blame that designing so great a matter as those reformes put all together comes to, I did not call such as in this age were known and reput to be the best judges and contrivers, for I never bestowed neither gold nor mony upon this head, and I look upon advice as verie necessarie to the most part of undertakers, and the not seeking and taking counsell is commonly the cause why things are found amiss in the most parte of designs that way, nor have I the vanity to consider my owne judgement as another cannot better, yet being resolved to performe what I have done with little noice and by degrees, and more to pleas and divert my selfe then out of any ostentatione, for I thank God I am as little envious as any man and am verie glad to behold things well ordered and contrived att other mens dwellings and never Judged anything of my owne small endeavour worthie to make so much noice as to call for or invit to either of my houses such publick Architecturs My work and projects lykways being complexed things and hardly ony man being to be found fitt to give advice in all I never Judged it worth the trouble of a convocatione of the severall artists such as masons who's talent commonly lyes within the four walls of a house, wrights, for the right ordering of a roofe and the finishing the timber work within, gairdners for gardens, orchards etc.

SOURCE: Miller, AH (ed) 1890 *The Book of Record: a diary written by Patrick first Earl of Strathmore and other documents relating to Glamis Castle, 1684–89.* Edinburgh, 35–42.

Sir Robert Kerr, First Earl of Ancram, to his Son, William Kerr, Third Earl of Lothian, 20 December 1632

The first earl of Ancram was a generously rewarded favourite of James VI and I who also prospered in the reign of Charles I. His service at court kept him often in London, and so in the early 1630s he transferred Ancram and other lands to his son, the recently married and ennobled third earl of Lothian (c.1605–75). In this document, the father gave detailed instructions to his son for the alteration of Ancram House, near Jedburgh.

It was my cair to give it a new frame, for it was only cast according to the forme of that tyme wel aneugh, but so out of square that I did lett the lower roomes decaye, having it always in my purpose to mend them; none of them being worth the keeping. But the Tower, which to beginne with, I would have yow for our present use, because yow meane to sommer there next yeare, God willing, to make the roome under the hall our ordinair eatting roome; not weakening the walls there, by stryking out new wyndowis, butt taking away the partitions, that all the 3 lights as there are, may meet in the center, and so yeild light aneugh, being only glas'd and kept as they are, strong in the out side, because the world may change again; and all the inside of the wyndowis lett them be enlarged doun to the floor with steps or some handsome way, iff neid by payring the insyde of the walls, or slopping them to the breadth to inlarge the light and so pave the floore and make a portall on the doore, and of the little place in the wall make a pantry or roome for the potts and glasses or cupps, or your plate, with a strong doore.

Then smooth the stares with lyme, and glaise it all, enlarging the wyndowes on the insyde, and sloping them doune to the bottome, as the chamber I spoke first of, so to the top of the stayres; and off that room above it, and is now the dyning room, make a fayre chamber, taking awaye these old long tables and put a round table only in it, which is to be used square most tymes; but may be lett out round when yow please to eate there with some extraordinare frend. Yow have hangings anew, and stooles and chayres for it: in the chimney put an yron chimney [fire basket]; a round yrone chimney will be best for it, that men may sit with it, and therein burne your Lothian coales; and iff yow, for lack of roome, or your pleasure, think fit to sett a bed in it, lett the head of it stand at that wall between the doore and the window lookes into the closse, which, thogh it be not a good place for a bedd, yet it is better then the other syde in my mynde, but in that use your fancy to have one or not, or sett it where yow will . . .

Of the wardrobe also, by enlarging the hight of the walls, and making handsome lights, make a chamber with a chimney, and, if yow can, joyne it handsomely to the little chamber on the top of the stayres, or of it yow may make a fyne cabinet for your bookes and papers, which is so necessary that it can not be wanting for a man that understands these things, and what it is to keepe any thing from the eyes and fingers of others.

By any meanes do not take away the battlement, as some gave me counsale to do, as Dalhoussy your nyghtbour did, for that is the grace of the house, and makes it looke lyk a castle, and hence so noblesse, as the other would make it looke lyke a peele [low-status defensive tower].

Out of the seller below take awaye the meale chests and make it seller all, with a partition for a wyne seller in the inmost corner.

And of the pitt yow are to have good consideration. My purpose was to joyne by it the building I was to make of the old hall, where I was to make eyther lodgings or a dyning roome with lodgings, and so from it having made a vault over the pitt to the sole of the window of the chamber under the hall in the touer to make a plattforme to goe off these lodgings in the tower to the other, without goeing upp and doune stairs and thorow the court . . .

Iff yow lyke better to lett the fore gate be built upp as ones it was, and make a gallery with some lodgings on the other syde, because all the bewty of the garden must be cast that waye, and it lyes to the sunne, which in Scotland is a mayne consideration; and therfor (but that is to be donne when yow have more monye and leasure) I would build on that syde the principall fyre roomes of the house, with a low hall, and the accesses in the fashion of this country [i.e. England] or France; and that to be kept sweet for interteyning my frends at solemne tymes, a whole bodye of a lodging with back staires, and easy lodgings to lodge a great man, and this to be joyn'd to the tower by a balcon or ship-gallery going about the tower to the entry above stayres, mentiond befor. For yow must alwayes remember never to weaken the tower, but leave it as strong as yow can, to keepe in a mister for a sure staying house, with the iron gate befor and another on the pitt door, and all the yron wyndowes kept in it. But yow are to make the best use of the present, and therefore keeping it to the best advantage as it is, and for the shortest cutt and the least charges, is eyther to eat in the high hall, making the chamber below it for your seruands, or a low dyning-room, or a warm winter chamber, or dyne in the old hall, and the chamber within it for a withdrawing roome; and housoever the rotten parte of claye over the stable yow must now build and make a back stair doun where the meill sellar was, or on the corner joining it with the new chamber, making on that corner a close staires to serve both, because the underchamber stayres goeth upp utterally. And indeed betyme, iff yow keep that room standing, because of the vault, yow must or may by tyme also draw your gallery from it and the gate to cum under it, and so on a straight levell not slopping uppuard as it doth now (because the passage turned to the right hand, which is now quyte away), and so building another tower lyke it, sett your fayr building, if ever I or yow do it, upp from it towards tower, and so between it and the tower have your garden gate. And iff you think it fit, a back passage to the towne, just forgaynst it, devyded with a wall from the garden on that syde next the toun, and all that even square besyd the old hall made into a backe court for wod, peates, coales, stables, landrys, and all sluttery to be hid from your principall court, which I would have paved.

Now for your utter court and the approaches to your house, which are most materiall; yow must have a speciall regard to them, to make them fayre and easye and noble and pleasand as the ground will afford you, for yow must not contract them now, but rather extend them to a form suttable to your quality; neither is it to be donne all together, butt as yow may overtake it, leaving alwayes place for a better resolution . . .

For yow must make all things of bewty and ornament and use, not only for your selff but other folk; and I love to see a house not straitted or minsed, but to have aneugh of roome in a large noble manner; nor is it all to be donne at ones, butt piece and piece, and to be disposed to that effect as yow may overtake it. I am so carefull to have it so that I am the longer on this; for or [before] it be donne it will cum to the volume of a booke, thogh it be but chalk and not sheawes, iff God will give us leave eyther of us that hath donne greater things for us, and iff wee dye by the way lett it be donne as they will who cum after.

SOURCE: Laing, D (ed) 1875 *Correspondence of Sir Robert Kerr, First Earl of Ancram, and his son, William, Third Earl of Lothian*. Edinburgh, i, 62–9.

Early Modern Art

While textual sources on early modern Scottish art are relatively scarce, the following documents illustrate the creation of art, the partronage of art and the motivations behind it.

DOCUMENT 138

William Dunbar's Description of the Court of James IV in the Early Sixteenth Century

Although probably exaggerated, the court poet William Dunbar's account of the court of James IV presents an image of a colourful, cultured and vibrant reign.

Schir, ye have mony servitours
And officiaris of dyvers curis; curis: occupations
kirkmen, courtmen, and craftsmen fyne;
doctouris in jure and medicyne; jure: law
divinouris, rethoris, and philosophouris, rethoris: rhetoricians
astrologis, artistis, and oratouris;
men of armes, and vailyeand knychtis,
and mony other gudlie wychtis; wychtis: strong men
musicianis, menstralis, and mirrie singaris;
chevalouris, callandaris, and flingaris; callandaris: obscure, but may refer to
cunyouris, carvouris, and carpentaris, those who kept calendars or archives;
beildaris of barkis and ballingaris; flingaris: dancers
masounis lyand upon the land, cunyouris: coiners
and schipwrichtis hewand upon the strand; barkis and ballingaris: ships
glasing wrichtis, goldsmythis, and lapidaris, glasing wrichtis: glaziers
pryntouris, payntouris, and potingaris; lapidaris: jewellers
and all of thair craft cunning, potingaris: apothecaries
and all at anis lawboring.

SOURCE: Small, J (ed) 1893 *The Poems of William Dunbar*. Edinburgh, ii, 220.

Artistic Activity at the Court of James IV

These accounts document payments made to two artists at the court of James IV, Sir Thomas Galbraith and a French painter named Piers. They show the purposes that art served for the royal court: the treaty for the king's marriage to Margaret Tudor was an important diplomatic document, the decorated banners for a royal tournament were to provide spectacle and entertainment, and the illuminated 'porteus' was a devotional text for the king's chapel. To give a flavour of the original language, the first two items have been reproduced in their original language, then a translation of the whole text follows.

December 1502
Item [the 9 day of December], to Schir Thomas Gabreth to pass to Edinburgh to illumyn the trewis and the conjunct infeftment, to by gold and to his expens   59s

July 1503
Item, to Schir Thomas Gabreth, to by gold for the Kingis armes on the foryet of Halyrudhous, 4 Franch crounis   summa 56s

* * * * * *

December 1502
Item [9 December], to Sir Thomas Galbraith to go to Edinburgh to illuminate the truce and the joint infeftment, to buy gold and for his expenses   59s

July 1503
Item, to Sir Thomas Galbraith, to buy gold for the king's arms on the foregate of Holyroodhouse, 4 French crowns   56s

January 1504
Item, to Sir Thomas Galbraith, in part payment for making the arms above the gate, 10 French crowns   £7

June 1507
Item, for 6 books of gold leaf to Sir Thomas Galbraith and Piers, for banners, standards, and decorated tabards for heralds, minstrels, the field, and pavilions £18
Item, to the said Sir Thomas for making of two decorated tabards and a banner, at 40s each £6

December 1507
Item, the third day of December to Piers, painter, for the rent of his house 56s
Item, to the said Piers, 1 book of gold leaf £3; 8 ounces of red ochre 20s; two pounds of white lead 4s; 1 quart of linseed oil 8s; half a pound of light azure 8s £5
Item, to the said Piers for a book and two quires of gold leaf £3 10s
Item, to the said Piers, which was obtained from John Mudie, a book of gold leaf £3
Item, to the said Piers, a book of gold leaf, obtained from and bought by Sir Thomas Galbraith £3 10s

May 1508
Item, to Sir Thomas Galbraith for illuminating the king's gospel book £10
Item, for two clasps of silver gilt for the same 41s

April 1512
Item, the same day and thereafter, to Sir Thomas Galbraith, in part payment for painting of a great parchment breviary ['porteus'] for the king with letters of gold and azure £18 12s

August 1512
Item, before this day, delivered by Master Thomas Dickson to Sir Thomas Galbraith, in part payment for painting the king's great parchment breviary mentioned above £3

SOURCE: Dickson, T (ed) 1877–1916 *Accounts of the Lord High Treasurer of Scotland*. Edinburgh, ii, 350, 383, 416; iii, 393; iv, 41, 87, 340, 358, 379.

James VI's Opinion on Religious Art

James VI planned to refurbish the chapel in Holyrood Palace for his return visit to Scotland in 1616–17, and carvings were in preparation in London by the sculptor Nicholas Stone, under the supervision of the royal architect Inigo Jones. James was well aware, however, that decorative religious images were not likely to go down well with presbyterians, and in this letter he attempted to forestall opposition by suggesting what kinds of imagery were and were not acceptable.

When we received and perused your letter of the 25th of February last, concerning the graven work of wood intended for decoring of our seat in our chapel at Holyrood House, we were at first afraid, that some of the directors or workmen had been Papists, and so without our knowledge had intended to erect there such idolatrous images and painted pictures as those of that profession had been in use to adore; but when we had better considered, and exactly tried what was done, we find but a false alarm, and that causeless fears have made you start at your own shadows. Yet seeing a change is commanded upon that work, upon notice given to us by our master of works here of the difficulty and longsomeness thereof, lest our silence, and not answering of your letter, might be interpreted for a kind of consent or approbation of what ye wrote thereanent – and to the effect that the command of that alteration shall not be thought to have proceeded from any such conceit in us as ye are possessed with – we have thought good hereby to certify you that we was not induced thereto by any such ground or consideration, but merely because of the misdoubt conceived that the work would have been so well or so soon done in that kind as in the form now directed. And therefore do not deceive yourselves with a vain imagination of anything done therein for ease of your hearts or ratifying your error in your judgement of that graven work, which is not of an idolatrous kind like to images and painted pictures adored and worshipped by Papists, but merely intended for ornament and decoration of the place where we shall sit, and might have been wrought as well with figures of lions, dragons, and devils, as with those of patriarchs and apostles. But as we must wonder at your ignorance, and teach you thus to distinguish the one from the other, so are we persuaded that none of you would have been scandalised or offended if the said figures of lions, dragons, and devils had been carved and put up in lieu of those of the patriarchs and apostles.

SOURCE: Burton, J 1897 *The History of Scotland*. Edinburgh, vi, 42–3.

List of Paintings in John de Medina's Studio at the Time of his Death in 1710

Half-length pictures:

Imprimis ane half length picture of the present Countess of Marischall
being ane originall   £40

Item another ditto of Lady Anne Keith her daughter, also an originall   £40

Item another ditto of Mistress Esther Home, daughter to Sir Andrew
Home, not finished   £18

Item another ditto of the Countess of Crawfoord and her sone togither
on the same picture, delivered up to the Earl of Crawfoord since Sir
John Medina's decease, by the relict [widow], for which he is to pay
£10 18s   £120 Scots

Item another ditto of the Prince of Nassau   £12

Item another ditto being ane coppey of the Lady Weem   £12

Item another ditto of Sir James Hall, only begun in the face, which is in
John Medina's custody   £1 10s

Three quarter pictures:

Imprimis a picture of Jerviswood for which the relict has received since
the defunct's decease   £43

Item a picture of his daughter Mrs Rachaell Baillie, which the relict has
received, for also   £43

Item a picture of his daughter, the Lady Stanhope, for which the relict is
also payed   £43

Item a picture of the Lady Jerviswood, for which the relict has received
since Sir John's decease   £43

Item a picture of James Drummond, wryter to the signet, his lady, not
wholly finished   £6

Item a picture of the master of Saltoun   £8

Item a picture of Lockhart of Carnwath's third son   £8

Item a picture, being originall, of Mr Abell, singing master   £8

Item a picture of Doctor Pitcairne not altogether finished   £12

Item a picture of Pluscardine, brother to the Laird of Grant, not
altogether finished   £8

Item a picture of the Laird of Keith   £12

Item a picture of the Lady Anne Keith	£12
Item a picture of John Adair	£18
Item a picture of David Fyfe, chirurgeon [surgeon], his wife, in John Medina's custody, not finished	£8
Item a coppie picture of the deceased Duchess of Queensberry, done by Andrew Hay	£3
Item a picture of My Lord Panmure, being a coppie for which the relict has received since Sir John's decease	£19
Item a picture of his Lady, being also a coppie for which the relict has also received	£19 7s
Item a coppie picture of Sir James Stewart, late Lord Advocat	£4
Item a coppie picture of the late King William	£3
Item a coppie picture of the late Duke of Gloster	£3
Item a coppie picture of Sir George McKenzie	£3
Item a coppie picture of the present Duke of Douglas	£3
Item a coppie picture of Queen Anne	£4
Item a coppie picture of the present Countess of Dundonald	£3
Item a coppie picture of the Lady Yester	£3
Item a picture originall of the present Countess of Home for which the relict received since the defunct's decease	£60
Item a picture originall of Sir Robert Blackwood, not finished, and sold by the relict since Sir John's decease for	£12
Item a coppie picture of Sir James Primrose	£3
Item a coppie picture of the late Duke of Argyll	£3
Item a coppie picture of Sir Hugh Dalrymple of North Berwick, Lord President of the Session	£4
Item a picture originall of Mrs Margaret Ballandyne, sold by the relict since Sir John's decease for	£36
Item a picture of Mr Francis Stewart's lady, being ane originall	£10
Item a coppie picture of Doctor Chamberland	£3
Item a coppie picture of the present Duke of Hamilton	£3
Item a coppie of his Duchess not finished	£3
Item a picture originall of Lockhart of Carnwath's second sone not yet finished in the custody of John Medina, the defunct's son	£3
Item a picture of Lady Grange Erskine not finished	£4
Item 9 pictures quhereof the face is only begune, which only serve for prive cloaths and are in John Medina's custody at £1 10s the piece is	£13 10s
Item a coppie picture, small half length of the Lady Marshall	£24
Item a half length landscape done by Van Dist	£15
Item a picture of Cleopatra, less than half length, originall	£18
Item a picture of Venus and a Satyre, being a coppie	£9
Item a coppie picture of ane English Lady, being half length	£12
Item a coppie picture of a Venus and a Cupid	£3
Item a coppie picture of Vanity, not yet finished, being a half length	£5

Item a coppie of Venus dead, colloured	£3
Item 3 quarter fruit pieces, picture being a coppie	£6
Item a picture of Adam and Eve driven out of Paradice, being a coppie done by Sir John himself	£26
Item a 3 quarter picture of Lucretia, being a coppie	£3
Item a picture of Rosamond with a cup in her hand, being ane originall	£12
Item a picture of Flora, being a coppie	£3
Item a 3 quarter picture of a Venus and a Satyre, being a coppie	£4
Itam a 3 quarter coppie picture of Charity	£6
Item a coppie picture of 3 quarters, of a Venus and Adonis	£3
Item a coppie picture of ditto length of a shepherd and a shepherdess	£3
Item coppie picture of ditto length of a landscape	£3
Item a coppie picture of Adam and Eve	£3
Item a picture of Lucretia, not finished, being ane originall	£9
Item a coppie picture of Cain and Abell, not finished	£3
Item a picture of a Venus and a Satyre, being a half length, an originall	£60
Item 2 three quarters pictures quhereof the head only finished	£18
A picture of Venus and a Cupidd, some larger than a three quarter	£5
Item a Cupid picture of a landscape	£3
Item a picture 3 quarter length of a Flora being ane originall	£12
Item a coppie picture, ditto length, of a landscape	£3
Item ane originall Venus and Cupid, being half length	£24
Item 7 little landscapes, all sold by the relict since Sir John's decease, at £12 Scots per piece is	£84
Item a paris plaister figure of Cain and Abell being broken	£1 16s
Item some paterns for painting, all worth	£30
Item 12 mazie tinto [mezzotint] prints in John Medina's custodie	£12
Item Van Dyk's postures	£16 4s
Item 5 half length postures in John Medina's custodie and the defunct's materials of his trade and instruments	£36

SOURCE: Marshall, R 1988 *John de Medina 1659–1710*. Edinburgh, 28–9.

Early Modern Music

A NOTE ON VOCABULARY

The following sources reveal that a huge variety of musical instruments and musical forms were familiar to the early modern Scottish audience. It is not possible to translate most of their names into modern English since few of them have comprehensible modern equivalents. For example, 'gittyrn' is cithern, an instrument similar to a lute, while a 'croude' was a bowed stringed instrument unlike any modern instrument. The message of these sources is clear, however: music played a prominent role in early modern Scottish culture.

DOCUMENT 142

Richard Holland, *The Buke of the Howlat*

Richard Holland was a churchman who spent much of his career in the far north of Scotland and the Orkney islands. His Buke of the Howlat *(owl) was composed between 1446 and 1450, and as a complex morality tale, it uses different species of birds as analogues for human society and politics.*

All thus our lady thai lovit, with lyking and lyst,
Menstralis and musicianis, mo than I mene may.
The psaltery, the sytholis, the soft sytharist,
The croude, and the monycordis, the gittyrnis gay;
The rote, and the recordour, the rivupe, the rist,
The trumpe, and the talburn, the tympane but tray;
The lilt pype, and the lute, the fydill in fist,
The dulset, the dulsacordis, the schalme of assay;
The amyable organis usit full oft;
Claryonis lowde knellis,
Portativis, and bellis,
Cymbaclanis in the cellis,
That soundis so soft.

SOURCE: Holland, R 'The Buke of the Howlat', in Amours, FJ (ed) 1897 *Scottish Alliterative Poems.* Edinburgh, 73.

Robert Henryson, 'Orpheus and Eurydice'

Little biographical detail is known of Robert Henryson (d. c.1490), one of the greatest poets of medieval Scotland. His 'Orpheus and Eurydice' drew on classical mythology and from Boethius's Consolation of Philosophy *to produce a fusion of myth, morality and romance. Orpheus was a famed musician whose talent is a major feature of the narrative. He married Eurydice, only for her to die shortly afterwards, and he pursued her through the underworld but was unable to bring her back with him.*

In his passage amang the planetis all,
he herd a hevynly melody and sound,
passing all instrumentis musicall,
causid be rollyn of the speris round;
Quhilk armony of all this mappamound,
Quhilk moving cesse unyt perpetuall,
Quhilk of this warld pluto, the saule can call.

Thair lerit he tonys proportionat,   lerit: learned
as duplar, triplar, and emetricus,
enolius, and eik the quadruplate,   eik: also
Epoddeus rycht hard and curious;
off all thir sex, suete and delicius,
rycht consonant fyve hevinly symphonyis
componyt ar, as clerkis can devyse.   componyt: composed

First dyatesseron, full sweit, I wiss
And dyapason, semple and dowplait,
And dyapenty, componyt with the dyss;
Thir makis fyve of thre multiplicat:
this mirry musik and mellifluat,
Compleit and full of nummeris od and evin,
Is causit be the moving of the hevin.

Off sic musik to wryt I do bot doit,
Thairfoir of this mater a stray I lay,
For in my lyfe I coud nevir sing a note;

bot I will tell how orpheus tuk the way,
To seik his wyfe attour the gravis gray,
hungry and cauld, with mony wilsum wone,   wilsum wone: dreary moan
Withouttin gyd, he and his harp allone.

SOURCE: Henryson, R 'Orpheus and Eurydice', in Smith GG (ed) 1906–14 *Poems of Robert Henryson*. Edinburgh, ii, 42–3.

William Dunbar's References to Music

William Dunbar (c.1460–c.1513) was a poet who received a pension from James IV between 1500 and 1513. The court was both his employer and his audience. 'Ane Ballat of Our Lady' has a meditative quality, while 'The Ballade of . . . lord Barnard Stewart' was written on the occasion of the embassy from France of Lord Bernard Stewart of Aubigny, a soldier and diplomat of Scottish descent, in 1508.

A) ATTRIBUTED TO WILLIAM DUNBAR, ROS MARY: ANE BALLAT OF OUR LADY

Haile, lamp lemand befoir the trone devyne,   *lemand: shining; trone: throne*
Quhar cherubim sweit syngis Osanna,
With organe, tympane, harpe, and symbalyne;
O mater Jhesu, salve Maria!

B) THE BALLADE OF . . . LORD BARNARD STEWART

Welcum, our Scottis chiftane most dughty:
With sowne of clarioun, organe, song and sence
To the atonis, lord, Welcum all we cry   To the atonis: to you together
With glorie and honour, lawde and reverence.

SOURCE: a) Mackay Mackenzie, W (ed) 1932 *Poems of William Dunbar*. London, 175; b) Small, J (ed) 1893 *The Poems of William Dunbar*. Edinburgh, ii, 60.

Gavin Douglas, 'The Palis of Honoure'

Gavin Douglas (c.1476–1522) was well connected in the Scottish church, aristocracy and royal family, and wrote all his poetry in the reign of James IV. 'The Palis of Honoure' was completed around 1501 and dedicated to the king. It was composed as an allegorical dream on the paths to honour, and eventually concluded that martial glory was the greatest route to honour, but not before devoting considerable coverage to the importance of the Muses, and the imagination.

In modulatioun hard I play and sing
Faburdoun, pricksang, discant, countering,
Cant organe, figuratioun, and gemmell,
On croud, lute, harp, with mony gudlie spring,
Schalmes, clariounis, portatiues, hard I ring,
Monycord, organe, tympane, and cymbell.
Sytholl, psaltterie, and voices sweit as bell,
Soft releschingis in dulce delivering,
Fractionis divide, at rest, or clois compell.

SOURCE: Small, J 1874 *The Poetical Works of Gavin Douglas, Bishop of Dunkeld.* Edinburgh, i, 20.

John Rolland of Dalkieth, 'The Seven Sages'

John Rolland was a priest who wrote 'The Seven Sages' in 1560 as the Scottish Reformation was played out in Edinburgh between the French and the English, although it was not published until 1578.

Als with him come divers grit kings & knichts
Duiks, Barrons, erls, & mony worthie wichts   wichts: people
With trumpet, schalme, drum, squasche & clarioun,
Harp, Lut, Organe, Symbal and Symphioun
Makand their mirth all into gude ordour . . .

SOURCE: Black, GF (ed) 1932 *The Sevin Seages*. Edinburgh, 27.

The Gude and Godlie Ballatis

The Gude and Godlie Ballatis *is a collection of poems that were composed in the decades before the Scottish Reformation of 1560, to promote Protestant ideas and attack the corruptions of the Roman Catholic church.*

Ye rychteous rejoyis and loue the Lord,
Just men to thank thair God dois weil accord.
Play on your lute, & sweitly to it sing,
Tak harpe in hand with mony lustie string,
Tyrle on the ten stringit Instrument,
And pryse your God with hart & haill intent.
Sing na auld thing the quhilk is abrogate,   the quhilk is abrogate:
Bot sing sum new pleasand perfite ballat: which is rejected
Blaw up organis, with glaid & hevinlie sound,
Joyfull in hart, quhill all the skyis resound.

SOURCE: [Wedderburn, J, J and R] 1897. Mitchell, AF (ed) *A Compendious Book of Godly and Spiritual Songs, Commonly known as the Gude and Godlie Ballatis* Edinburgh, 93.

Act of Parliament, 1579

This act of parliament highlights the importance of music to the Scottish commonwealth.

For instruction of the youth in the art of musik and singing, quhilk is almost decayit, and sall schortly decay, without tymous remeid [timely remedy] be providit, our Soverane Lord James VI with avise of his thrie estatis of this present parliament, requeistis the provest, baillies, counsale, and communitie of the maist speciall burrowis of this realme, and of the patronis and provestis of the collegis, quhair sang sculis are foundat, to erect and set up ane sang scuill, with ane maister sufficient and able for instruction of the yowth in the said science of musik, as they will answer to his hienes upon the perrel of their foundationis, and in performing of his hienes requeist do unto his Majestie acceptable and gude plesure.

SOURCE: quoted in Millar, P 1949 *Four Centuries of Scottish Psalmody*. London, 109.

'Vox Borealis', or 'The Northern Discovery'

In this satire of 1641 the Governor of Edinburgh Castle keeps a fiddler and a fool who . . .

. . . goe to singing Scots jigges in a jearing manner at the Covenanters, for surrendering up their Castles as followeth, The fiddler hee flings out his heeles And dances and sings: Put up thy dagor, Jamie, the parliament is ended . . . Then the Foole hee flirts out his folie, And whilst the Fidler playes hee sings:

'Put up thy dagor Jamie, and all things shall be mended: Bishops shall fall, no not at all, when the parliament is ended. Which never was intended but only for to flam thee, we have gotten the game, we'll keep the same, put up thy dagger, Jamie . . .'

SOURCE: Vox Borealis, or the Northern Discovery, reprinted in 1809 *The Harleian Miscellany*, iv, 422–41.

Anonymous Account of the Music of John Abell

John Abell (1653–c.1716) was a celebrated Scottish musician in the courts of the Restoration monarchs Charles II and James VII and II, known for his violin and lute playing, but most particularly for his vocal talents. This document gives insights into the activities of the court only days after the birth of the Prince of Wales, James Francis Stuart, in June 1688. This was the occurrence that provoked the Revolution of 1688, with the invasion of William of Orange in November.

Mr Abell, the celebrated musician, and one of the Royal band, entertained the publick, and demonstrated his loyalty on the evening of the 18th June 1688, by the performance of an aquatic concert. The barge prepared for this purpose was richly decorated, and illuminated by numerous torches. The musick was composed expressly for the occasion by Signor Fede, Master of the Chapel Royal, and the performers, vocal and instrumental, amounted to one hundred and thirty, selected as the greatest proficients in the science . . . The first performance took place facing Whitehall, and the second opposite Somerset House where the Queen Dowager then resided. Great numbers of barges and boats were assembled, and each having flambeaux on board, the scene was extremely brilliant and pleasing. The music being ended, all the nobility and company that were upon the water gave three shouts to express their joy and satisfaction; and all the gentlemen of the musick went to Mr Abell's house, which was nobly illuminated and honoured with the presence of a great many of the nobility; out of whose windows hung a fine machine full of lights which drew thither a vast concourse of people. The entertainment lasted till three of the clock the next morning, the musick playing and the trumpets sounding all the while, the whole concluding with the health of their Majesties, The Prince of Wales, and all the Royal Family.

SOURCE: quoted in Farmer, HG 1952 'John Abell', *Hinrichsen's Musical Year Book*. London, vii, 445. Farmer's source has yet to be identified.

Tobias Hume, *Introduction to the First Part of the Ayres*

Tobias Hume was a soldier and a composer of music for the viol. Here he outlines the contrast between his two professions, and describes his musical style.

Alwaies thus to the Reader. I do not studie Eloquence, or professe Musicke, although I doe love Sence, and affect Harmony. My profession beeing, as my Education hath beene, Armes, the onely effeminate part of mee, hath beene Musicke; which in me hath beene alwaies Generous, because never Merecenarie. To praise Musicke, were to say, the Sunne is bright. To extoll my selfe, would name my labours vaine-glorious. Onely this, my studies are farre from servile imitations, I rob no others inventions, I take no Italian Note to an English Dittie, or filch fragments of Songs to stuffe out my volumes. These are mine owne Phansies expressed by my proper Genius, which if thou doest dislike, let me see thine . . . Now to use a modest shortnes, and a briefe expression of my selfe to all noble spirits, thus, My Title expresseth my bookes Contents, which (if my hopes faile me not) shall not deceive their expectation, in whole approvement, the crowne of my labours resteth. And from henceforth, the statefull instrument Gambo Violl, shall with ease yield full various and devicefull Musicke as any other instrument. For here I protest the Trinitie of Musicke, parts, Passion and Division, to be as gracefully united in the Gambo Violl, as in the most received Instrument that is, which here with a Souldiers Resolution, I give up to the acceptance of all noble dispositions. The friend of his friend, Tobias Hume.

SOURCE: Hume, T 1605 *Introduction to the First Part of the Ayres*. London.

William Drummond of Hawthornden, Sonnet

Scotland's foremost poet of the seventeenth century, William Drummond's Poems *appeared in print in 1616, and included sixty-eight sonnets as well as a variety of other poetic forms.*

Sound hoarse sad Lute, true Witnesse of my Woe,
And strive no more to ease selfe-chosen Paine
With Soule-enchanting Sounds, your Accents straine
Unto these Teares uncessantly which flow.
Shrill Treeble weepe, and you dull Basses show
Your Masters Sorrow in a deadly Vaine,
Let never joyfull Hand upon you goe,
Nor Consort keepe but when you doe complaine.
Flie Phoebus Rayes, nay, hate the irkesome Light,
Woods solitarie Shades for thee are best,
Or the blacke Horrours of the blackest Night,
When all the World (save Thou and I) doth rest:
Then sound sad Lute, and beare a mourning Part,
Thou Hell may'st moove, though not a Womans Heart.

SOURCE: Ward, WC (ed) 1894 *The Poems of William Drummond of Hawthornden*. London, 62.

Sir John Clerk of Penicuik on Musical Taste, Early 1700s

Sir John Clerk of Penicuik (1676–1755) is best known as a supporter of the Union of Parliaments of 1707. However, he also had a great enthusiasm for music, gained during the extensive periods of time he spent on the Continent in his youth. He played harpsichord, and produced his own musical compositions. He had strong opinions on musical taste, as these comments illustrate.

This custom of breaking notes into smaller as the voice ascends or descends or makes cadences, is very frequent amongst the skilful performers, for these knowing nothing of the laws of Harmony fall into gross irregularities. The best of all graces is to sett them in notes and consider them with the counterpoint, whereby the faults will plainly appear. Some very short breakings and lesser faults, may be allowed, but those long Graces used by some are intollerable and especially in the worship of God.

SOURCE: Clerk Papers, GD18 4541, quoted by kind permission of Sir John Clerk of Penicuik.

Early Modern Literature

Gavin Douglas, Prologues to the Twelve Books of the *Eneados*

Gavin Douglas's most significant work is his translation of Virgil's Aeneid, *the* Eneados, *completed in the summer of 1513. As a humanist work, it was intended to cultivate knowledge of and interest in Classical literature, as well as to enrich the literature of the Scots language. Douglas's Prologues and Epilogues took a variety of metrical forms, and historians and critics have questioned their relevance to the translation as a whole. However, they stand alone as examples of Douglas's most creative work, in which he pondered the reception of his translation, and the nature of poetry itself.*

A) PROLOGUE I, LINES 105–12

First I protest, beaw Schiris, be your leif,
Beis weill advisit my werk or ye repreif,
Considdir it warllie, reid oftair than anis;
Weill at ane blenk slee poetry nocht tane is;
And yit, forsuith, I set my besy pane
As that I suld, to mak it braid and plane,
Kepand na sudroun bot our awin langage
And speikis as I lernit quhen I was page.

beaw Schiris: beautiful sirs
or ye repreif: before you reprove
warllie: warily; oftair than anis:
   more than once; it is best not
   to take poetry at face value

sudroun: English
page: a boy, when I was young

B) PROLOGUE I, 193–98

And, wnder the cluddes of dirk poetry
Hid lyis thair mony notable history
For so the poetis be ther crafty curis,
In similitudis, and vnder quhent figuris,
The suthfast mater to hyde, and to constrene;
All is not fals, traste wele, in caice thai fene.

curis: deceits
quhent: quaint
suthfast: truthful
fene: lie, deceive

C) PROLOGUE VI, 9–16

Quhat wenis fulis this sext buke bene but japes
All full of leis or ald idolatreis?
O hald your pece, ye verray goddis apis!
Reid, reid agane, this volume, mair than tuise;

What fools believe this sixth
   book is but japes

Consider quhat hid sentence tharin lyis:
Be war to lak, les than ye knaw weill quhat;
And gif yow list nocht wirk eftir the wise,
Heich on your hed set wp the foly hat.

Be wary to disparage things that you don't know well.
If you do not wish to work towards wisdom, set the dunce's cap high on your head.

SOURCE: Small, J (ed) 1874 *The Poetical Works of Gavin Douglas, Bishop of Dunkeld*. Edinburgh, ii, 6–7, 9; iii, 1.

John Bellenden's Preface to his Translation of Hector Boece's *Chronicles of Scotland*

In the early 1530s John Bellenden produced a Scots translation of Hector Boece's Scotorum Historia, *or* Chronicles of Scotland, *which had been published in 1527. The following is an English translation of Bellenden's Scots text. Bellenden's translation, like Boece's Latin text, was strongly concerned with using the example of history to cultivate the virtue and civic spirit of the king, the nobility, and the people of Scotland. The Preface, dedicated to James V, reveals the same priority.*

Erasmus of Rotterdam [a Dutch humanist philosopher], most noble Prince, shows that there is nothing the people admire more than the actions of kings, for their lives are so public that all people discuss whether they should be commended or reproved. Therefore, there is nothing so fruitful to repress the common vices of the people as a clean-living prince . . .

Of the behaviour of princes and noble men I find nothing more useful than the reading of histories. Noblemen shall find in them not only martial deeds, but also many documents concerning their fame, their honour, and perpetual memory, and seeing every state appraised for their merits and demerits. The fruits of history are so necessary that, if they did not exist, the valiant deeds of strong champions would be lost and forgotten. On the other hand, the effect of history causes long ago events to appear recent in our memory, as if they were instantly done. Therefore Cicero said 'He that is ignorant of such things as have been done before his time, for lack of experience, is but a child'. For these reasons, most noble prince, I, your native and humble servant, impelled by the love and vehement affection that I bear to you, have translated 'The History of Scotland' since its first beginning, into vulgar language.

Your Highness will find in this present history, many grave sentences, no less pleasing than profitable, wherein your Highness may gain understanding of how this realm shall be governed in justice, and what sorts of people should bear authority or office. Your Highness shall find how once illustrious princes have degenerated from virtue, because they were accompanied by avaricious people and vain flatterers. Such men are more set upon the pursuit of wealth than princely reverence, yet through their corrupt advice, some of your Highness's noble ancestors were abused in this way, and suffered misery because of it. Some lost not only their lives and their power, but remain infamous in the memory of their people. I doubt not, most noble Prince, but that in the same manner many of those who depend on your Highness, are more interested in their own profit, than in the commonwealth.

Your Highness shall shortly have a perfect understanding of who are abusers and who are lovers of the commonwealth, because your Majesty, through your strength and manhood, has gained full control over the country and brought your subjects to peace and tranquillity. This feat could not have been achieved by the nobles during your Majesty's minority.

Therefore, my sovereign, I dare to boldly affirm that no other business will be as useful to your Highness as the frequent reading of our, and of other, histories. For this activity impels the readers not only to perform actions that will be remembered, but also inspires experience and wisdom, as if the reader has travelled the world, or been alive for many years, having seen so many examples of virtue and vice, and so many illustrious military deeds.

Who is he that will not rejoice to hear the martial feats of our strong champions King Robert the Bruce and William Wallace? The first, by a natural desire to recover his realm, was brought to such hardship, that at times he might be distant from the sight of the people. Instead he lived in remote places, and ate roots and herbs, in the hope of better fortune. At last by his manhood and prowess he came to such glory, through victory over the English, that he is now admired the most valiant and noble prince of Scotland, either before or since his own time. The other [William Wallace] came from small beginnings to great courage and physical strength. He not only expelled the English from Scotland, but the fear of his presence put King Edward to flight. His sword and the rage of his fury were so awful that the English were not strong enough to repel his invasion. Similarly, there have been many other valiant princes of his realm, such as Caratak, Galdus, Gregoure, Fergus the Second, with many others, as may be known by the reading of this history. Some of your noble predecessors degenerated from virtue, and are not to be admired. I could name Roman Emperors who turned to vice, such as Nero, Caligula, Heliogabalus, Domicus, Commodus, Vitellius, and others, but for the sake of space I will pass.

SOURCE: Chambers, RW and Batho, EC (eds) 1938–41 *The Chronicles of Scotland*. Scottish Text Society, i, 15–20.

John Knox's *History of the Reformation*

John Knox's History of the Reformation, published in part in 1587 and in full in 1644, looms large for the historian of the Scottish Reformation and the reign of Mary Queen of Scots. Knox had four audiences with Mary Queen of Scots between 1561 and 1564, and accounts of these meetings were written up retrospectively for the History. This may lead us to question whether these episodes can be read simply as accounts of conversations, or whether Knox manipulated the narrative and sharpened the portraits of himself and the queen to achieve the desired polarisation between the masculine Protestant preacher and the feminine and fickle Catholic queen.

The Quene, in a vehement fume, began to cry out, that never Prince was handled as she was. 'I have,' said sche, 'borne with you in all your rigorouse maner of speaking, bayth against my self and against my Uncles; yea, I have sought your favouris by all possible meanes. I offered unto you presence and audience whensoever it pleased you to admonishe me; and yitt I can nott be quyte of you. I avow to God, I shalbe anes revenged.' And with these wordis, skarslie could Marnock, hir secreat chalmer-boy, get neapkynes to hold hyr eyes drye for the tearis; and the owling [howling], besides womanlie weaping, stayed his speiche.

The said Johne [Knox] did patientilie abyde all the first fume, and att opportunitie answered, 'Trew it is, Madam, your Grace and I have bein att diverse controversies, into the which I never perceaved your Grace to be offended at me. Butt when it shall please God to deliver you fra that bondage of darknes and errour in the which ye have been nurisshed, for the lack of trew doctrin, your Majestie will fynd the libertie of my toung nothing offensive. Without the preaching place, Madam, I think few have occasioun to be offendit at me; and thair, Madam, I am nott maister of my self, but man obey Him who commandis me to speik plane, and to flatter no flesche upoun the face of the earth.'

'But what have ye to do,' said sche, 'with my mariage?'

'Yf it pleise your Majestie,' said he, 'patientlie to hear me, I schall schwa the treuth in plane wordis. I grant your Grace offered unto me more than ever I required; but my answer was than, as it is now, that God hath not sent me to await upoun the courtes of Princesses, nor upoun the chamberis of Ladyes; but I am send to preache the Evangell of Jesus Christ, to such as please to hear it; and it hath two partes, Repentance and Fayth. And now, Madam, in preaching repentance, of necessitie it is that the synnes of men be so noted, that thei may know whairin thei offend; but so it is, that the most parte of your Nobilitie ar so addicted to your affectionis, that neather God his word, nor yitt thair Commounwealth, ar rychtlie regarded. And thairfoir it becomes me so to speak, that thei may know thair dewitie.'

'What have ye to do,' said sche, 'with my mariage? Or what ar ye within this Commounwealth?'

'A subject borne within the same,' said he, 'Madam. And albeit I neather be Erle, Lord, nor Barroun within it, yitt hes God maid me, (how abject that ever I be in your eyes) a profitable member within the same: Yea, Madam, to me it apperteanes no lesse to foirwarne of suche thingis as may hurte it, yf I foirsee thame, then it does to any of the Nobilitie; for boyth my vocatioun and conscience craves playness of me. And thairfoir, Madam, to your self I say that whiche I speak in publict place: Whensoever that the Nobilitie of this Realme shall consent that ye be subject to ane unfaythfull husband, thei do as muche as in thame lyeth to renunce Christ, to banishe his treuth from thame, to betray the fredome of this Realme, and perchance shall in the end do small conforte to your self.'

At these wordis, owling was heard, and tearis mycht have bene sein in greattar abundance than the mater required. Johne Erskin of Dun, a man of meak and gentill spreit [spirit], stood besyd, and entreated what he could to mitigat hir anger, and gave unto hir many pleasing wordis of hir beautie, of his excellence, and how that all the Princes of Europe wold be glaid to seak hir favouris. But all that was to cast oyle in the flaming fyre. The said Johne [Knox] stood still, without any alteration of countenance for a long season, whill [until] that the Quene gave place to hir inordinat passioun; and in the end he said, 'Madam, in Goddis presence I speak: I never delyted in the weaping of any of Goddis creatures; yea, I can skarslie weill abyd the tearis of my awin boyes whome my awin hand correctis, much less can I rejoice in your Majesties weaping. But seing that I have offered unto you no just occasioun to be offended, but have spocken the treuth, as my vocatioun craves of me, I man sustean (albeit unwillinglie) your Majesties tearis, rather than I dar hurte my conscience, or betray my Commoun-wealth through my silence.'

Heirwith was the Quene more offended, and commanded the said Johne to pass furth of the cabinet, and to byde farther of his pleasur in the chalmer. The Laird of Dun taryed, and Lord Johne of Coldinghame cam into the cabinet, and so thei boyth remaned with hyr neyr the space of ane houre. The said Johne stood in the chalmer, as one whom men had never sein, (so war all effrayed,) except that the Lord Ochiltrie bayre him companye: and thairfoir began he to forge talking of the ladyes who war thair sitting in all thair gorgiouse apparel; whiche espied, he mearlie said, 'O fayre Ladyes, how pleasing war this lyeff of youris, yf it should ever abyd, and then in the end that we might passe to heavin with all this gay gear. But fye upoun that knave Death, that will come whitther we will or not! And when he hes laid on his areist, the foull wormes wilbe busye with this flesche, be it never so fayr and so tender; and the seally sowll, I fear, shalbe so feable, that it can neather cary with it gold, garnassing, targatting, pearle, nor pretious stanes.' And by suche meanes procured he the cumpany of women; and so past his tyme till that the Laird of Dun willed him to departe to his house quhill new advertisement.

SOURCE: Laing, D (ed) 1846–8 *The Works of John Knox*. Wodrow Society, ii, 387–9.

James VI to Henry Howard, Earl of Northampton, Spring 1605

This document illustrates the range of tones and rhetorical techniques that James used to communicate with those who served him. It gives insights into how he exercised his power and demonstrates that, even after two years in England, he retained a strongly Scots prose. In the letter, addressed to the earl of Northampton, James began with praise and grateful thanks for his service in confidential matters, before abruptly changing tack, and expressing anger with Northampton's conduct as constable of Dover Castle and warden of the Cinque Ports. Evidently he had been dealing harshly with Scottish merchants and seamen.

[External address] To our right trustie and right welbeloved cousin and counsellor the E. of Northampton

If I hadde hadde any particulaire occasion worthie the troubling you with to have recommendit unto you all this tyme of my absence, youre lettirs shoulde not have bene ansourles. But if for fault of other matter I hadde desyred you to have bene diligent and cairfull in my affaires thaire, it hadde bene but to bidde a running man goe faster, quhiche [which] is both unnecessarie and injuriouse, for I may easielie judge of your diligence by your accounte. For if the injust stewarde in the Gospel coulde have gevin as good a *reddere rationem* [reasonable return] for his diligence as ye have gevin to the cheif of the Stewardis, he had never bene castin in utter darkenes. And yett my eyes saw all youre lettirs consumed with fyre, thoche [though] without weeping or gnashing of teethe. My reading of thaim carieing lykewayese that other Acherontide [gloomy] qualitie with it that, lyke as I hadde dronkin of Lethe flood, quhen [when] any pointe contained in any of thaime is told me by any other personne, I can never remember to have hearde of it before.

But now I must turne my penne to a farre contrarie style, repenting me of that epithet I give you in the first wordes heireof. For quhat can I thinke of youre affection to me and the union, quhenas [when] youre workes declaire the contrarie? I must judge of youre mynde by youre actions and not by youre wordis. Your orations in parliament in advancement of the union are but wordis, but your officers' severitie in Dover are actions. A strainge thing, that your naturall avarice, and innate hatred to me and all Scotlande for my cause, shoulde make you to cause youre officers at suche a tyme pyke [pick] shillings from poore Scottismen. Well, I proteste to God, I thocht you at my pairting from you as honest a servande as ever king hadde, but quhat now, I thinke of you since the discoverie of this youre greate hipocrisie, judge ye and, according to youre faithe, so be it unto you, as ever it be. I am glaid that I have gottin this grounde to paye you hoame upon for youre often crewall and malitious speachis against babie Charlis and his honest father. But I knowe ye are now so proud of youre new patrone as ye littill care your old friendis.

I knowe this lettir willbe the more wellcome that it is my precursoure, being schortlie to follow who, like the sunne in this season, ame mounting in my sphære and aproching to shyne upon youre horizon. And so, praying you to beleeve the contraire ather [either] of the first or last pairte of this lettir, I bid you hairtelie fair well for all this great querrell [quarrel].

James R.

SOURCE: British Library, Cotton MSS, Titus C VI (MS1605), fo. 178.

DOCUMENT 158

'As Phoebus in his Spheres Hicht', from the Maitland Quarto Manuscript, *c.*1586

This poem appears in a collection known as the Maitland Quarto Manuscript and has been attributed to Marie Maitland, daughter of Sir Richard Maitland, the courtier who put the collection together around 1586. Textual evidence suggests that the author was indeed female, and in the poem the speaker regrets that she cannot change her gender and marry a woman, comparing their love favourably with the love of famous couples from Classical literature. The poem is now seen as a significant text in lesbian literature.

As Phoebus in his spheres hicht
Precellis the kaip crepusculein   Excels the cap of twilight
And Phoebe all the starris licht
Your splendour so madame I wein   wein: believe
Dois onlie pas all feminine
In sapience superlative   sapience: wisdom
Indewit with vertewis sa devine
As leirned Pallas redivive.   redivive: revived

And as be hid vertew unknawin
The adamant drawis yron thairtill   The magnet draws iron to it
Your courtes nature so hes drawin
My hairt youris to continew still
Sa greit joy dois my spreit fulfil
Contempling your perfectioun
Ye weild me holie at your will
And raviss my affectioun.

Your perles Vertew dois provoike   perles: peerless
And loving kyndnes so dois move
My mynd to freindschip reciproc   reciproc: reciprocal
That treuth sall try sa far above
The auntient heroicis love
as salbe thocht prodigious
and plaine experience sall prove
Mair holie and religious.

In amitie Perithous
To Theseus wes not so traist   traist: faithful
Nor till Achilles Patroclus
nor Pilades to trew Orest
Nor yit Achates luif so lest   lest: last/endure
to gud Aenee nor sic freindschip
David to Jonathan profest
nor Titus trew to kind Iosip.

Nor yet Penelope I wiss   wiss: believe
so luiffed Ulisses in hir dayis
Nor Ruth the kynd Moabitiss
Nohemie as the scripture sayis
nor Portia quhais worthie prayiss
In Romaine historeis we reid
Quha did devoir the fyrie brayiss   Who did eat the hot charcoal
To follow Brutus to the deid.

Wald michtie Jove grant me the hap   hap: chance
With yow to have your Brutus pairt
and metamorphosing our schap   schap: shape
My sex intill his vaill convert
No Brutus then sould caus was smart
as we doe now vnhappie wemen
Then sould we bayth with joyfull hairt
honour and bliss the band of hymen.

Yea certainlie we sould efface
Pollux and Castoris memorie
and gif that thay desservit place
amang the starris for loyaltie
Then our mair perfyte amitie
mair worthie recompence sould merit
In hevin eternall deitie
amang the goddis till inherit.

And as we ar thocht till our wo
nature and fortoun doe conjure
and hymen also be our so
Yit luif of vertew dois procuire
freindschip and amitie sa suire
with sa greit fervencie and force
Sa constantlie quhilk sall induire
That not bot deid sall us divorce.

And thocht adversitie us vex
Yit be our freindschip salbe sein
Thair is mair constancie in our sex
Then ever amang men hes bein
no troubill, torment, grief, or tein
nor erthlie thing sall us dissever
Sic constancie sall us mantein
In perfyte amitie for ever.

SOURCE: Craigie, WA (ed) 1920 *Maitland Quarto Manuscript*. Scottish Text Society, 160–2.

William Drummond of Hawthornden, 'For the Magdalene'

Drummond here uses sacred diction to describe temporal and emotional experience.

These Eyes (deare Lord) once Brandons of Desire,
Fraile Scoutes betraying what they had to keepe,
Which their owne heart, then others set on fire,
Their traitrous blacke before thee here out-weepe:
These Lockes, of blushing deedes the faire attire,
Smooth-frizled Waves, sad Shelfes which shadow deepe,
Soule-stinging Serpents in gilt curles which creepe,
To touch thy sacred Feete doe now aspire.
In Seas of Care behold a sinking Barke,   Barke: ship
By windes of sharpe Remorse unto thee driuen,
O let mee not expos'd be Ruines marke,
My faults confest (Lord) say they are forgiuen.
     Thus sigh'd to Jesus the Bethanian faire,
     His teare-wet Feete still drying with her Haire.

SOURCE: Kastner, LE (ed) 1913 *The Poetical Works of William Drummond of Hawthornden*. Scottish Text Society, i, 12.

Zachary Boyd, Sermons

Zachary Boyd (1585–1653) was a minister and dedicated administrator of the University of Glasgow who strongly supported the National Covenant of 1638 and the brand of presbyterianism that it stood for. He was also an author of religious poetry, although this has not always been well received by literary critics. His staunch Calvinism provides a counterpoint to other examples of sixteenth- and seventeenth-century Scottish literature that are often more classical and worldly in their tones and concerns.

A) AN EXPOSITION OF THE EPISTLE OF ST PAUL TO THE HEBREWES, CHAPTER I

Let us never in word or worke that seemeth great in our eyes gaze upon the instrument. Heares thou a man make an excellent sermon whereby all the powers of thy soule are shaken, so that thou is forced to quite they sinne? Say not, O the preacher! O the wonderfull man! Love the man the meanes of thy mercy. But saye not, O the man! But say rather, God is mighty in the man. Lok over the man & gaze upon God; fixe they eyes upon him & wonder at his word . . .

The hand of God hath wrought wonders. As thou should neither gaze on him whose word thou heares & whose worke thou sees, so neither should he that speakes the word admire him selfe, neither he that hath wrought a good worke vaunt him selfe thereof, but saye, it is the Lord & not I . . .

He must be a holy man that is minded to be an interpreter; otherwise he shall evanish in his imaginations . . .

B) THE CHRISTIAN HIS PILGRIMAGE PREACHED THE NINTEENE DAY OF AUGUST 1627

What ever good wee have, it is not of our selves. By grace are yee saved through faith, saith the apostle, and that not of your selves. It is the gift of God [Eph. 2:8], not of workes lest any man should boast [Eph. 2:9] . . . It is by grace that wee are saved, not of our selves, not of workes . . .

Man is like a house of three house height . . . As for the deepest part of the dungeon where the affections dwell, God no fewe wordes declares, who dwelleth there, viz the affections, the thoughts, & imaginations of the heart, which are evill at all times [Gen. 6:5] . . .

So from the highest mind to the lowest affection, there is no soundness in the soule but wounds & bruises & putrifying sores [Isa. 1:6] . . .

SOURCE: Atkinson, DW (ed) 1989 *Selected Sermons of Zachary Boyd*. Scottish Text Society, 10–12, 36–9.

George Mackenzie of Rosehaugh, 'An Apologie for Romances', Preface to *Aretina*, 1660

A jurist, philosopher and royalist political theorist, the polymath George Mackenzie of Rosehaugh (1630–1714) features here as author of Aretina, *which has been seen as the first Scottish novel, defending the value of the romance.*

I am confident, that where Romances are written by excellent wits, and perused by intelligent Readers, that the judgement may pick more sound information from them, then from History, for the one teacheth us onely what was done, and the other what should be done; and whereas Romances presents to us, virtue in its holy-day robes, History presents her only to us in these ordinary, and spotted sutes which she weares whilst she is buried in her servile, and lucrative imployments: and as many would be incited to virtue and generosity, by reading in Romances, how much it hath been honoured; so contrary wise, many are deterred by historical experience from being virtuous, knowing that it hath been oftner punished than acknowledged. Romances are these vessels which strain the christal streams of virtue from the puddle of interest; whereas history suffers the memory to quaff them of in their mixt impuritie; by these likewise lazy Ladies and luxurious Gallants, are allured to spend in their Chambers some hours, which else, the one would consecrate to the Bed, and the other to the Bordell [brothel]: and albeit essayes be the choicest Pearls in the Jewel house of moral Philosophy, yet I ever thought that they were set off to the best advantage, and appeared with the greatest lustre, when they were laced upon a Romance; that so the curiosity might be satisfied, as well as the judgement informed, especially in this age wherin the appetit of mens judgements is become so queasie, that it can relish nothing that is not either vinegared with satyres, or sugared with eloquence.

SOURCE: Mackenzie, G 1660 'An Apologie for Romances', preface to *Aretina; or, The serious romance.* Edinburgh, 5–11.